FUTURE OF THE UNITED NATIONS IN THE 21ST CENTURY

FUTURE OF THE UNITED NATIONS IN THE 21ST CENTURY

by

Lt Gen (Dr) VK Saxena, AVSM, VSM

(Established 1870)

United Service Institution of India

New Delhi

Vij Books India Pvt Ltd

New Delhi (India)

Published by

Vij Books India Pvt Ltd
(Publishers, Distributors & Importers)
2/19, Ansari Road
Delhi – 110 002
Phones: 91-11-43596460, 91-11-47340674
Fax: 91-11-47340674
e-mail: vijbooks@rediffmail.com

ISBN : 978-93-84464-69-1

Contents

PREFACE

My purpose of undertaking this work is to delve into the exciting world of the UN with an aim to try and perceive the future of this World Body in the tumultuous times of the 21st Century. With an analytical eye towards the future, I have basically researched the question, 'whether the UN, in times to come, will get further marginalized and doomed to irrelevance or will it eventually be scaled up to a status of indispensability'. The thrust of my book has been to bring out very useful inputs on how the UN, which reflected the main political concerns, threats, perceptions and the distribution of power of the World War II victors in 1945, must now re-position and re-align itself in the current framework of threats, challenges, aspirations, power plays, economics and the security perceptions of the new world pegging order of the 21st Century. The outcome has been a fruitful, fresh and original addition to the existing body of knowledge on the future of the UN in our lives and our times.

Driven by the above basic premise, the main issue under examination is as stated below :-

> "Given the current state of the UN pitched against the framework of multifarious threats that our Planet faces currently, or is likely to do so in the foreseeable future, what is likely to be "The Future of this only hope of the mankind (The UN) in the 21st Century?"

The analysis commences with an attempt to figure out the contours of the emerging face of the 21st Century. For this, and in order to build a good depth of the perspective, the start point is pegged somewhere mid way in the last Century, when the war victorious nations sat over the cataclysmic and gigantic destruction of humanity staring at the huge challenge of how to save the successive generations from the scourage of a bloody war. The period that followed saw the crumbling of the erstwhile colonial-imperial empires, the Cold War peaked and ebbed and then followed the strong global urge of a rightful representation of a New World Order. From the foregoing, precipitated a sense of what may lie ahead in the present Century which announced its arrival through the gruesome destruction and the smoking rubble of the Twin Towers on Sep 11, 2001.

The search reveals that 21st Century indeed presents a whole new set of challenges. The 'array of concerns' that led to the foundation of the United Nations way back in 1945 have shifted, expanded and changed colour. Besides the need for a proportional representation of the New World Order, the compulsions of collective security of humanity from a panoramic spread of the threat continuum from economic and social threats to inter-state conflicts, from the curse of civil wars, genocides and ethnic clearing (sic) to international terrorism and transnational organized crimes. All these grave challenges stare us in the face, in the current times.

Against the backdrop of the above threat profile, the book tries to ask a straight question - Can the UN (in its current dispensation) address the challenges of the 21st Century. In search of the answer, the analysis interplays the perceived strengths and weaknesses of UN against the emerging threats in the foreseeable future. In that, the strengths of visibility, universality, peacekeeping capability and the social care, foot print of the world body in healthcare, food security, spread of education, rights protection and crises management are pitched against many its failures and weaknesses, like failure to prevent genocides, marginalization of UN, disregard by members and above all, the existential crisis of keeping the organization financially alive.

The above interplay throws up a large agenda of 'to do' list if the world body is to have a viable future in the 21st Century and beyond. Issues like the need for global governance, solving the sovereignty vs intervention dilemma, need for a finality to the concept of R2P and the multifarious effects of Global Compact have been discussed. Alongwith this, the Charter deficits and the curse of veto in the context of the foundational need for equitable representation with several seating options on the high table of UNSC has been presented.

Towards curing the administrative, management and co-ordination related ailments, issues like right - sizing, the need to adopt the best management practices and cutting out corruptions/duplications/ overlapping amongst various agencies of UN have been analysed.

The book thereafter moves from 'ideas' to 'actions points', wherein, from the host of 'ideas for good' generated thus far, specific action points have been identified. Some of these include, the roller coaster of US-UN relationship and the desired end-state in the role of major powers, middle powers, small and developing States, coalitions, blocks and caucusing States. The role of the Secretariat and the growing influence of the good offices of the Secretary General have also been discussed. Visiting the Millennium Development Goals (MDG), the pertinent question of what after the MDG has been analysed by bringing to focus the run up of MDG till now and what lies ahead in each area of specific target.

The book also discusses in detail, the Report of the Secretary General's High Level Panel on Threats, Challenges and Change, bringing to focus how the recommendations of this important Report on the need for collective security, challenges of prevention, use of force, structural, organizational and administration reforms for a more effective UN can be realized over time. Also, how we can overcome many a sub-optimalities in the field of Peace Building, Peacekeeping and Peace Enforcement.

The Book thereafter brings to focus the UN Secretary General's Report on 'In Larger Freedom' in all its three dimensions of 'Freedom from Want' 'Freedom from Fear' and 'Freedom to Live in Dignity'. It highlights how the three verticals - Economic Development, Human Rights (including Women Rights) and Environmental and Health need to be addressed if the major recommendations of the Report are to be implemented. The ideas on Economic Development have led to a discussion of the New International Economic Order or NIEO, Women and Development and development as a MDG agenda. On Human Rights, the journey of evolution leading to the Universal Declaration, normative foundation, putting into place a regime of Treaties and Covenants and a Report Card of successes and failures in preservation of International Human Rights around the globe in the decades gone by, have been discussed. Under environment and health, the relevant aspects of the Earth Summit, UNEP, The Kyoto Process et. al, have been discussed.

Towards the end, the book highlights the role of United Nations in maintaining global peace. The perspective is set by examining the UN Report Card in ending wars and preserving peace in various parts of the Globe - Rwanda, Srebrenica, Iraq, Somalia and others. This is followed up with an examination of UN Peacekeeping efforts over time. Building up the chronology from the early years of Peacekeeping, the compulsions of the same during the Cold War years and the surge thereafter, have been highlighted. Reflecting on the Peacekeeping Report Card, various shades of Peacekeeping from the traditional to the complex and multi-dimensional have been flagged. This has led to the discussion on the Challenges of Peacekeeping in the 21st Century, wherein, issues like success criteria, sovereignty vs intervention, mandate inadequacies, resource crunch and guiding rules for the use of force have been included.

Basically, the book has dealt with the bottom line - where are and where we need to go if the UN has to have a viable meaning and a serious future in the times ahead.

I am of the view that my humble effort has added fresh thoughts and new inputs to the existing body of knowledge on the subject and the reader will find something worthwhile in my book.

LIST OF ABBREVIATIONS

1	AIDS	Acquired Immune Deficiency Syndrome
2	AU	African Union
3	BTWC	Biological and Toxin Weapons Convention
4	CTBT	Comprehensive Test Ban Treaty
5	CWC	Chemical Weapons Convention
6	ECOSOC	Economic and Social Council
7	FAO	Food and Agricultural Organization
8	FMCT	Fissile Material Cut Off Treaty
9	GNP	Gross National Product
10	HIV	Human Immunodeficiency Virus
11	HLP	High Level Panel (Report of the United Nations Secretary General's High Level Panel on Threats Challenges and Change – 'A More Secured World: Our Shared Responsibility')
12	IAEA	International Atomic Energy Agency
13	ICAO	International Civil Aviation Organization
14	ICC	International Criminal Court
15	ICJ	International Court of Justice
16	ICT	International Criminal Tribunal
17	ICTR	International Criminal Tribunal for Rwanda
18	ICTY	International Criminal Tribunal for the Former Yugoslavia

19	IDSA	Institute of Defence Studies and Analysis
20	IMR	Infant Mortality Rate
21	IMTFE	Intenational Military Tribunal for the Far East
22	IPCC	Intergovernmental Panel on Climate Change
23	LDCs	Least Developed Countries
24	MDGs	Millennium Development Goals
25	NDC	National Defence College
26	NPT	Non Proliferation Treaty
27	NWFP	North West Frontier Province
28	NWS	Nuclear Weapons States
29	SARS	Severe Acute Respiratory Syndrome
30	ODA	Official Development Assistance
31	ONUC	The United Nations Organization in Congo
32	OSCE	Organization for Security and Cooperation in Europe
33	PSI	Proliferation Security Initiative
34	RDF	Rapid Deployment Force
35	ROE	Rules of Engagement
36	SOMA	Status of Mission Agreement
37	UN	United Nations
38	UNAIDS	United Nations Programme on HIV/AIDS
39	UNAMIR	United Nation Assistance Mission for Rwanda
40	UNCD	United Nations Conference on Disarmament
41	UNCTC	United Nations Counter Terrorism Committee
42	UNDP	United Nations Development Programme
43	UNEF	United Nations Emergency Force

44	UNEP	United Nations Environment Programme
45	UNFCCC	United Nations Framework Convention on Climate Change
46	UNGA	United Nations General Assembly
47	UNMOGIP	United Nation Military Observer Group in India and Pakistan
48	UNOSOM	United Nation Operation in Somalia
49	UNPKO	United Nations Peace Keeping Operations
50	UNPROFOR	United Nation Protection Force
51	UNSC	United Nation Security Council
52	UNSG	United Nation Secretary General
53	UNRDF	United Nation Rapid Deployment Force
54	USI	United Services Institution
55	WHO	World Health Organization
56	WMD	Weapons of Mass Destruction

1

Emerging Face of 21St Century

Cataclysmic Changes in the Last Half of the Century

The 20th Century can convincingly be characterized as the bloodiest period of hundred years in the history of mankind. Carrying on its forehead, the blood-stained scars of the two World Wars, complete with their gigantic destruction and decimation of millions of human beings and material, 20th Century is indeed a period of some cataclysmic changes in the course of time. It is against the backdrop of these changes and events, that the birth of the United Nations, its infancy and growth over the years to adulthood, maturity and beyond, right up to the close of the 20th Century, and into the emergence of the 21st Century, need to be studied and analysed.

Though the United Nations was established at the end of World War II, its evolutionary roots can be traced back to the 16th Century European ideas about international law and organizations, followed by a series of developments in the 19th Century, leading on to the establishment of the League of Nations soon after World War I[1].

True to the fears and aspirations of many a nations freshly blooded in the war, the League of Nations truly reflected the environment in which it was conceived. Almost half of its twenty six provisions focused on preventing war. Two basic principles were paramount. Firstly, the member States agreed to respect and preserve the territorial integrity and political independence of States. If they failed, the League had the power under Article 16 to enforce settlements through sanctions. Secondly, all the members States embraced the principle of collective security, in that, the aggression by one State was agreed to be countered by all members acting together as a League.

Besides all this and more, the League proved to be ineffective. It failed to act decisively against the aggression of Italy and Japan in 1930. Collective security failed as Britain and France pursued their own verticals of national interests while the US, in the face of congressional opposition, failed to join the organization. Most importantly, the League could not prevent the out break of World War II[2].

And then followed the cataclysmic and unprecedented destruction of mankind, the one that the humanity had never seen before. Just sample these figures related to World War II casualties, put out on the internet :- [3]

(a)	Estimated Military Deaths	-	22,000,000 to 30,000,000.
(b)	Estimated civilian deaths due to military activity and crimes against humanity	-	38,000,000 to 55,000,000.
(c)	**Total deaths**	-	**60,000,000 to 85,000,000.**

In the above 60 to 85 million deaths (amounting to about 2.5-3.5% of the world population), one single country, Japan alone counted for a figure of 393,367 dead only through US strategic bombing which included 210,000 killed in one stroke during the Atomic bombing of Hiroshima and Nagasaki. Germany lost 8-10.5% of its population while the erstwhile USSR lost around 13.5%. The worst was the Holocast, the mass murder and genocide of approximately six million Jews through a programme of systematic state-sponsored murder by Nazi Germany, led by Adolf Hitler and Nazi Party throughout the German Reich and German occupied territories.[4]

Wounded and bleeding from the catastrophic destruction of the World War II the victorious nations of the war, namely, the USA, UK, USSR and China pledged above all, to save the succeeding generations from the scourge of war and to ensure that the horrors of the World War were never repeated. This thought and resolve has been the defining nature and the raison d'être for the establishment of the UN[5].

The story of UN, post birth has been one of sugar-n-spice, of success and failures, of fears and aspirations, and of bouquets and brickbats, in all, a mixed bag. Bumming along on the roller - coaster drive on the journey of humanity, this world heritage of mankind has been a witness to all that has happened in the last half of the Century after its birth, be it as a mute bystander, or as an active controller, driver or a moderator. A glimpse is provided at succeeding paras.

Crumbling of the Erstwhile Colonial-Imperial Empires

In the first 30 years of UN, many new States emerged from the colonial system through UN facilitation. The sustained work of the UN General Assembly (UNGA) and its Committee on 'Non Self Governing Territories' began to bear fruit. At the close of World War II, few would have predicted the end of colonial rule in Africa and Asia. Yet twenty five years later, most of the former colonies had achieved independence with relatively little threat to international peace and security. The membership of UN more than doubled from 51 in 1945 to 118 in 1965. These numbers tripled by 1980 to 156 and the same stands at 193 today[6]. In 1960, UNGA adopted a 'Declaration on Colonialism' which called for granting independence to all colonial territories[7]. This declaration catalysed the pace of de-colonialism.

The vast majority of the above member States were newly independent States which came into being as the UN endorsed the principle of self-determination calling for an end to the erstwhile colonial-imperial regimes. As the time passed, already independent colonies like India, Egypt, Indonesia and Latin American States used the UN forum to advocate an end to colonialism and independence of territories still colonized by Great Britain, France, The Netherlands, Belgium, Spain and Portugal.

In this way, the UN provided an important international forum for collective legitimization of a change in international norms in which, colonialism and imperialism were no longer the acceptable patterns of State behaviour and that the colonised peoples had the right to self determination[8].

Cold War and Beyond

The World War II coalition of great powers (US, Soviet Union, Great Britain, France and China), whose unity had been the key to UN's founding, were nevertheless a victim of rising tension even before the first General Assembly Session could commence in 1946[9]. Developments in Europe and Asia between 1946-1950, soon made it clear that the emerging Cold War would have fundamental effects on UN. How could the collective security system operate when there was no unity among the great powers on whose co-operation it depended? Even the admission of new members was affected between the period 1950-1955, because each side vetoed application from States that were allied to the other block[10].

The Cold War made the actions of the Security Council on threats to peace and security in the world extremely problematic with repeated sharp exchanges and frequent deadlocks. Some conflicts, such as the French and American Wars in Vietnam and Soviet interventions in Czechoslovakia and Hungary were never brought to UN for fear of veto. In fact, the UN was able to respond to North Korean invasion of South Korea in 1950 only because the Soviet Union was boycotting the Security Council at that time. Over the years, the power-political and ideological confrontation between the two power blocks dominated the debates and negotiations in UN, most of the time dead-locking the Security Council in bitter debates.

Another fall out of the breakdown of great-power unity was the innovation of peacekeeping as act of prevention, containment and moderation of hostilities by the 'representatives of the willing'. It effectively meant an act to promote order in troubled spots by keeping the 'Great Powers' out of such situations[11].

With the end of Cold War in 1990s, there was indeed a noticeable improvement in the climate among the Permanent Five (P-5) at the UNSC. The Council discussed amicably, the successor of UNSG Javier Perez de Cuellar, discussed ways to bring to an end the murderous Iran-Iraq War[12] and a system of regular P-5 informal meetings was set in place. While all this was happening on one side, the world was changing fast. There were resurgence of nationalism, civil wars and ethnic conflicts, and an emergence of a new phenomenon of failed-states along with its curse of humanitarian crises. The consequence of these developments showed up as greater demands than ever before on United Nations to deal with threats to peace and security, as well as, environmental and developmental issues, democratisation, population growth, humanitarian crises and more. The UN peacekeepers were called on to re-build Cambodia; create peace in Bosnia; organise and monitor post conflict operations on Nicaragua, Namibia and many other places; monitor human rights violation in El Salvador provide humanitarian relief in Bosnia, Somalia, Rwanda, Kosovo, Congo, East Timor as well as Afghanistan.

Faced with such multifarious challenges, the early Post Cold War optimism faded by around 1995 as the UN members displayed a lack of political will to provide military, logistical and financial resources needed to deal adequately with multifarious tasks and complex situations.

The Crises and Challenges as on Date

From the above details, the challenges of the Cold War Legacy, as it exists today have been summarised below:-

(a) Though the Cold War has long ended, its euphoria of P-5 co-operation and synergy has also long faded since a host of new problems like civil wars, ethnic conflicts and humanitarian crises have taken over the world.

(b) Though Cold War duals have reduced, the selfish and narrow national interests of big five still decide UNSC responses, often blocking viable proposals to draw geo-political advantage to one's country. Case in point is the Russian and Chinese veto of UN Resolution on Syria in Feb 2012 calling President Assad to step down, thus letting the Syrian imbroglio to go on.[13] Unfortunately, it continues till date.

(c) There is a wide spread acceptance that the Security Council is in a conundrum. With only five of the erstwhile war-victor States out of 193 sovereign nations of the world today occupying the 'High Table', the new world order is not represented. There is a general sense of frustration and discontentment leading to a strong yearning for change.[14] Only time will tell whether the desired changes will ever come about, and if so, when and to what extent?

The New World Order

One of yet another major dilemma that confronts the UN in the 21st Century is the need to reshape itself in consonance with the new world order. For good or bad, the Cold War years of blow hot-blow cold maintained a semblance of balance between two identifiable power blocks with their place at the world (read UN) leadership platform fairly clear. All the above changed over the years and especially so in the early years of the 21st Century. Some of the drivers for this change are summarised below :-

(a) Apart from the erstwhile two (and now one) super powers, there are many 'prominent players' today, who have the capability (and therefore the aspiration) to dominate the world stage today.[15] Take the case of G7 (US, UK, Japan, France, Germany, Italy and Canada), who collectively constitute 50.4% of global nominal GDP and 39.3% of global GDP (PPP).[16] Similarly, international experts now hold the view that the 'Big Four' (Brazil, Russia, India and China) are the emerging power houses whose economies will collectively overtake G-7 economies by 2027. These will now demand their rightful share in the pie of world leadership. And then there is G-20 (19 major economies and the EU) which account for 80% of the global GNP and 80% of the world trade.[17] Most of these strong countries opine that theirs is not a rightful representation on the world's highest power forum, the UNSC. And lets not forget the G-77, the largest Inter Governmental Organization of the world holding great leverage and power sway in the UN General Assembly. Their aspirations of having their due representation in the world leadership caucus also beckons attention. Lastly, a great numbers of NGOs and IGOs, that have international presence (ICRC, Amnesty International...) are also viable contenders in the claim for representation in the world leadership. With all the above as ground reality, the five war-victorious nations deciding on the fate of 193 sovereign States does not gel anymore. The world leadership has got to have a new face.

(b) Despite the phenomenal rise of China in particular and BRIC (G4) in general, USA with a GDP more than two and a half times of China and military expenditure almost half of the entire world, also with the lions share of 22% of the total UN budget and 27% of the total peacekeeping budget, willy-nilly gives the US a status of 'bound to lead.[18,19]However in the changed world realities, the style of leadership required in a world marked by multilateralism is not of unilateral action but one geared to building coalitions and consensus besides achieving active consultation and co-operation. Unfortunately, the status of this deserved end-state is still far from reality. In fact, the history of US engagement with UN is one of 'mixed messages' and considerable variations.

(c) The cases of American unilateralism hegemony and dominance are very visible all along the UN's six decades of existence. The most prominent example of US 'go it alone' policy is its military intervention in Iraq in 2003 with no UN endorsement. This act marks the biggest marginalisation of UN, where the US reduced it to irrelevance. In the late 1990s, US opposition to the creation of International Criminal Court, the Convention banning anti-personal land mines, the Comprehension Test Ban Treaty and the total indifference to the Kyoto protocol on climate change signalled its continued adherence to its 'go it alone' policy that continued unabated well into the early years of the 21st Century with Bush administration's opposition to international treaties and invasion of Iraq[20]. Various acts of US hegemony and unilateralism are making many countries less and less willing to accept US dominance.[21]

(d) With the mounting human disaster of unemployment (the percentage of long term unemployed workforce, i.e, 6 months or more, has risen from 0.8% in 2007 to 4.2% in 2010)[22], burgeoning trade deficits (US trade deficit starting from near negligible figs in 1980s has climbed to 817.3 billion dollars)[23] and a debilitating cost of the Global War on Terrorism or GWOT in short (US $ 1.283 Trillion as of 18 Mar 2011)[24] the erstwhile 'go it alone' right and arrogance attached to it, has somewhat taken a 'reality beating'. As time passes, many countries are becoming less and less willing to accept US dominance. Consequently, the US has lost a good deal of its soft power and the ability to lead. In any case, with the huge budget deficit (US $1.327 Trillion for 2011 - 2013)[25] as well as Republican majority in the House of Representatives following the 2010 elections, US payments to UN are again targeted for cuts.

Extracted from the above facts, the challenges to the UN in the context of new world order are summaried as under :-

(a) The emerging world order demands a changed face of world leadership at the UN. This face is certainly starkly different from the face of war victorious nations of 1945 that adorned the high table at the birth of UN.

(b) In the world of emerging powers, the likelihood that the US can lead, even when it chooses to, is inevitably diminished. The irony however is, that the alternative rising powers may not be willing or as yet, be able to assume centre stage leadership.

The US-UN pas de deux (as Ramesh Thakur puts it)[26] will therefore go on, and the outcome of which will decide much of the future of the UN in the 21st Century.

Resultant Emerging Face of the 21st Century

> *"In the 21st century, I believe the mission of the United Nations will be defined by a new, more profound awareness of the sanctity and dignity of every human life, regardless of race or religion. More than ever before in human history, we share a common destiny. We can master it only if we face it together. And that, my friends, is why we have the United Nations."*
>
> *- Kofi Annan*

On Sep 11 2001, the United Nations was due to convene the 56th Session of the General Assembly in the New York city. That meeting would have opened, as it had every September since 1981, with a moment of silence in recognition of the Assembly's self-proclaimed International Day of Peace. That act of reverence for 20 years had commemorated 'the ideals of peace both within and among all nations and peoples'. At the appointed moment of 3PM, however, the Assembly Hall stood silent and empty, as an injured Nation, and a 'shocked world' tragically focussed on the gruesome events unfolding just 50 Blocks South, where the smoking rubble from the Twin Towers of the World Trade Centre lay as reminders that peace was hardly secure at the beginning of the new millennium. 21st Century had announced its arrival.[27]

The terrorism from the air that wrecked the terrible calamity was a very different insult to the world peace than the ashes of war, out of which the United Nations was born. And like this harrowing experience which marked the globalisation of terrorism, the 21st Century presents a whole new set of challenges which were either non-existent, or inconceivable, to Franklin Roosevelt, Joseph Stalin and Winston Churchill when they laid the foundation of the UN over the smouldering ruins of the Second World War. It is not to save the successive generations from the scourge of another World War that is worrying the humanity today, it is the multiple challenges of rescuing disintegrating States, addressing economic dislocations, extending human rights, aiding environment, containing arms races, resolving border disputes, calming ethnic and religious hatreds and more that stare us in the face. How the UN will be able to take on the above challenges will actually decide the future of this world body. The purport of this Chapter is to examine the challenges that we face today.

International institutions are often forged in the fire of experience and response to events that demonstrate what can happen when international co-operation breaks down. In the wake of two catastrophic World Wars within a thirty year period, the victims of World War II convened 51 countries to fashion a collective security arrangement that would prevent in the second half of the 20th Century, a repeat of horrible events of the first half. Not surprisingly, the founders in establishing the UN, put into place an organisation that reflected the main political concerns and the distribution of power of the 1940s. Today the 'array of concerns' that led to the foundation of the UN have shifted and expanded. Essentially, while 'Collective Security' continues to be a central issue, our answers to the questions - 'Security from What?' and 'Security for Whom?' has changed drastically, over time[28].

While the wartime orientation of saving humanity from Great Power Wars was the main threat in 1945, civil wars and terrorism are much more likely to disrupt global security today. Small arms and 'dirty bombs' are much greater concern than missiles and warheads. The major threat to security of countless people is not violence or conflict, but poverty, disease, inequality, forced migration or environmental degradation. A broad goal of development 'demands to co-exist' besides World collective security. As UNSG has rightly observed, "We will not enjoy development without security, we will not enjoy security without development and we will not enjoy either without respect for human rights"[29].

The answer to the question 'Security for whom?' has also changed. On the forefront is not the security of soldiers/civilians in Great Power Wars, it is security of innocent hapless civilians against genocide and ethnic cleansing. If Balkans, Rwanda, Darfur and many others are horrific examples, saving humanity against atrocities and large scale loss of life must be a major concern overriding all obstacles that come in the way (State sovereignty Vs intervention, Responsibility to Protect (R2P), explained later).

Besides the changed answers to the question 'Security from what?' and 'Security from Whom?', the constellation of powerful actors on the global stage has also changed beyond recognition. In fact, the World moves on... Sweden and Spain were major players in 1648, minor actors by 1814 and barely involved at all by 1918-1945. The balance of global economic and military weights are alternating swiftly, giving rise to a set of systemic threats and challenges that the national leaders have not even began to contemplate, let alone tackle. According to a Goldman Sachs Policy Paper, "Dreaming with BRICS: the Path to 2050", if no major catastrophe strikes Asia, following points are reasonably clear[30]:-

(a) By the time the UN celebrates its Centennial in 2045, China could well constitute the largest economic and productive force in the World, bigger than the US.

(b) India may possess the third largest economy in the world, larger than Japan and that of any individual European State.

(c) Brazil, Indonesia and possibly a revived Russia could be advancing fast, overtaking the traditional European States in economic clout.

The unanimous opinion amongst scholars of UN has it, that the future of the UN in the 21st Century will largely depend on how the rights, fears and aspirations of the new world order are accommodated by the World Body.

Conclusion

This Chapter traces the background, history and the origin of the UN on the heels of a failed League of Nations and in the aftermath of World War II that brought unprecedented death, destruction, genocide and catastrophe, the likes of which the humanity had never seen before. The raison d' être of the founding fathers of the UN was therefore an emphatic resolve to save the successive generations of humanity from the scourge of another global war.

The Chapter also highlights, how, post the birth of UN, cataclysmic changes took place in the Second half of the 20th Century. These include the crumbling of the erstwhile colonial imperial regimes, the Cold War imbroglio and the new world order shaping the emerging face of the 21st Century. The question now arises is that 'Can the UN address the challenges of the 21st Century'?

Endnotes

1 F.S. Northledge, "The League of Nations : Its life and Times, 1920-1946", New York : Homes and Meier, 1986.

2 FP Wallers " A History of the League of Nations", New York, Oxford University Press,1952.

3 www.http://en.wilipedia.org/wiki/world-war-II-casualies. Accessed on 20 Sep 2011.

4 www.http//:en.wikipedia.org/wiki/The Holocast. Accessed on 25 Sep 2011.

5 Norman Lowe, "Mastering Modern World History", New Delhi; Macmillan Press, 1997, page 47.

6 www.http://undp.org/en/statistics. Accessed on 20 Oct 2011.

7 2, ibid; Volume1 . Pages 1 and 2.

8 Report of the "UN Open Ended Committee on Reform of the UN", New York, 1994.

9 http://www/dadalos.org/uno-int/grundkurs-2/un-entwicklung-2.htm. Accessed on 31 Oct 2011.

10 http://www.en.wikipedia.org/wiki/cold_war. Accessed on 06 Nov 2011.

11 Irus L. Claude Jr; "The Changing United Nations", New York: Random House, 1965, page 32.

12 Cameron Hume, "United Nations, Iran and Iraq: How Peacemaking Changed", Bloomington: University of Indiana Press, 1994, pages 81-82 and 88-100.

13 "Russia and China Veto UN Resolution in Syria", The Telegraph, 08 May 2012.

14 Paul Kennedy, "The Parliament of Man, The Past, Present and Future of United Nations", Vintage Book, Random House INC, New York, 2006 page 51.

15 http://www.en.wikipedia.org/wiki/G7.Accessed on 20 Nov 2011.

16 http://www.thedailybeast.com/newsweek 2009/03/20/power-up. Html quoted in http://en.wikipedia.org/wiki/BRIC. Accessed on 27 Nov 2011.

17 Thomas Axworthy,"Who Gets to Rule the World", Toronto Star (Canada) 2007, quoted in http://en.wikipedia.org/wiki/G-20. Accessed on 04 Dec 2011.

18 Karen A. Mingst and Margaret P Karns, "The United Nations in the 21th

Century" Fourth Edition 2012 Chapter1

19 http://www.better_world_campaign.org/issues/funding. Accessed on 18 Dec 2011.

20 Steward Patrick and Shepharad Foreman, ed. "Multilateralism and US Foreign Policy: Ambivalent Engagement" Boulder: Lynne Rienner, 2002)

21 David M. Malone and Yuen Fong Khoong, ed "Unilateralism and US Foreign Policy: International Perspectives" (Boulder: Lynne Rienner 2003)

22 http://www.topics.mytimes.com/top/.../u/united-states economy/index.html. Accessed on 15 Jan 2012.

23 http://www.en.wikpedia.org/wiki/Balance_of_trade. Accessed on 22 Jan 2012.

24 http: www.fas.org/sgp/ers/natsec/r133110.pdf. Accessed on 29 Jan 2012.

25 http:/www.en.wikipedia.org/wiki/2012-united-states-federal-budget. Accessed on 05 Feb 2012.

26 Ramesh Thakur. "The United Nations Peace and Security", Cambridge University Press, 2006, page 350.

27 John Allphin Moore, Jr, and Jerry Pubantz "Encyclopedia of the United Nations," Facts On File, Inc, 2002, pix.

28 Paul Hienbecker, Patricia Golf, "Irrelevant or Indispensable? The United Nations in the 21st Century", Wilfred Laurier University Press, 2005, pages 1-2.

29 Kofi Annan, "In Larger Freedom : Towards Development, Security and Human Rights for All" Report of the Secretary General (New York : UN document A/59/2005, 21 Mar 2005) para. 17.

30 Report of the US National Intelligence Committee, "Mapping the Global Future", London 2003.

2

Can the UN address the Challenges of 21st Century

"The UN was not built to confront many of the challenges that face the world today."

—Thomas G. Weiss

Strengths and Weaknesses of UN

Before we can take on the main question contained in the title of this Chapter, it would be worthwhile to have a brief look at the UN Report Card over its nearly seven decades of existence aggregated in terms of its strengths and weaknesses. Such an analysis is likely to give a fair idea as to what the UN (keeping its history and track record in line) will be able to do/ not do in the foreseeable period of the 21st Century wherein, it will be called on, time and again, to take on the multifarious challenges that lie ahead. Let us start by recounting some of the strengths and achievements of the UN over time

Strengths

"I want to begin by talking for a few minutes about what a world without the UN would be like, or rather it was like until not so long ago... The UN's ill-fated precursor collapsed without the outbreak of War."

—Malcolm Templeton[1]

Within eleven short years of its existence, the authority of the 'League of Nations was challenged by the Japanese Invasion of Manchuria (1931) and the Italian invasion of Abyssinia (1935). Further, upon its failure to prevent the World War II, the League was dissolved in 1946[2]. Compared to this, the longevity of UN since 1945 is in itself an achievement.

A World without Global War. The defining sentence of the UN Charter reads 'To save the succeeding generations from the scourge of war and to ensure that the horrors of the World War were never repeated' The experiment has been successful since over the subsequent sixty years, many parts of the world have enjoyed unparalleled peace and prosperity and the world has been spared the horror of another conventional global war[3].

Inter State Wars. There have been fewer interstate wars in the last half of the 20th Century than in the first half, in spite of the fact that in the former period, the number of States grew almost four fold. UN has certainly contributed to that result.

De-Colonization. As brought out in Chapter 1, in the first 30 years of UN, many new States emerged from colonial system though UN facilitation. The sustained work of UN General Assembly (UNGA) and its Committee on 'Non-Self Governing Territories' began to bear fruit in 1960 when seventeen former colonies achieved independence and became members of UN. This process of enlargement of the area of freedom has continued apace enhancing the present UN membership from 51 in 1945 to 193 today[4]. In 1960 UNGA adopted a 'Declaration on Colonization', which called for granting independence to all colonial territories[5].

Universality. UN has provided a sense of 'universality', 'recognition' and a 'voice' to its member States many of which could not even dream of sustaining a nominal independence[6].

Visibility. UN has provided international visibility to the human rights issues. The expression 'Human Rights' did not figure in the covenant of the League of Nations. The UN Charter considered human rights as a proper subject for international concern. This led to its inclusion and elaboration in the Universal Declaration, International Covenants on Human Rights and the development of International Humanitarian Law (IHL)[7].

Peacekeeping. Notwithstanding its many imperfections, the UN deserves credit for its ingenuity in inventing peacekeeping. Initially not included in the Charter, peacekeeping was created to respond to conflicts between states. Former UN Secretary General (UNSG) Dag Hammarskjold described it as Chapter VI ½ of the Charter, i.e, action between peaceful techniques of moderation and fact-finding (Chapter VI) and more robust tools such as intervention (Chapter VII)[8].

Peacekeeping Achievement During Cold War Era. As Secretary General Hammarskjold saw it, 'UN peacekeepers were a 'buffer' between warring factions'[9]. Their objective was not to defeat an aggression but to prevent fighting, keep order and monitor violation of cease-fire agreements. Quite a few successes can counted during this period; UN Emergency Force (UNEF) in the end 1950 restrained Britain, France, and Israel from invading Egypt; UN Organization in Congo (ONUC) prevented fragmentation of a newly independent African country etc.

Invocation of Chapter VII. Notwithstanding the crippling effect of the veto, UN successfully invoked Chapter VII provisions of intervention in several cases during the cold war years. The prominent ones include sanctions against Southern Rhodesia to end the minority rule and against South Africa for its racial policy of Apartheid[10,11].

Unipolar Moment. In the brief demise of the 'reciprocal game of veto' post cold war, saw some swift intervention actions by the UN. Within hours of the Iraqi invasion of Kuwait in 1991, UN Security Council (UNSC) adopted Resolution 668 condemning invasion and authorizing other nations to intervene in Iraq. Even in Yugoslavia, the UNSC successfully enforced sanctions under Chapter VII despite the fact that the conflict involved parties within one member State[12]. The ceasefire in Croatia in 1992 and maintenance of peace through 14,000 peacekeepers under UN Protection force (UNPROFOR) was another achievement.

Further Peacekeeping Achievements. Post the Cold War the UN undertook many peacekeeping missions in Croatia, former Yugoslavia, EI Salvador, Angola, Mozambique, Cambodia and Namibia etc, albeit with a mixed degree of success.

World Economy. Under the UN auspices, the world economy has grown faster than in any comparable period in history especially between 1945 to 1974[13].

Health Care and Education. Quite a lot has been achieved by the UN in the field of immunization, health care, nutrition and basic education. The Infant Mortality Rates have more than halved. This is due to improved sanitation and availability of vaccines against six killer diseases of children. Moreover ill nutrition, which was a major cause of ill health and death, has reduced drastically. Consequently, life expectancy has risen in all parts of the world[14].

Major Diseases. A thirteen-year effort by the WHO has resulted in the complete eradication of small pox from the planet. This has saved an estimated $ 1 billion a year in disease control[15]. Similarly the ongoing efforts of the World Health Organization (WHO) in completely eradicating leprosy, its success in effectively halting the spread of Severe Acute Respiratory Syndrome (SARS), and finally, the global initiative to control the spread of HIV/AIDS and the menace of tuberculosis are noteworthy, though much still needs to be done. UN Programme for fighting parasitic diseases has similarly saved millions of lives.

Poverty And Hunger. FAO has been leading a global campaign to eradicate proverty and hunger. IFAD has developed a system of providing credit in very small amounts for the poorest and the most marginalized groups. This has benefited over 230 million people in nearly 100 developing countries.

On Environment. UN has played a vital role in providing global visibility and concern for environment. The 'Earth Summit' and the Conference on Environmental Development have resulted in treaties on biodiversity and climate change. UN Intergovernmental Panel on Climate Change (IPCC) is making consistent efforts to bring global awareness of the potential disastrous effects on global warming.

UN Development Programme (UNDP) Achievement. UNDP, in close co-operation with over 170 member States and other UN agencies, has designed and implemented projects for agriculture, industry, education and the environment, with a budget of over $ 1.3 billion. It is the largest multilateral source of grant for development assistance in the world[16].

Towards Sustainable Development. UN has been in the forefront of the campaigns for sustainable development and proper use of world's oceans, space, air space, as well as, Arctic and Atlantic lands. UNCLOS is a landmark achievement. Over 300 international treaties on topics as varied as human rights conventions to agreements on the use of outer space have been enacted through the efforts of UN.

Weaknesses

The salient weaknesses of the UN in its six decades plus of existence will act as pitfalls and booby traps for its further survival in the 21st Century. These will have to be addressed and rectified as a contributing factor in UN's future. The same are briefly enumerated in the succeeding paras.

Disregard by Member States. UN is nothing but the cumulative confederation of member States. Though experts believe that there are three UNs viz, the Nation States, the UN bureaucracy and the Peoples, essentially it is the Nation States which decide what UN will or will not achieve. If the Nation States themselves, start to disregard/ bypass/boycott UN, that will be a sure recipe of its demise, in the times to come. Iraq's invasion by US in 2003 without UN endorsement was not the first time when the world body had been marginalized. Way back in 1948, the blatant disregard of UN Resolution 181 recommending the partition of the Jewish State by the parties to the conflict was probably the first instant of trashing the cumulative will of the people and the recommendations of the world body[17].

Corrosive Moral Equivalence. UN has suffered from this failure time and again. It has a history and tendency of drawing no distinction between the attacking and defending armies, e.g by failing to condemn the Arab Aggression in 1948 during the first Arab Israeli War in 1948, it betrayed Israel. Later by failing to condemn Pak marauders that invaded Kashmir in 1948 it revealed a false symmetry between the aggressor and the victim. It failed to brand Pakistan as an aggressor and hence failed to recognise and condemn aggression. By doing that, it did not resolve the conflict but merely froze the two antagonists in their respective positions, thrusting a now defunct, irrelevant and superfluous observer gp (UNMOGIP) along the 500 mile long cease fire line[18]. This betrayed and disillusioned India. Resultantly, India no longer recognised the UN monitoring authority in 1971 as it had agreed to in 1949.

Cold War Freeze-Still Counting. That the Cold War Freeze created a complete Soviet-American deadlock in the UNSG is a history, what is worrisome, is the continuing trend of under-cutting and blocking moves/ proposal among the big five in pursuance of narrow national interests and with a view to gain comparative geo-political mileage. Not only the does UNSC not represent the emerging world order, it continues to be plagued with the same old crippling and debilitating disease, which it has suffered right from its birth.

Intervention –Sovereignty Pendulum. Swinging between the eternal debate of intervention vis-à-vis sovereignty, and keeping the decision on R2P in an eternal hanging balance, the UN has many times been only a by-stander when ghastly acts took place. Some examples:-

(a) **Kurd Genocide.** Saddam Hussein's offensive against Iraq's Kurdish minority in Mar 1998 when the infamous 'Chemical Ali' slaughtered some 100,000-200,000 Kurds in bloody chemical attacks[19].

(b) **Liberia and Sierra Leone**. A civil war raged in Liberia from 1990 to 1995 which forced more than 800,000 people into exile. Many countries were affected by these masses of refugees but the UN did not get involved. Between 1991 to 1996 in Sierra Leone some 50,000 people died which was about half of the country's population; UN remained a passive by-stander, inextricably involved in the eternal debate of intervention vs sovereignty. Only by 2000, it could send a peacekeeping force. 'Too little, too late'.

(c) **Rwanda**. There is perhaps no more damaging indictment of UN than its failure to prevent genocides. In the Rwandan genocide, when thousands of Rwandans were being slaughtered in the Hutu-Tutsi clashes, UNAMIR stood by, taking shelter under their mandate that their mission was only to monitor Arusha Accords, i.e, to make the Rwandan capital a weapon secure area. The 'impotency' of the mission in trying to maintain the so called 'neutrality' and 'impartiality', ended up in the massacre of 10,74,017 Rwandans by Feb 2002 out of which, 94% were Tutsis.

(d) **Srebrenica**. In the terrible genocide and massacre of Bosnian Muslims at the hands of Serbs in 1992, another dimension of UN failure come to fore. Not only had the massacre taken place in so called 'Safe UN Areas', the Dutch Peacekeeping force was grossly under manned. The Peace keepers put up no fight to save the Bosnian Muslims, worse still, the UN Force did not get any support from the NATO Forces based in Italy. UNPROFOR remained a by-stander as scenes of unimaginable savagery unfolded[20]. The UN's failure in Srebrenica spread chaos in former Yugoslavia as another UN Safe Area came under assault. Sarajevo was shelled by Siberian Artillery and Kosovo and Croatia were subjected to ethnic cleansing[21].

(e) **Failure in Iraq**. In the aftermath of liberation for Kuwait, when the Iraqi Army launched genocide operations to crush the Kurdish rebellion in Northern Iraq and Shia uprising in Southern Iraq, UN failed to prevent the disaster. It just adopted resolutions after resolutions, which were simply ignored by Iraq.

(f) **Self Contradiction**. In the wake of Sep 11, UN adopted Resolution No 1373, which unambiguously denounced international terrorism. Within a week, the UNGA overwhelmingly elected Syria to sit on the UNSC, knowing fully well, that Syria had been a known sponsor of terrorism for more than 20 years.

(g) **Impartiality and Neutrality**. In many cases, UN forces, under the myth of maintaining impartiality and neutrality, have corrosively ended up equating the aggressors and the victims (e.g Rwanda). In 1995-96 in Afghanistan, the UN forces betrayed the domestic opponents of Taliban by maintaining neutrality towards Taliban despite their brutalities and the aidit was getting from Pakistan[22].

(h) **Somalia**. The long story of suffering, gross human rights violations and mass casualties in the famine struck Somalia is a standing testimony of how an intervention can be rendered impotent and can result in a failed mission when the interest of the sole superpower determines the course of events. The failure of UN operations in Somalia (UNOSOM), as well as, the intervention and atrocities by Ethiopian force finally de-generating into a US led offensive against Al Qaida, all point towards a terrible growth of events over time and the increasing ineffectiveness and exploitation of the UN[23].

(j) **Biggest Marginalisation**. As stated earlier, 2003 was to witness the unprecedented marginalisation of UN, when USA and UK unilaterally invaded Iraq without any UN authorisation. The events that followed are history.

(k) **Human Rights Failures**. While the space constraint prohibits the detailed description of scores of Human Rights abuses, it can be stated in essence that UN has stood by, acted impotently or weak-kneed in many cases of genocide, ethnic cleansing and other human rights disasters. The list of live examples is long and blood-soaked; Rwanda, Srebrenica, Sierra Leone, Anfal, Somalia, Darfur, Abu-Gharib, Hiditha, Guantanamo Bay, Chechnya.... all pointing to an irrefutable truth that the UN, for whatever may be the reason, has been more or less unable to prevent human rights violations, genocides and mass humanitarian disasters.

I sum the future of the UN in times ahead will depend much on how it avoids its past failure and converts its shortcomings into enabling strengths.

Threats and Challenges of the 21st Century

Economic and Social Threats

Hunger and Poverty.

(a) **The Scene Then**[24]. The Report of the High Level Panel (HLP) on Threat, Challenges and Change brought out some grim facts about world poverty status. It stated, that in the period 1990 – 2004, the number of people living in extreme poverty has increased in some regions by more than 100 million. In at least 54 countries, the per capita income has declined. Every year, about 11 million children die from preventable diseases and more than half a million women die during pregnancy or child birth. In Sub-Saharan Africa, which is worst hit by poverty, the average life expectancy has declined from 50 to 46 years and the number of people living off $ 1 or less everyday, has multiplied. Stark poverty added to ethnic or regional inequalities have compounded the grievances.

(b) **The Scene Now**. Besides many effects (covered later), the world hunger and poverty scene remains grim. As per a 2010 report, about 1395 million out of the world population of 6.8 billion are in the grip of hunger and poverty[25]. The developing countries are worst hit which have 98% of world's malnourished[26]. 1.4 billion people in developing countries live on $ 1.25 a day or less[27], out of which 75% live in rural areas[28]. 22,000 children die each day due to conditions of poverty andhunger[29]. The factual details quoted above show the magnitude of the challenges which exist today and need to be overcome.

Infectious Diseases.

(a) **The Scene Then**. The HLP report states that in the last three decades of the 20th Century, there has been a strong resurgence of infectious diseases, polio is again showing its ugly face defying claims to its eradication. The international response to HIV/AIDS has been sluggish. The number of deaths per year from HIV/AIDS in Africa outstripped the combined number of battle deaths in all the civil wars in ninetees. WHO had reported in 2005 that if the current trends continue, nearly one billion people will be infected by TB, 150 million will develop the disease, 36 million will die[30].

(b) **The Scene Now**. The situation remains grim. Take the case of the AIDS, world's No 1 killer. As per the UNAIDS report of 2010[31].35 million people are living with HIV/AIDS out of which 65% are women. The area worst affected by the disease is Sub-Saharan Africa which accounts for 90% of all children and 60% of all the women population with AIDS. In addition to the above, it is estimated that more than 11 million children die each year from preventable health issues such as malaria, diarrhoea, and pneumonia[32]. As regard water-borne diseases, statistics show that about 2.3 billion suffer from such diseases. The scholars convincingly talk about water-wars in future since it is 12% of the world population that uses 85% of world's water[33] and none of the 12% live in developing countries.

Food Insecurity. Current trends indicate persistent and possibly worsening food insecurity in many countries, especially Sub-Saharan Africa. Loss of arable land, water scarcity, over fishing, deforestation and alteration of eco systems pose daunting challenges for sustainable development. According to a Report titled, 'State of Food Insecurity in the World 2011', the number of hungry people in the world has increased. The current estimates put the hungry people at 945 million out of the world population of 6.8 billion. Food insecurity emanates from the fundamental state of hunger and malnutrition in the world population. Very briefly, the main reasons for the growth of hunger are as under :-

(a) **Growing Poverty**. Rising poverty figures (as stated above) for whatever reason (lack of resources, unequal income distribution, conflict and more) leads to increased inability of people to buy food. While the overall world poverty figures have reduced (from 1900 million in 1981 to 1345 million in 2005), the corresponding figures in Sub-Saharan Africa has increased[34].

(b) **Harmful Economic and Political Systems**. The principal underlying causes of poverty and hunger are operation of economic and political systems. Essentially, the control over resources and income is based on military, political and economic powers of a Nation, which typically ends up in the hands of a minority who live well, while those at the bottom, barely survive. The economic and political grind makes the rich richer and the poor poorer.

(c) **Conflict**. Inter and Intra state conflicts are also causes of hunger and poverty. Large scale destruction of resources, infrastructure and people disrupts food generation activity and causes large scale repatriation and refugees, bereft of food and bathed in misery. By 2008, the total number of refugees under UNHCR'S mandate exceeded 10 million. By the end of the same year the number of conflict induced Internally Displaced Persons (IDP) reached some 26 million[35].

(d) **Climate Change**. Climate change is increasingly being viewed as a current and future cause of hunger and poverty. Increasing drought, flooding and changing climate patterns require a shift in crop and farming practices, that may not be easily accomplished. Climate change inflicts severe damages which affect the poor and deprived the most. Increased rain floods, droughts, cyclones, typhoons etc cause wide spread loss of agriculture and other food resources. Food insecurity stands as a stumbling block to sustainable development for the millions of poor, hungry and deprived populations in the world. This insecurity is threatening to become more severe as the world population climbs (expected to rise from the current 6.8 billion to 8.9 billion by 2050).

Environmental Degradation[36]. Environmental degradation has enhanced the destructive potential of natural disasters and in some cases has hastened their occurrence. The dramatic increase in major disasters witnessed in the last 50 years provides worrying evidence of the trend. As per one estimate, more than 2 billion people were affected by such disasters in the period 1990-2000. Floods, droughts, storms and heat waves which take million of lives are a result of environmental degradation. The 2011 Human Development Report warns that the development progress in the world's poorest countries could be halted or even severed by mid Century because of environmental degradation. Jeri Klingman, the lead author of the report says that poor countries in Sub-Saharan Africa are at a particular risk where the main problems are de-gradation of land and desertification.

While drought in Sub-Saharan Africa is of concern, the rising sea levels in low lying nations in South Asia and Pacific will put more than 100 million people at risk in the decades ahead.

Challenges to Sustainable Development. The economic and social threats enumerated above constitute threats to sustainable development. Since security and sustainable development are implicitly interlinked, the challenges to the latter constitute a serious threat to global security. Unfortunately, international institutions and states continue to treat such challenges as stand alone threats and try to deal with them in a fragmented sectoral approach. Though the UN has an unparalleled advantage of convening, drawing attention and rallying international communities to recognize such global threats and challenges, its global programmes, e.g, World Summit on Sustainable Development, Millennium Development Goals with such laudable aims as halving extreme poverty, protecting the environment, achieving greater gender equality, as well as, halting and reversing the spread of HIV/Aids by 2015 remain only partially fulfilled. Hence there is a grave challenge to somehow get the international community and global organisation to rally its cumulative power in addressing the monster of social and economic threats described above. We now see the wisdom in the following words.

> *"Sustainable human development is the essential pre-condition and the essential foundation of collective security".*

—Bruce Jones

Threat of Inter State Conflicts Threat Alive

Threat Alive. Very simply, the UN charter is premised on the fundamental thought of saving the successive generations from the scourge of war (the driving thought was World War and resultant destruction of humanity). The impetus in 1945 therefore not only outlawed war, but unlike the League, gave the UN the authority to enforce the peace through diplomatic, economic and even military actions[37]. 67 years down the line, though the threat of interstate war has reduced, it has not vanished. Suffice to say, that even after the end of cold war, the world has seen 35 major wars[38]. Some of these continue today. Unresolved regional disputes in South Asia, North East Asia and Middle East continue to threaten international peace and security. Worse, interstate rivalry in lawless regions have fuelled and exacerbated internal wars, making them more difficult to bring to close.

Deadly Spill Effect. The ongoing interstate wars like in Palestine or Afghanistan fuel extremism in the parts of Muslim/Arab world and the West, fostering perceptions of cultural and religions antagonism between them. Such potential dangers give weight to the theory of clash of civilizations as proposed by Political Scientist Samuel P Huntington, stating that people's cultural and religious identities will be the primary source of conflict in present Cold War World[39].

New Prospects for Inter State Conflict. Many scholars have brought out that one of the potential causes of inter-state conflicts in the future could be conflicting demands on the shrinking strategic natural resources of the world like water, hydrocarbons, minerals etc[40]. If the desire to build world empires, subjugate/colonise humanities or be a master of large tracts of the planet is not a likely raison d'être for inter state conflict, the desire to own/control/deny precious natural resources against burgeoning demand will surely stand in, as a valid reason.

The Threat of Internal Conflicts

The Changing Nature of War. The nature of wars and conflicts have changed in significant way in the last 50-60 years. Studies show that since 1992, while the threat of interstate wars has declined by 40%, the dangers of intrastate conflicts; the ones arising from the collapse of an already weak (failed) State, ethnic conflict or civil wars have dramatically increased to more than 95%[41]. Civil wars that have become internationalised through the intervention of other states or groups represent another problem.

Ongoing Conflicts a Live Threat[42]. A wikipedia download quoting figures from Uppasala Conflict Data Programme[43] recognised by UN have put out the following update:-

(a) **1000 + Deaths/Year.** There are more than 10 internal conflicts going on in the world today accounting for 1000 or more violent deaths per year. These are in Columbia, Afghanistan, Somalia, Iraq, NW Pakistan, Mexico, Sudan (2), Yemen, Syria and Egypt. In fact, in some cases the fatalities in 2011 have crossed more than 10,000, Syria (6000-10,100 -13,000 and counting), Mexican Drug War (19,396).

(b) **Small Scale Conflicts.** Besides the above, there are 28 other small scale conflicts going on in the world today. While per year casualties in these conflicts is between 10-1000, the cumulative fatalities upto 2012 have crossed many crores; Korea (4,770,000+), Baluchistan (1,672-25,000) Khurdish-Turkish (45,000-1,00,000) etc.

Threat of Nuclear, Radiological, Biological And Chemical Weapons

A Live Threat. While it has been over twenty years since the end of the Cold War, the existence of thousands of nuclear weapons continues to pose a serious global threat requiring international action for collective security. Primarily, this threat arises in two ways. Firstly some countries under the garb of NPT (signatories) acting in letter, but not perhaps the spirit of the Treaty, illegally develop full scale weapon programme keeping the option to withdraw from the Treaty when ready for weaponisation. Secondly, there is a threat of erosion or possible collapse of the Treaty itself. Not only the countries have scant regard for the Treaty per se, countries outside the Treaty are going ahead to acquire nuclear (weapon) capability overtly and covertly[44].

Ever Growing Numbers. In 1963, there were only four States that had nuclear weapons. By 2004, while the established nuclear players went up to eight, the clandestine ones reached 15-25. As of date, besides the five nuclear weapon States (NWS) under NPT [US, Russia, UK, France, China], there are three non-NPT nuclear powers (India, Pakistan and North Korea) and some other States that are believed to have nuclear weapons (Israel, Iraq, Iran ?? and Syria ??). The entire non proliferation regime are at risk due to withdrawals/threats of withdrawal from NPT. We are approaching a point where the erosion of non-proliferation will become irreversible.

Existing Stockpiles. Irrespective of the fact whether more countries acquire nuclear weapons or not, the existing stockpiles of weapon are a threat large enough. As per a 2007 estimate, the world stockpiles of nuclear weapon countries (US, Russia, China, France, UK, India, Pakistan and Israel) stand at 7300 strategic nuclear weapons, 4700 – 11,700 non strategic nuclear weapons amounting to 12,000 – 19,000 weapons in all [45]. Worse still is the fact that many stockpiles are inadequately secured. As of Aug 2011, there have been more than 250 reported incidents of nuclear material diversion and illicit trafficking[46]. Experts suggest that if a simple nuclear device is detonated in a major city the number of death would range from tens of thousands to more than a million. And then there is a whole new dimension of nuclear terrorism (covered later). The contours of this threat can be visualised clearly. It is for no small reason therefore, that the world leaders gave a clarion call for nuclear safety at the 2012 Seoul Nuclear Security Summit.

Radiological Weapons

A different threat is posed by radiological weapons which are sure weapons of mass disruption than weapons of mass destruction. Radiological weapons can use plutonium or highly enriched uranium or can rely simply on radioactive materials of which there are millions of sources used in medical and industrial facilities worldwide. The immediate destructive effect of a radiological or a 'dirty bomb' is only as great as its conventional explosive, and even the radiation effects of such a bomb are likely to be limited. The more harmful effects of disruption and economic damage would be prompted by public alarm and the necessity of evacuating and decontaminating affected areas. The ubiquity of radiological materials and the crude requirements for detonating such a device suggests a high likelihood of its use given the fact that trafficking/pilferage/diversion of radioactive material is a high probability.

Chemical and Biological Weapons

The Threat Dimension.[47] Chemical and biological materials also pose a growing threat. They share with nuclear weapons the awful potential of being used in a single attack to inflict mass casualties. Chemical agents are widespread and relatively easy to acquire and weaponise. One only has to recall Saddam Husain's offensive against Iraq's Kurdish community in 1988 where the infamous 'Chemical Ali' slaughtered some 100,000 - 200,000 Kurds in bloody chemical attacks (sic).

Destruction of Stockpiles. Despite being signatories to the CWC or BTWC, the Chemical Weapon States have lagged behind in destruction of their chemical arsenal as mandated by the Treaty. Out of a total of 70,000 million tons of reported chemical weapon agents, only a small portion stands destroyed. The balance stands like a deadly threat.

Technology Fuelling the Threat. While rapid growth and scientific advances in the biotechnology sector hold out the prospects of prevention and cure for many diseases, these also increase the opportunities for development of deadly new ones. Dramatic advances in recombinant DNA technology and direct genetic manipulation raise the prospect of 'designer bugs' which may be developed to reconstruct eradicated diseases and to resist existing vaccinations, antibiotics and other treatments. There are countless fermentation medical and research facilities equipped to produce biological agents. Such agents can be manipulated to cause deliberate outbreaks of infectious diseases which could prove as lethal if not more than nuclear detonation. Under worst-case assumption, an attack using only one gram of weaponised small pox could produce between 10,000 to 10,00,000 fatalities. The magnitude of this threat thus becomes quite evident. The fact that the Turkish analyst are passing sleepless nights in trying to analyse Syria's (A non signatory to CWC) chemical weapons stockpile due to the current days of uprising, lends a degree of contemporary relevance to this threat[48].

The Threat of Terrorism

> "*Terrorism has become the systematic weapon of war that knows no border or seldom has a face*".
>
> —Jacques Chinac

Refusing to Ebb. If there is one threat on the world scene which is refusing to ebb, it is the ugly face of international terrorism. A few days after the tragic attacks on New York and Washington in Sep 2001 which killed 3000 civilians – twice the number of combatants who died during the attack on Pearl Harbour in Dec 1941, the UNSG outlined the relevance of the topic. 'Terrorism' is a global menace. It calls for united global response[49]. 9/11 was followed over the next three years by equally horrific terrorist outrages in Bali, Madrid and Beslan. Iraq saw more terrorist attacks than anywhere else in the world in 2004-05. If Afghanistan, much of the Arab world and the Sub-Saharan African nations are any evidence, international terrorism as an assault on the fundamental human values continue to bleed the world endlessly[50].

The Weapons of Mass Destruction (WMD) Dimension. The possibility that any terrorist group could get their hands on WMD is yet other critical security concern on the world body's agenda. Also worrisome is the role of State as sponsors and supporters of international terrorism. Terrorism flourishes in environments of despair, humiliation, poverty, political oppression, extremism and human rights abuse. It also flourishes in the context of regional conflicts and foreign occupation and it profits from a weak State's incapacity to maintain law and order. Terrorism is acquiring gigantic proportions; a global reach, complex world wide connectivity, sophisticated weaponry providing lethal capabilities not to mention the looming threat of WMDs falling in their blood-stained hands. The threat is live and the threat is enormous. It calls for a firm and a coherent international response.

Threat of Transnational Organised Crime

A Menace. Transnational organised crimes like trafficking of drugs, narcotics and human beings are a menace to States and societies eroding human security and fundamental obligation of States to provide for law and order. One of the core activities of organised crime-drug trafficking has major security implications. It is estimated that criminal organisations gain billions of dollars annually from narcotics trafficking-their single largest source of income. Drug trafficking has also fuelled the spread of HIV/AIDS virus in some parts of the world.

Designer Drugs[51]. The Annual Report of the UN International Nations Control Board (INCB), 2011, states that with the increased influence of the internet, the production of so called 'designer drugs' is soaring out of control across much of the world. Designer drugs are often produced by slightly modifying the molecular structuring of controlled/banned drugs making a new drug with similar effects which can elude national/ international ban.

Poor Response. The international response to the above crimes has been poor and sluggish and the actions to contain them have been decentralized and fragmented. Other impediments in containing the threat have been an insufficient co-operation among States, weak coordination among international agencies and inadequate compliance by many States.

Human Trafficking. Similar to drug/narcotics menace, the threat of human trafficking stands upfront as a slur on human fundamental right to be free from all types of commercial sexual exploitation, forced child labour and other forms of human exploitation.

With the strengths and weaknesses of UN, as well as, the major threats of the 21st Century defined, the book will now try to interplay the two to proceed further.

Inter Play of Strengths and Weaknesses against the Threats and Challenges so Identified

Having been through the paces of first identifying the strengths and weaknesses of the UN systems in terms of its past successes and failures and thereafter, highlighting the multifarious threats that we face in the 21st Century, the future of the UN in times to come will essentially be an interplay of its strengths and weaknesses against the threats and challenges so identified.

Let us now ask the fundamental question contained in the title of this Chapter, i.e 'can the UN address the challenges of the 21st Century?' Unfortunately, there are neither any binary (Yes/No), nor simple answers. There are two major reasons for the same. Firstly, the multi-dimensional threats that confront our planet in the 21st Century are vastly different in context and content to the ones, which the world faced at the time, when the UN was born in 1945. Secondly, the political and geo-strategic realities of the current tumultuous times are starkly different from 1945 when the victors of the Second World War established the UN on the central thought of saving the successive generations from the scourge of another World War. While this thought process runs deep and controls the entire infrastructure and ethos of the UN as of date, unfortunately, this thought is no longer the main issue facing the world in 2013, hence the misfit. That is to say, that since this basic orientation in the thought process itself has undergone a sea change, there are contradictions in terms. The experts today are asking the question, can the UN with its war-time orientation take on the challenges that confront us in the 21st Century?

The book has already briefly analysed the threats that we face in the 21st Century. Whether the UN will be able to address the same or not will be the litmus test to its continued survival or death into irrelevance. Essentially, the future of the UN in the 21st Century will hinge on its ability to address what ails the humanity in 2013 and beyond and not what it cured or didn't, in the last Century. While the UN has had a mixed bag of successes and failures over the last sixty-five years, it is the dilemmas, challenges and threats of today and beyond, that must be taken on by the UN squarely, if it hopes to have a future in the 21st Century.

Finding the answer to the question

In essence, the answer to the basic question, whether UN will be able to address the challenges of the 21st Century will largely depend on how the UN addresses some of the major issues that stare us in the face today. Some of these are elucidated at succeeding paragraphs.

Need for Global Governance

The Felt Need. The multifarious challenges of the 21st Century call for an macro-umbrella organisation that could provide 'global governance' a governance, whose domain, jurisdiction and writ must cover the entire planet. Today there is no 'World Govt' or 'World Parliament' though there are increasing demands to provide peacekeeping and peace building to initiate international regulations, to halt environmental degradation, alleviate poverty and inequality in the world, promote greater human economic and social well-being, provide humanitarian aid to the victims of natural disasters and violence, protect human rights for various groups... the list goes on. All these raise the felt need for a mechanism to provide 'global governance'. A set of rules, norms and organisational structures to manage trans-boundary and inter dependence problems that the Nation States acting alone cannot solve – problems, threats and challenges without boundaries; terrorism, crime, drugs, environmental degradation pandemics and human right violation, to name a few[52].

Global Governance: Responsibility and Challenges. No single Nation however big and strong, can take on the onerous responsibility of global governance. Thomas G Weiss and Ramesh Thakur argue in their book 'Global Governance and UN: An Unfinished Journey' that this great task of 'Governance without Govt' has to be provided by the UN[53]. But that is easier said than done, can the UN meet the new demands of Global Governance with simply adding more programmes? How various initiatives can be funded? Can the UN be more effective in coordinating the related activities of various institutions, States, NGOs? Can it improve its own management and personal practices? Can it adapt to deal with the changing nature of conflict and persistent poverty and inequality? Will it be able to reformat the UNSC which represents the power realities of 1945 to new Global World order of the 21st Century. Will the member States abide by their committed funding of UN programmes and empowering the Secretariat?

Complex Question : Difficult Answers. All the questions listed above are complex challenges which demand solutions. The key to all these and more lies in the capacity and willingness of the Nation States to commit themselves to international co-operation and the capacity of the UN to optimise its cumulative strength made up by its membership. The big question is, 'Will it happen?' Experts opine that for it to happen, UN has to shed the rigidity of its Central Structures, get over its slowness to accommodate non-state actors and adapt to the changing realities of geopolitics[54]. For the UN to succeed, the States will have to have a rethink on the concept of State Sovereignty.

The Concept of State Sovereignty

Westphalian Order Still Alive. When the Peace of Westphalia essentially ended European religious wars in 1648, powerful political structures accepted that the world should be divided into territorial states. The emergence of the territorial state was accompanied by the notion that the State was sovereign. Accordingly, the sovereignty of all other social groupings was legally subordinated to the States sovereignty[55]. State sovereignty was thus an idea that arose in a particular place at a particular time. The same however came to be widely accepted as European political influence spread around the world. As time passed, States guarded their sovereignty strongly, sharply resisting any interference to the same.

Charter Position in State Sovereignty. The above well-entrenched principle of State sovereignty and non-intervention in the domestic affairs of the State got affirmed in the UN charter. However, faced with the challenges of the contemporary world, the concept of State sovereignty has evolved on many fronts. Some illustrations are as under :-

(a) **Challenges without Boundaries.**[56]**21st Century World scenario presents problems and challenges without boundaries**; international terrorism, drug-abuse, human trafficking, environmental degradation human right violations... the list is endless. Addressing these challenges calls for actions that essentially transgress national boundaries. This international action is seen by member States as intervention in their sovereign rights to govern their States and resolve their issues. This contradiction in terms is a major issue.

(b) **Effect of Globalisation.** Global tele communications, world wide web, economic interdependence, global financial activities, international election monitoring, international environmental regulation are among many developments that infringe on State sovereignty and traditional areas of domestic jurisdiction. The growing activities of IGOs and NGOs have ended the centrality of States as primary actors in world politics. Multinational co-operation with operations in several countries and industry groups, such as oil, steel, textiles, automobiles have sometimes more resources and influence than an individual State. Their operations across boundaries are sometimes an affront to a State's perception of its own sovereign rights on deciding the fate of its business processes.

(c) **Global Compact**. Partnerships between the UN and the private sector including multinational co-operations have become increasingly important for a variety of governance challenges. The 'UN Global Compact initiative' by Secretary General Kofi Annan in 1999, is one suchstep[57].Since the UN partners in businesses are spread across nations boundaries, it sort of diminishes the control, the States can exercise over them in their domestic domains, i.e, Hyundai based in DPRK is aligned one-on-one to UN, and thus, to its international businesses globally through UN Compact. This to some extent, diminishes the exclusive control of DPRK over Hyundai in purely domestic domain.

(d) **Double Edge**. Nation States by ratifying various international treaties and conventions exercise their sovereign rights to accept a particular 'world position'. At the same time they loose a bit of their sovereign rights in allowing international monitoring of their activities assured to check adherence to the ratified Treaties and Conventions. The latter is generally resisted.

(e) **Humanitarian Intervention**. There is yet a very important dimension of humanitarian intervention. What the world community is to do when the State itself becomes enemy of its people? When it fails to alleviate human sufferings during violent conflict, when it fails to provide basic life sustaining needs or establish civil order, when it itself engages in genocide, mass killing, ethnic cleansing etc. While the worst act of domestic criminal behaviour by a State is large scale killing of its own people, the worst acts of international criminal behaviour is to attack/invade/ annex another country[58]. All these need to be deplored and the State is to be reigned if for nothing else, but to protect innocent human life. From this thought is born the concept of 'Responsibility to Protect' (R2P) which simply makes the world community 'responsible' to protect human life when the same is endangered by 'Excessive State Violence[59]. The actions pursuant to R2P are expectedly seen by the States as an intervention by the world on their perceived exclusive rights to State sovereignty. The conflict therefore rests between State Sovereignty and Humanitarian Intervention in the name of R2P. The call for international action against genocide in Darfur in 2005-06 was in pursuance of R2P. Similar drivers existed in world community's call to end suffering in Libya (2011) and in Syria (2012).

(f) **World Acceptance of R2P.** The 2005 World Summit endorsed the R2P norm but many States, particularly the developing countries feared its consequences for the norms of non-intervention and sovereignty. The dilemma continues.

It is on the outcome of this direct confrontation between the Westphalian roots of State sovereignty and non-interference vis-a-vis the challenges of globalization, 21st Century perils and R2P, that will decide the fate of the UN in the 21st Century. Another fact to note is that since the capacity to mobilise resources necessary to tackle global problems also remains vested in States, the tools to R2P are to come if the Nation States agree to pitch in[60].

Conclusion

This Chapter opened with a fundamental question, '**Can the UN address the challenges of the 21st Century**'. The answer is not an easy Yes or No but is contingent on a whole gamut of attendant factors and competing priorities. It is for the Nation States to either enable and strengthen the world body by looking beyond their narrow verticals of national interests or to doom the heritage of mankind into the black hole of irrelevance and marginalization. In addition, there are a host of 21st Century dilemmas to be addressed, as well as, the looming traps of past failures, that must be avoided.

Endnotes

1 Malcolm Templeton in Ramesh Thakur,ed. "Past Imperfect Future Uncertain: the UN at Fifty" UK Macmillan Press Ltd 1998, page 16.

2 Norman Lowe, "Mastering Modern World History" New Delhi, Macmillan Press, 1997, page 47.

3 Report of the Secretary General's High Level Panel on "Threats Challenges and Change : A More Secure World-Our Shared Responsibility" UN Document Number A/59/565 dated 02 Dec 04.

4 Report of the "UN Open Ended Committee On Reform Of The UN", New York 1994, page 12.

5 FP Watters, "A History of the League of Nations" (Oxford University Press), 1952, Vol 1, page 1-2.

6 Ramesh Thakur. op cit, page 16.

7 "UN, Human Rights-A Compilation of International Instruments" Volume 1, 1995, pages 51-54.

8 http:/nobelprize.org/nobel_prizes/peace/laureates/1988un_history.html. Accessed on 10 Mar 12.

9 Bijayalaxmi Misra, "UN and Security Challenges in New Millennium", New Delhi, 2004, page 48.

10 UN Monthly Chronicle, Nov-May, 1965, pages 38-39.

11 MP Vorster, "UNSC Resolution 418 (1974), South Africa Yearbook of International Law" 1978, Pretoria, pages 130-152.

12 Adam Roberts, "Humanitarian War, Military Intervention and Human Rights", New York 1993, pages 190-193.

13 Jonathan Power, "A Vision of Hope : The Fifteenth Anniversary of UN", London 1995, page 67.

14 Jonathan Power. Ibid, page 11.

15 Gold and Connolly, "Developments and the UN: Achievements and Future Challenges", page 71.

16 Gold and Connolly.ibid, page 23.

17 26 ibid, page 350.

18 UN, "The Blue Helmets : A Review of UN Peace Keeping" New York : Dept of Public Information 1996, page134.

19 David Mc Dowd, 'A Modern History of the Kurds", London : IB Tauris 1996,

pages 357-363.

20 UN General Assembly "Report of the Secretary General Pursuant to General Assembly Resolution 53/35 : The Fall of Srebrenica".

21 Richard Holbrooke, "To End a War" New York, Random House, 1998, page 99.

22 William Mallay, "The UN and Afghanistan : Doing its Best in Failure of Mission" in William Mallay, ed, "Fundamentalism Reborn! Afghanistan and Taliban" New York, NYU Press 2011, page 195.

23 'UN Chronicle' Volume 13 No 1 Mar 1993, pages 13-16.

24 "Report of the Secretary General: High Level Panel on Threats Challenges and Change: A More Secure World-Our Shared Responsibility", UN Document A/59/565, Dec 2004, pages 24-26.

25 "US Census Bureau, International Data Base"(http://www.census.gov/ipc/www/ibd/worldpopinfo.php.Accessed on 10 Mar 12.

26 "FAO News Release 2010" (http://www.fao.org/docrep/012/a1390e/.pdf. Accessed on 15 Mar 12.

27 "IFAD Rural Poverty Report 2011"(http://www.ifad.org/rpr2011.pdf. Accessed on 15 Mar 12.

28 "Human Development Report 2007/2008" (http://hdr.undp.org/en/reports/global. Accessed on 15 Mar 12.

29 "UNICEF State of the World Children, 2010" (http://www.unicef.org/rightsite/SOWC/pdf. Accessed on 15 Mar 12.

30 24 ibid paras 45 to 50, pages 24-25.

31 "UN AIDS Report in Global Epedemic, 2010" (http://www.unaids.org/global report). Accessed on 15 Mar 12.

32 "MDG Report – Goal 4, 2010" (http://mdgs.un.org/unsd/mdg/Resources/Stake/ Products/ Progress 2010/2010.Addendum Goal 14.pdf.Accessed on 15 Mar 12.

33 "WHO:Unsafe Water Sanitation and Hygiene" (http://www.who.int/publications/cra/chapters).Accessed on15 Mar 12.

34 Food and Agriculture Organisation 2011, "The State of Food Insecurity in the World 2011" (http ://www.fao.org/drcrep/013 /i1683e.pdf.) Accessed on 08 Apr 12.

35 International Food Policy Research Institute 2010, "2010 Global Hunger Index". Accessed on 08 Apr 12.

36 Report, "Environmental Degradation Threatens Global Progress For Poor", (http:/www/voonews.com/English/news/science-technology/environment.) Accessed on 08 Apr 12.

37 Thomas, G. Weiss and others, "The United Nations and Changing World Politics", Westviao Press, 2010, page 4.

38 "World Bank's Mini Atlas of Human Security", available at www.miniatlas of human security.info. Accessed on 06 May 2012.

39 htpp://www.en.wikipedia.org/wiki/the-clash-of-civilisation. Accessed on 06 May 2012.

40 Brahma Chellaney, "Water, Asia's New Battle ground", Georgetown University Press, Aug 2011.

41 "The Human Security Report 2005", New York Oxford University Press 2005, (www.Human security report.Info). Accessed on 06 May 12.

42 http://www.en.wikipedia.org/wiki/list-of-ongoing-military conflicts. Accessed on 06 May 12.

43 "A Definition Uppasala Conflict Data Programme" (http://www.pcr.w.se/research/vcdp/defects). Accessed on 06 May 12.

44 http://www.heritage.org/research/reports/2010/the-threat-of-nuclear-weapons. Accessed on 27 May 12.

45 http://www.edi.org/nuclear/database/nukestab.html, "Current World Nuclear Arsenal". Accessed on 27 May 12.

46 http://www.nti.org/analysis/reports/nis-nuclear-traficking-database. Accessed on 27 May 12.

47 David Mc Dowell, "A Modern History of the Kurds" London I.B Tauris 1996, pages 357-363.

48 Sunday's Zaman, 13 Apr 12.

49 UN Press Release SG/SM/7962/Rev.1 Sep 18 2001.

50 26(Chapter1) ibid, page 181.

51 http://www.guardian.co.uk/world-drug-trade. Accessed on 27 May 12.

52 Margeret.P.Karns and Karen A. Mingst. "International Organisations : The Politics and Processes of Global Governance", 2nd edition (Boulder : Lynne Rienner, 2009).

53 http://www.unhistory.org/briefing/15globalgovt.pdf. Accessed on 27 May 12.

54 http://www.fes-globalization .org/dept-publications/global-governance.htm. Accessed on 27 May 12.

55 Thomas G.Weiss and other, "United Nations and Changing World Politics". West views Press, 2010, pages i-iii.

56 "Problems without Borders" http://www.worldmapper.org/articles/variety-facs.pdf. Accessed on 27 May 12.

57 http://www. un global compact.org. Accessed on 27 May 12.

58 26 (Chapter 1) ibid. page 244.

59 14 (Chapter 1) ibid.

60 http://en.wikipedia.org/widi/responsibility.to.protect. Accessed on 27 May 12.

3

Curing the Ailments

> *"The United Nations today leads what seems at times alike a double. Pundits criticise it for not solving all the world's ills, yet people around the world are asking it to do more, in more places than ever before"*
>
> —Ban-Ki-Moon[1]

The preceding chapters have shown that the future of our 'World Heritage' in the 21st Century is contingent upon the complex outcomes of the multifarious actions it takes to address the many challenges, perils and dilemmas of our times in the foreseeable future. While, what the UN can do, or will be able to do, to address the above challenges are the 'action points for implementation', the first question is, 'Will the UN survive in the first place' or be 'relevant enough on the world stage' so as to take the action that we are envisaging it to take ? In this context, UN as a World Body is to be seen 'distinctly different' from the 'action' it takes (and outcomes thereof). The first question is the survival/intended relevance of the UN as a world body itself.

Dilemmas to Survival. In the context of above thought, the contemporary realities of the world present a few 'musts' which beckon to be addressed if the UN has to survive and remain relevant in the future. There are however, any numbers of obstacles in dealing with these 'musts' (read reforms). Conflicting national interests vis-a-vis the common good of humanity, deep political divides and vested interests of the 'share in the world pie' to name a few. These are the stumbling blocks to reforming the UN and make it survive/remain relevant so as to exist to take the actions, we are assigning to it. These 'musts' are discussed at succeeding paras.

Representation of the New World Order

The Basic Issue[2]. The first and the fundamental position of great discomfort and endless debate for the member States, is the fact, that the highest decision making body of the UN, the seat of power in world affairs, the UN Security Council (UNSC), represents a world of 1945 and not a world of 21st Century. The permanent five (P-5) which rule the UNSC today, may have been the major victor nations of World War II, some of them are no more the world leaders and economic power houses of the world today. The veto power of the P-5 on substantive world issues has been viewed by the rest of the world as something of an anarchism. The P-5 under-represent the majority of the world's population and principal financial contributes to UN. The legitimacy of the UNSC as the authoritative validator of international security action has been subjected to a steady erosion as it has been perceived to be unrepresentative in composition, undemocratic in approach and unaccountable to anyone below (General Assembly) or above (the World Court)[3].

The Many Faces of the Challenge[4]. While there is a near global acceptance of the need of UNSC re-structuring as the key to UN's future relevance, this challenge has many facets; Should the Security Council membership be expanded and diversified in line with the 'representative principle'? What arrangements can satisfy the criteria of representation and efficiency? Should voting be modified to alter the undemocratic bias of the veto power? How to bring a geographical balance at the top table where Europe is over-represented at the expense of Latin America, Africa and Asia? How the membership criteria could be made representative of the contributors to the regular budget, voluntary contributions to the UN activities, agencies and troop contribution? How can we achieve a position wherein those who contribute the most, should have a commensurate say in decision making?

Multi Deficits. Experts opine that UNSC suffers from quadruple legitimacy deficit; performance, representation, procedure and accountability. The performance deficit is represented by an uneven and selective record. Un-representation is glaring; in 1945, 51 member states were represented by P-5 and six non-permanent members; in 2012, 191 states are represented by the 'same' P-5 and 10 non-permanent members[5]. Its procedural legitimacy is suspect on grounds of lack of democratisation and transparency in decision making. Accountability is of course non-existent in the face of unchallengeable status of the High-5.

The Charter Position. The founders of the UN conferred primary responsibility on the Security Council for maintenance of international peace and security. The council was designed to enable the world body to act decisively to prevent and remove threats. It was created to be not just a **'REPRESENTATIVE'** body but also a **'RESPONSIBLE'** body, one that had a capacity for decisive action. The Charter (Article 23) established the membership in the Council as a whole and explicitly linked the same, not just to the geographical balance, but also, to the contributors to maintaining peace and security in the world at that point in time.

What is the Challenge? The challenge is to increase both the effectiveness and credibility of the Security Council. It is because of the following main reasons that this challenge has become the order of the day (Researcher's inputs) :-

(a) **Changed World Order**. It is very clear that the world order represented by the war victorious nations of 1945 which founded the UN is totally different from the world of 2012, and more precisely, from the world of 21st Century. This world demands that the new pegging order be represented on the high table. The hierarchy of world order must flow out, not only from the military might (as in 1945), but also from a host of other determinants of the Comprehensive National Power (CNP). These include economic power, industrial power, demographic power, power of natural resources (water, oil, minerals, etc) and also the interse position (acceptability) of a Nation State among the comity of Nations.

(b) **The Status-Quo Issue**. When the UN was formed in 1945, 51 Nation States were represented by five permanent members. It is only paradoxical that even in 2013, when the numbers of Nation States are 193, these continue to be represented by the same five nations. Nothing can be a more skewed representation.

(c) **Responsibility-vs-Representation**. Clearly, the criteria for the P-5 in 1945 was not representation but responsibility and capability/ capacity of victorious nations to keep order in international peace and security. The world demands representation. It is ironic that the entire African continent with 53 nations has no representation at all in P-5. Also, the entire Asia and Pacific with 56 countries and Americans with 35 countries have only one representative while the continental Europe with just 47 countries have grabbed 60% (3 out of 5) of all the seats of UNSC. How unreasonable is this, is well understood by the world today, which is demanding change on the basis of representation.

(d) **Veto- A Curse of Anarchy**[6]. That the veto by the five permanent members has been the biggest stumbling block in the actions of the UN, requires no explanations. A total of 257 vetoes by the P-5 from a period of 1946-2004 shows the power-play of narrow natural interest and a dirty game of one-upmanship in the erstwhile bipolar world (total vetoes from 1946 to 2004 are 257, out of which 239 vetoes relate to Cold War period, 1946-89). The overwhelming world opinion strongly favours abandoning the curse of veto, and if that is not possible, at least diluting it or expanding its base.

One Challenge-Multiple Solution[7]. In order to address the near insurmountable challenge of a truly representative, responsible and democratic Security Council, multiple solutions have been put forward. There is an overwhelming consensus that the Council needs greater representation of Africa, Asia and Latin America and that the permanent members must better reflect geopolitics and economics. Proposed additions to P-5 perhaps include Germany, Japan (and possibly India). Another view proposes an addition of one member each from Asia and Latin America and two from Africa. The problem is how to select ? Another school of thought calls for no permanent members/no new permanent members. Recommendations on the veto issue have many shades-eliminate/increase base/give it only to sole-super power/no veto to new members. The bottom line is, '**EQUITABLE REPRESENTATION**', but also a size small enough to preserve the ability to act[8].

A Possible Solution. The Report of the Secretary General's High Level Panel (HLP) on Threats, Challenges and Change suggests two models of solutions for re-structuring of the Security Council. These are briefly described below :-

(a) **Model A.**

Regional Area	**Number of States**	**Permanent seats (continu-ing)**	**Proposed New Per-manent Seat**	**Proposed Two-Year Seats (non-re-newable)**	**Total**
Africa	54	0	2	4	6
Asia & Pacific	57	1	2	3	6
Europe	47	3	1	2	6
Americas	35	1	1	4	6
Totals Model A	**193**	**5**	**6**	**13**	**24**

This model depicted below, basically aims to correct the representative anomaly of the UNSC. This is proposed to be achieved by granting two new member vacancies to Africa and one additional to Asia Pacific region. The increase of three is partially to be offset by down scaling Europe from three to one thus correcting its over representation. None of the six members have any veto. In addition, the Model calls for new, two year non renewable seats, again fully representative of all the regions proportionally, as described above.

(b) **Model B.**

Regional Area	**Number of States**	**Permanent seats (continuing)**	**Proposed New Per-manent Seat**	**Proposed Two-Year Seats (non-re-newable)**	**Total**
Africa	54	0	2	4	6
Asia & Pacific	57	1	2	3	6
Europe	47	3	2	1	6
Americas	35	1	2	3	6
Totals Model A	**193**	**5**	**6**	**11**	**24**

In recognition of the difficulties of shaking the current status-quo of the P-5, this Model proposes eight four year renewable seats and 11 two year non-renewable seats, proportionally representing the regions of the world described above. Clearly, this model aims to address the representation anomaly with creation of counter-weight seats without disturbing the P-5[9].

A Curious Oddity[10]. Ramesh Thakur, the noted UN Scholar in his seminar work 'The United Nation Peace and Security' (2 ibid) opines, that the UNSC reform is held hostage to a curious oddity. While there is consensus on the need for reform, the agreement breaks down as soon as any one formula or package is proposed. This is so because once the people see the details of a concrete proposal, losers and opponents always seem to outnumber the winners and supporters. One possible reason for this is, that the concept of 'equitable representation' has many meanings and interpretations depending on how a State looks at it from its own national interest point of view. The noted scholar suggests five parameters on which the representation issue can be decided. These include, the strength of the elected parliamentarian or population distributions (India's population is more than whole of Africa and almost double of Latin America), or the quantum of financial burden borne (Germany and Japan bear heavy burden with no representation) or the representation could be made reflective of cultures, religions and civilisations of the world[11].

Based on the analysis of the facts, the following is brought out:-

(a) **A Major Factor**. One of the major deciding factor in keeping the UN effective and relevant in the 21st Century would be to correct the anomaly of an unrepresentative, undemocratic and a skewed UNSC.

(b) **The Likely Eternity of the Current P-5**. The above notwithstanding, given the realities of the world and the complex and inter-twined interests of geopolitics of major players, it will be most unlikely to drop any of the exiting P-5 for the sake of representative correction. The answer would probably lie in creating counter weights of proportional representation.

(c) **Representation Dilemma**. The best way of resolving the representation paradox is to be governed by Nation States and Geographical Regions. This is so, because the 'Westphalian Order' still reigns supreme (Tuvalu, a Nation State of 11810 people[12] is as much a full member of UN as China with 1,347,350,000 people[13]); and secondly our sensibilities of world distribution are driven by geographical entities (Africa, Asia, Europe, Americas, etc).

(d) **On Veto Power**. It is most unlikely that the P-5 will let go their veto. The ideal solution (which is a no go) is 'No veto' but a practical solution will be an enhanced veto base spread across new members (albeit with diluted effect) or ratification of P-5 veto across new members.

(e) **Possible Way Out**. The only possible way out will be through a constructive dialogue process conducted in a spirit of give and take outside the corrupting influences of narrow national interests or group opinion pressures of various caucuses (indeed an utopian thought !). Ramesh Thakur flags the degree of difficulty quote, "If 16 distinguished world citizens acting as individuals (referring to HLP, 10 ibid) cannot choose between Model A and Model B, can 191 separate Governments do so?", unquote[14].

World is standing on hope and the hope is that some day we will have the world order represented proportionately, democratically and un-biasedly at the UNSC – a requirement crucial to the future of the United Nations in the 21st Century.

Financing – Keeping The Un Alive

"*When the scope of our responsibilities and the hopes invested in us are measured against our resource, we confront a sobering truth*"

—UN Secretary General[15]

Financing – An Existentional Issue. All debate on the future of the UN in the 21st Century must take the second place to the most fundamental question - 'Will the UN 'survive' as an international institution in the first place?' The future debate only comes later. The problem of UN survival is directly related to the member States (especially US), meeting up their obligations to fulfil their budget obligations.

Some Peculiar Facts About UN Budget. In order to make viable recommendations on the future of UN financing, some peculiarities about the UN budget/financing need be highlighted. These are as under :-

(a) **Complex Budgets.** The UN Budget comprises of three separate budgets, A regular budget to cover its administrative machinery, major agencies and their auxiliary agencies; a budget for peace-keeping organisations; and a budget to fund economic and social programmes.

(b) **Sources of Funding.** The above budgets are funded in three different manners; compulsory subscription by member States to ordinary budget; compulsory subscription by member States to Peace Keeping budgets and voluntary contributory payments to special agencies and programmes[16].

(c) **Budgets Have Soared. Over time, all the above budget figures have soared.** Normal budget has grown from $20 million in 1946 to $ 2.4 billion in 2009. Peace Keeping Budget has swelled to $ 7 billion in 2009.

(d) **Payment Liabilities.** The scale of contribution is worked out based on a special key (formula) which takes into account the Gross National Product for the last six years, per capita income, economic destructions (such as war) and the country's international debt liabilities.

Financing Woes. The UN financing woes are due to non-payment of compulsory dues by the member States, that too the main culprits are large debtors, led by USA. In the late 1990's the UN faced its most serious financial crises with member States owing more than $2.5 billion for the current and past assessments. In 2009, the arrears to UN regular budget amounted to $ 829 million out of which 93% was owed by the US alone.

Volunteerism[17]. The irony is, that the UN lacks the financial muscle or mechanism to enforce what is desired. The route to solve every issue is anchored in the concept of 'volunteerism'. It is for this reason that UN Reforms always remain an elusive goal. Even if a Nation State does not pay its compulsory contribution, the only way out is through persuasion. The dilute measures of putting restriction in the voting rights in the General Assembly or the act of naming and shaming is unlikely to have the effect of ensuring that the dues are indeed paid.

Possible Way Out. The researcher feels that a fresh exercise of ODA liabilities be undertaken by the UNSC based on current realities and payment capabilities. Interests should be charged on late payments except for a few very low income countries in genuine financial difficulties/debt trap. Deliberate non-payment should attract sanctions. In the new exercise, the cost of ending the Single-State-Dominance by the sole-super power and hence the feeling of living 'in mercy' or as a 'financial hostage', should be ended, by the financial burden being shared by middle order economic powers based on their respective economic capability, as assessed by the UNSC.

Actions at the UN. While the above, (which is indeed a very tall order, essentially based on the pure willingness of the many States to resolve this issue) is recommended to be put into effect, the UN, led by the UNSC must undertake a massive exercise of introspection with an aim to reason and realign its priorities and learn to manage their finances within regular budgets. If rampant corruption, huge wastages and gross spending on non-essentials can be controlled, the same will be possible. In this context, there is also a case for winding down non-essential UN bodies/ committees/ commissions/agencies where independent and vertical tasking patterns can be dual/multi-hatted to a fewer essential ones.

Finding Ways and Means of Alternate Funding.In addition to the above exercise, an expert group under UNSC should examine in a time-bound manner, various proposals for providing to the UN access to autonomous/ alternative sources of funding. Many practical financing options have been put forward by experts. These could include, taxes in currency speculations (Tobin Tax) etc. Paul Hawken has made the viable suggestions in his book "Ecology of Commerce" to put a tax on missiles, planes, tanks and guns sold (ie. Tax on international arms sale)[18]. The main problem with implementing such a tax would be funding acceptance. Although such a system might find acceptance within some nations, particularly those with a history of neutrality or without an active military (Costa Rica) or with lower levels of military spending (Japan 1% of GDP), it would be unpopular among many consumers of arms. Other likely opponents will be nations engaged in ongoing military conflicts. Arms producers are likely to oppose the idea too. Another tax which the UN might promote is **Global Resource Dividend** by which, the Nation States are made to provide financial support to the UN based on their assessed possession of Global Resources[19].

Some Corrections Required Within. In the current scheme of things some corrections are required within the system. Firstly, the unwarranted favouring of States which are not held to account in a manner appropriate to their economic efficiency by the system of subscription must end. Imagine the share of China to the rate of contribution to the ordinary UN budget since 2002 standing at a mere 1.55% and that of Russia at 1.20%, compared to the US share of 22.0%. There is a strong case for reviewing this rate.

Another sub-optimality which must come under the anvil is the non-satisfactory resource management in the UN and the need to cut down the unnecessary flab of non-essentials Committees/Organisations etc. There is also a need to curb the cumbersome administrative processes that eat up disproportionate financial resources. In fact, sustaining the non-essential flab of the UN along with poor efficiency of work doubles the intensity of financial crisis. For a practical and a lasting solution to this crisis, it is necessary to take the following actions[20] :-

(a) **Mountains of Debt.** Reduce the mountain of debt in the form of non-payment of subscription dues by member States, most notably by USA, the largest single debtor.

(b) **Address the US Imbroglio.** The above is not going to happen unless the persistent demand of US to reduce its subscription rate is addressed in some manner. The only way to arrive at a viable solution would be to re-visit the rates of contribution of the Nation States both to the Ordinary Budget, as well as, Peacekeeping Budget; and adjust/correct/re-order the same, based on current ground realities, economic power and share of global resources owned by a State. We might end up reducing the US share at the cost of others, who need to pay. Ironically, the route to this salvation is through a difficult, tunnel of persuasion and consensus, which is more absent than present in international negotiations and are invariably eclipsed by perceived national interests/vulnerabilities/inter-state rivalries.

Reforming Adminstration, Management And Co-Ordination

A Major Factor. Another major factor impinging upon the future of the UN in 21st Century is the administrative viability of the organisation and the management and co-ordination of its processes, and finances in a cost-effective manner. This is a huge and a mammoth task and a very tall order to implement. Much of the research content is dedicated to addressing various aspects of this main issue. At the overall macro level, a few important issues need to be flagged :-

(a) **Right Sizing the UN Secretariat**. The UN Secretariat has continuously grown. From a mere 300 in 1946 to 14,691 in 1994. It was cut down to less than 8000 in the early years of the millennium but has grown again. This huge bureaucratic and secretarial monolith needs to be right-sized and kept in check through cutting down non-essential posts/programmes and duplications[21].

(b) **Best Management Practices**. The first five Secretary Generals paid little attention to introduction of best management practices like internal audits, performance evaluations, programme reviews, expenditure oversight committees, checks on recruitments/ promotion practices in the UN activities and procedures. The result felt over many years are huge wastages/duplications and sub-optimal expenditures[22]. The **'Quiet Revolution' started by Kofi Anan** in 1997 to merge departments, cut costs and build a code of staff conduct needs to be carried forward with vigour. There is a need to bring greater 'accountability and responsibility' for expenditures vs. results in all UN endeavours[23].

(c) **Cutting Out Corruption**. As a part of the world-wide phenomenon, the corrupt practices have also made inroads in the UN structures . The investigation report of the infamous scandal of 'Oil for Food Programme' ripped away the curtain and showed the unsightly corners of UN. There is a need to clean the mess, make people accountable, and achieve the bang for each buck. The establishment of Internal Oversight Services with a degree of operational independence in 1998 is a step in the right direction. There is a need to introduce measures to improve the performance of senior management, monitor individual performances, deal with frauds and corruption, ensure whistle blower protection and ensure financial disclosure and enhanced transparency in procurements/contracts/ payments etc.

(d) **Cutting Out Duplications**. The problem of multiple agencies engaged in similar tasks has plagued the UN from the beginning. There is a huge lack of co-ordination in the areas of economic and social development and in humanitarian crisis. Clearly, there is a need to review the operations of the ECOSOC end–to–end, to include appropriateness of rule, flushing out duplicity through ruthless cutting on non-essential organisations, programmes, projects and optimally knitting in the numerous NGOs so that they do not become blood-suckers/parasites or financial drag blocks but act as effective force-multipliers/whistle blower/support agencies.

Conclusion

The pie of the UN resources is very finite and in fact shrinking. The future of this body will depend on how this pie is cut skilfully and exploited optimally. Failure to do this will make the huge structure of UN, crumble under the dead weight of financial liabilities, wastages, duplications, over-size, as also, deep-rooted corrupt practices.

Endnotes

1 UN Secy General Ban Ki Moon, quoted in Sidney Morning Herald, Dec 31, 2010.

2 Peter Weltensleen, "Representing the World; A Security Council for 21st Century "Security Dialogue 25 No (1994) page 67.

3 Aryeh Neier, " The Quest For Justice", New York Review, 8 Mar 2001, page 34.

4 2 (Chapter 1) ibid, Page 302.

5 Ramesh Thakur, ed, "What is Equitable Geographic Representation in the 21st Century?", Tokyo, United Nations University 1999.

6 26 (Chapter 1) ibid. page 308.

7 James A. Paul, "Security Council Reform's Arguments about the Future of the United Nations (1995)" http://www.globalpolicy.org/security/pubs/secret.htm. Accessed on 10 Jun 12.

8 Edward C. Luck, " The UN Security Council; Irrelevant or Indispensible? The United Nation in the 21st Century", ed. Paul Heinbeacker and Patricia Golf (Water loo, Canada, Wilfred Laurier Press, 2005, page 148.

9 24 (Chapter 2) ibid, page 81.

10 26 (Chapter 1) ibid.

11 Amy Gutman and Dennis Thompson, "Democracy and Disagreement", Cambridge MA Harward University Press, 1996, page 4.

12 http://www.ask.com/questions_about/least_popular_UN_Member. Accessed on 10 Jun 12.

13 http://en.wikipedia.org/wiki/list_of_countires_by_population. Accessed on 10 Jun 12.

14 26 (Chapter) ibid page 305.

15 Secretary General Kofi Anan, quoted in Millennium Report "We the Peoples".

16 "The UN Financial Crises", http://www.dadalos.org/uno_int/grundkurs_5/finanzen.htm. Accessed on 17 Jun 12.

17 Margel P. Karns and Karen A Mingst, "The United Scales as Dead Beat?" US Policy and "UN Financial Crises, Boulder" Lynne Rienner 2002, pages 267-294.

18 Paul Hawken, " The Ecology of Commerce". Harper Collins, 1993, ISBN 978-0-88730-704-1.

19 http://www. en.wikipedia org/wiki/Reform-of-the-United-Nations. Accessed on 17 Jun 12.

20 http ://www.dadalos.org/uno_int/grundkurs_5/finanzen.htm. Accessed on 17 Jun 12.

21 http://www. en.wikipedia.org/United-Nations. Accessed on 17 Jun 12.

22 http://www.unescap.org/.../full_report_on _the_inspection_of /20 rbm_practice. Accessed on 17 Jun 12.

23 United Nations, "Report of the Panel in United Nations Peace Operations (Brahimi Report)",

4

From Ideas To Action

"This is an opportunity which may not occur again until another generation has passed, to transform the UN by aligning it with, and equipping it for the substantive challenges it faces in the 21st Century".

—Mr. Kofi Annan,UNSG[1]

How the UN must adapt to the 21st Century

The book so far has highlighted the contours of the threats which confront us in the 21st Century and has enumerated and the major dilemmas that face the UN on the successful resolution on which, hangs its future in the 21st Century. The stage is now set to transform ideas into actions. Quite obviously, the content that follows forms the heart of the entire research work.

The approach that has been followed to deal with this portion is as under :-

(a) It has been premised that for many good reasons towards the preservation of the civilised world order, the UN has to survive and flourish in the 21st Century.

(b) Keeping the above as the term of reference, what needs to be done in various macro level functional domains of the UN has been analysed.

At the macro level, the action areas identified are as under :-

(a) How the UN must adapt to the 21st Century?

(b) The Millennium Project – from words to action.

(c) Implementing the recommendations of the High Level Panel on

'Threats, Challenges and Change'.

(d) Implementing the Secretary General's Report on 'In larger Freedom'.

(e) Steps to achieve 'Freedom from Want' and 'Freedom from Fear'.

(f) Towards Effective, Efficient and Equitable Security in the Emerging World Order.

The UN is a complex system consisting of multiple actors. For the UN to adapt to the 21st Century, its multiple actors must do likewise. Who are these actors and how they need to adapt to the 21st Century has been analysed in the succeeding paragraphs.

Who Are the Actors? Undoubtedly, the 'Member States' are central to the UN since the organisation was formed by the States. UN depends on the States for its sustenance and is directed by the States in a complex interplay of interests which may either be purely national, i.e, focussed on a particular State, or may belong to a group/community or race, or may have religious overtures and compulsions. Over the years, it was the States that remained central to what the UN did, or did not do. As the years rolled by, the international world order got shaped by the complex interplay of human destiny playing out through the instruments of geopolitics and geostrategy. What emerged from the oblivion were the middle powers, emerging powers, small States, neo-independent States coming out from the shackles of their colonial past, blocks, coalition and NGOs and more. Each of these has a face, an identity and its own propulsion today. The desired end state that each of them may pull the UN boat in cohesion, is at best a utopian dream, still far into the horizon[2]:-

(a) **The Secretariat.**[3] Quite distinct from the Nation States, the members of the UN Secretariat, particularly the Secretary General and other major officials have, over time, acquired authority, influence and legitimacy which enables them to act at times, without the explicit directions of the governing bodies and a majority of member States. Consistent with the constructivist views, the UN professional staff may influence the actions of the member States and others because of their expertise and role as important sources of ideas. Therefore the actions of this group consisting of the UNSG and other specialized agency secretariats are material to the UN and will decide what the UN would achieve/

not achieve in the 21st Century.

(b) **NGOs.**[4] The other players in the reckoning as a force who will decide the destiny of the UN in the 21st Century, are the NGOs whose numbers have mushroomed over the years. Increasingly, the peoples in whose name the UN charter was drafted are exerting their voices through these very NGOs and other civil society groups. External experts, scholars, consultants and committed citizens. Certain NGOs have worked with the UN bodies and Secretariat for long but their roles as actors in the UN system has grown in the recent years. Members of the NGOs frequently provide new ideas, advocate new policies and mobilise public support for UN activities[5] .

The Three UNs. It therefore becomes clear that the major players which have an important role in shaping the destiny of the UN in the 21st Century are basically the member States, the Secretariat and the NGOs. These are loosely referred to as the 'Three UNs'. This distinction was given by Iris Claude in his 1956 classic work 'Swords into Ploughshares'[6].

Relevance of Actors (Three UNs) in the Current Research. Since the entire body and spirit of the UN is contained and represented by the three actors, namely the member States, UN and Secretariat and the NGOs, the complex interplay of their roles and the positions that they take in times to come, will be critical in deciding what will be the future of the UN in the 21st Century. This makes a detailed examination of each player in this trio, central to my research. The takeaway from this examination will be some recommendations which would emerge for each of the constituents to follow, if the UN is to remain relevant in the 21st century.

Role of States – The Likely and Desired

A Broad Classification. For the purpose of discussion and research, the member States can be broadly divided into four broad identifiable groups. Besides the US as the only surviving super-power (though with many dents now) in the uni-polar world, there are major powers (Russia, China, France, UK, Germany and Japan), middle powers (representing a whole lot of traditional and emerging power), as well as, small and developing States. Besides this, there is a cumulative entity represented by Coalitions, Blocks and Caucusing Groups, both with regional and multilateral forces. Since the likely/desired role of each of thesecountries/groups depend very much where they belong to, it is appropriate to discuss them along these lines.

United States

Ramesh Thakur in his seminal work '*The United Nations, Peace and Security*' describes the US-UN relationship as 'pas de duex'. He states that because of the sustaining belief in being a virtuous power, the US is basically averse to domesticating international values and norms. Many Americans seem to want to use the UNSC as a forum of concentrated power to control the actions of all other countries[7]. Notwithstanding a plethora of views, for and against the US-UN relationship, the purpose of the research will be served by examining the following two questions:-

(a) What has been the broad pattern of US-UN relations over the six decades plus of UN's existence?

(b) What does this pattern indicate and what is desired of US to ensure a healthy future of UN in the 21st Century?

The Roller-Coaster of US-UN Relationship

(a) **Ambivalent Rules.** True to the coinage of Ramesh Thakur, the US-UN 'pas de deux' has a prominent signature of ambivalence with noticeable highs and lows along the sands of time. It will be right to say that as a dominant power post World War II, US was the anchor-pin in the establishment of the UN. The Bretton Woods Conference of 1944, which aimed to create a new international monetary and trade regime, opened world markets and promoted a liberal economy, is considered to be the most important US contribution in laying the foundation of UN[8].

(b) **The Highs.** To start with, the UN Charter was consistent with US interests and there was a time up to, say 1960s, when US could count on majority support on major issues. US used the UN in gaining collective legitimisation of its own actions - Korean War 1950, Cuban Missile Crisis 1963, Iran Hostage Crisis 1979, Gulf War 1990-91, international support post 9/11, etc. A golden era of uni-polar moment arrived for US post the fall of Soviet Union in 1991 to about the beginning of financial crisis in 2008. This period saw the US support to the UN peace keeping challenges and Clinton administration's short-lived policy of assertive multilateralism to share the responsibilities for global peace by supporting an invigorated UN. This however remained short-lived as US soon turned to unilateral actions. Even in the current times, there have been mixed bag of 'highs' and 'lows' in US-UN relationship. For the 'highs', the Obama administration gives an indication of taking UN seriously. In 2009 US has paid its peace keeping arrears and has signed the convention on Rights of Persons with Disabilities. US joined P-5 in protecting Libyans against their Govt with the use of force. It also remains supportive of Kofi Annan's Peace Plan on Syria[9].

(c) **The Lows**. After around the 1960s, with the emergence of many developing countries, blocks/coalitions/caucusing groups, the majority support of US actions in the UN started to wane. US withdrew from ILO in 1978 (rejoining it later), from UNESCO in 1984 (rejoined in 2003). With a demand for the New International Economic Order, and linking of Zionism with racism, the opposition to US unilateralism grew sharply and there was a tangible drop in the majorities voting with US in UNGA. This alienation of US grew over time, as US perceived UN to be a 'hostile place' and consequently, around 1985, the Congressional support to paying UN dues declined[10]. By mid 1990's, the problems with UN missions in Somalia, Bosnia and Rwanda had a devastating effect on US-UN relationship. Unilateral actions followed - convention banning anti-personal mines (1997), refusal to sign Kyoto Protocol (1997), opposition to International Criminal Court (1998), rejection of CTBT (1999). The lowest ebb came when the US reduced the UN to irrelevance by going to war against Iraq in 2003 without the latter's authorisation. The tide again turned upwards as the US returned to UN seeking Security Council's help in the post-war challenges in Iraq and Afghanistan.

(d) **US-Internal Scene and UN**. Internally, the US-UN relations get affected by a host of other factors which include, domestic policies, the approach of presidential leadership, executive legislative relations, lobbying by domestic groups, public opinions and a sharp partisan divide between the Democrats and Republicans. Overall, the US has generally supported the idea of UN reforms (though many hold counter view). A 2008 poll in US reported that 79% respondents want the UN to be strengthened to investigate human rights violations, arrest genocidal leaders and organise a permanent peace keeping force. About 40% feel that UN was doing a good job[11].

(e) **The Perception of the 'West' – Some Reflections.** Despite the 'US-UN sugar and spice', American preferences on many issues embodied in US policies and backed by US power have explained a great many public policies emanating from the UN or its associated specialized agencies managing the institution of Global economy[12].

Following points are deliberated:-

(a) **US Still Very Much There in the Lead.** Despite all the financial downturns, rising credits, tough global competition and negative effects of Global War on Terror (GWOT) on the country's economy, US still has solid strengths. It is near certain that its economy will upturn in coming years, its military and technological strengths, which are unmatched even today the world over, are only going to grow maintaining a clear lead. Essentially, US will remain a formidable and a deciding strength in what the UN does, or does not do, in the 21st Century.

(b) **The Flip Side.** While the above is stated, it is for US to realize that the type of global dominance it enjoyed in the uni-polar heaven from about the demise of the erstwhile Soviet Union in 1991 to the economic shocker in 2008, no longer exists[13].

(c) **The New World.** The US must also realize the fact, that the type of world that was in the sixties and seventies when the US could count on majorities almost as a 'right' or 'given', no more holds. The new and the emerging world realizes its growing strengths, clouts and intense equations vis-a-vis US, which may perceive as a fading/declining/defaulting force in many areas that define comprehensive national power and world stature. The reality that the UN is no longer its 'backyard' of the type it used to be, must dawn on us.

(d) **Unilateralism Won't Hold.** With the major portion of the world community standing in rebellion, the US must realise the fact that unilateral actions (of the type in 2003) will become largely unsustainable. These will only end up isolating the US and alienating it more and more from the 'World Today'.

(e) **In Essence.** The bottom line is that US requires the UN as much as, vice-versa. If only the US could realize that the route to success today is through consensus and coalition rather than hegemony/ unilateralism/ superpower card, the UN will be secure and flourishing in the 21st Century.

Role of Other Major Powers as Actors

Soviet Union/Russia.

(a) **Basic Attitude : Cold War Years.** Much of the history of six decades of the once formidable USSR (and now resurgent again: Russia) has been anchored on an adversial reciprocity with its one time peer – USA. In the early years of the UN's existences and right through the Cold War period (say 1945-1975), USSR used its veto power 113 times. Many a times it sided with the majority blocks opposing US unilateralism/hegemony/big-brother attitude. It never was a part of Bretton Woods institutions and basically followed an anti US stand[14].

(b) **Demise : Post Cold War.** With the demise of USSR and the Cold War winding up, Russia's need for a comeback became inevitable. Standing on a weak and shaky platform, its once formidable and nearly granted opposition to US stance, mellowed. It allowed UN watch over its withdrawal from Afghanistan, abandoned its long term ally (Iraq) and supported the US-UN action. As the reality of its dismemberment became more and more telling, Russia aligned more and more with US[15].

(c) **Today's Scene.** Today a resurgent Russia, riding on its recoiling economy and drawing strength from its vast oil reserves besides a turning-around arms sale is no more a down-and-out erstwhile super power that it used to be. It is very much on the comeback trail. The veto stance in awareness of its P-5 exclusivity has started returning (veto on Yugoslavia, veto-US action in Iraq 2003 and now Syria). A little softening to give more latitude to US, was seen as its own house caught fire (Chechnya)[16]. A mixed sugar and spice relationship continues.

(d) **The Desired End State.** According to the **Researcher's sense,** the desired end state of Russia-UN relation that will be conducive to the healthy future of the UN in the 21st Century is stated below :-

(i) **Growing Stature**. The growing stature of Russia is good both as a damper of uni-polar dominance, as well as, for bringing in a more balanced international order.

(ii) **Increased Financial Responsibility**. As Russia recoils back, it must pick up its financial responsibility towards UN (currently at a paltry 1.6%[17]) commensurate to its comprehensive national power. Its contribution must be reversed upwards.

(iii) **New International Order**. The World is eager to see a more accommodative stand from Russia on the P-5 table when it comes (if ever) to recognising and accommodating the new international order.

France and Britain

(a) **Power States.** The once War-victorious huge colonial powers have had a prominent role and position in the six plus decade of UN's history. Both as permanent members of the P-5 have opposed re-structuring based on NIEO. Both have sufficient clout of 'ownership' flowing out of their share in the UN budget (6% and 8% respectively).

(b) **World Positions**. Both the countries have extended umbrellas of their influences through their continued links/influence in their erstwhile colonies and a flourishing 'commonwealth' lineage. Since both belong to the 'North', they have showed the expected and traditional resistance to the North-South divide. They have stood with the US mostly, rarely in the opposite camp, though France has always opposed US stance in intervention with the UNSC authorization. Both countries have strong and permanent positions in UN structures (UNESCO, ILO, ICJ, ECOSOC, WHO etc)[18].

(c) **Desired End State.**

(i) **More Accommodation**. While both the countries are likely to retain their position of centrality and prime influence, in the UN, it is only to be hoped that as a part of 'North Camp' both these countries show a bit more accommodation to the restructuring demands of South, based on NIEO.

(ii) **Counter Weight Stance.** The French Stand, in defiance of uni-polar hegemony/dominance is a good counterweight to irrationality of US. This brings a semblance of a balance. The same is hoped in future as well. May be, more strengthened by like-minded countries.

China

(a) **Deserved to be Counted.** With a second largest economy just behind the USA as of 2010, huge foreign exchange reserves, largest holder of American debt, largest donor to African Countries, a home to more than 1/6 of all the humanity and the only non-Western member of the P-5, China demands to be counted and deserves to be counted in the first-rank countries of the world and a key factor in the UN[19].

(b) **China's Coming of Age.** Wresting and occupying the once sleepy and inactive seat of the Republic of China (ROC) in P-5, the Peoples Republics of China (PRC), after a long non-interfering and non-participating status in the UN spanning nearly 50 years (which many scholars call a 'deep learning course') and mediated by its ambitions, changing perceptions and unique perspectives, has indeed come on the front stage by its own achievements and with a rising national pride[20]. As regards its historical positions, China has traditionally sided with G-77 and NAM and has selectively used its veto where its various national interest (oil) demanded (US action in Iraq-2003). It has only very reluctantly supported Darfur, sanctions against Iran in 2010 and the UN sanctioned intervention in Libya 2011.

(c) **Growing Assertiveness.** China's growing assertiveness in UN affairs is eminently visible. Paying an enhanced share in UN budget (3% up from 0.1%); pressurising world community to hold the Fourth World Conference on Women in China; calling for a new international currency to replace the dollar; taking strong participative position at the UN high table, China is and will be a key factor in the destiny of the UN in the 21st Century[21].

(d) **Desired End State (Researcher's Inputs).** In the view of the Researcher, the desired end state of the PRC that is conducive to the future of UN is as under:-

(i) **Continued Support**. China's continued support and backing of various blocks and caucuses (like G-20, G-77, NAM etc) are desirable to bring a semblance of balance and a support of at least one of the P-5 on this side of the divide.

(ii) **On Growing Assertiveness**. China's growing assertiveness, its one-on-one with the US in dominance on the world stage (especially economic forums) and its power projection through the veto route, is a good counter balance to US (read big power block) one-sided dominance. The same is a desired stance.

(iii) **India's Chances**. It is only to be hoped (actually with no hope) that PRC will ever support India's ambition for a permanent seat in the UNSC. Given the blow hot - blow cold attitude in the Sino-Indian relations, China will continue to be the biggest hurdle in the Indian dream of a chair at UNSC (even in extended P-10/P-15 etc).

Germany and Japan

Initially keeping a low profile as defeated powers of World War II, both the countries endeavoured a rebound on the world stage by joining the UN (Japan-1956, Two Germanys-1973). Actually it was the self-propulsion of the growing economic might of these resurgent power houses that gave them a 'natural calling card' in UN affairs. One of the most amazing things is, that in order to get adequate leverage in the UN system in consonance to their financial load bearing of the UN hostilities both countries have amended their respective constitutions so as to permit the members of their armed forces to be a part of UN peacekeeping programmes[22,23,]. Accordingly, Japan contributed 2000 Japanese troops in Cambodia while Germany has sent more than 7000 soldiers to UN and UN-Mandated operations in Kosovo, Ethiopia, Georgia, Liberia, Lebanon, Sudan and Afghanistan. Both the countries have shown their desire to be a permanent members of the United Nations Security Council. In many ways the claim is well justified given their growing clout, huge economic progress and a lion's share in their contribution to the UN Budget. Undoubtedly, these claims to their desired end state will be as subjected to the same huge resistance by the present P-5 as is faced by the rest of the world.

As regards the above two countries, the following inputs are relevant:-

(a) **Conducive to UN Interests.** The continued all-round growth of these two countries is conducive to the growth and future of the UN in the 21st Century, for not only it signals a continued and healthy fund flow into the UN budget kitty, but also, provides on the world platform, two strong and mature members in the international opinion/action debates.

(b) **UNSC-Seat Remote.** There are very remote chances of the two countries making it to the P-10/P-15, however the debates will go on.

(c) **UN Peacekeeping.** Will continue to get a good filling with regular troop/fund inflow.

Middle Powers

Which Countries are Implied. By middle powers are implied those countries which lie between the superpower and small/developing nations. These are strong, matured, self-sustaining developed countries which are strong/emerging economies. Countries like Canada, Australia, Brazil, India, Turkey, South Africa, Nigeria, Norway, Sweden, Argentina, etc, fall in this grouping. Following points are stated as regards to the middle powers:-

(a) Central Mass/Followers/Leaders. These countries constitute the 'central mass' of the UN body politic. This self-propelling force can be the 'followers' or may provide 'leadership' on many counts, viz, diplomatic skills, negotiating resources or intellectual leads, etc. The researcher is of the strong view that such countries and their positive opinion/contribution is a life-line for the UN's future in the 21st century.

(b) Role in UN Peace Keeping Operations. Their strong role and presence in the UN Peacekeeping Operations is likely to continue and remain a main resource base for this international venture (Canada -120,000, Australia-5500+peacekeepers, Nigeria-peacekeepers in Liberia, Sierra Leone, Darfur, Brazil-Haiti and other places)[24 25].

(c) Strong Voices. Middle powers are, and likely to be, the strong and relevant voices in world debates (climate change, GATT, disarmament, sanctions, war fighting). These are and will be essential for opinion making, as well as, providing effective counter to one- way traffic (unilateralism) or super power hegemony.

(d) **Rising Aspirations**. Though legitimate, the world in general and P-5 in particular, will have to come terms with aspirations of few (Brazil, Australia, Canada, India) for a place on P-10/P-15. These initiatives are likely to keep the debate on NIEO alive.

Small and Developing States

Major Gainers. Small and developing states have been the major gainers for the UN systems. Short of diplomatic resources and economic power, many such nations have used the UN forums and its multifarious agencies and platforms to gain recognition on the international stage, push their national agendas, seek economic rewards and in general get their otherwise obscure voices heard. Also, by receiving membership/ leadership on various UN bodies and agendas these countries have gained recognition and political mileage/clout disproportionate to their national power. Malaysia, as a leader of NAM and OIC in 2003 is an example[26]. Most of these nations choose various coalitions/caucuses/groups which serves their interest the best. This phenomenon is called 'Forum-shopping'. The same is likely to continue. For voting favours for support in opinion making, such States try to extract reciprocal rewards from great powers or opinion stake-holders. For example, Ethiopia extracted a promise from the US to broker a peace between the government and Eritrean rebels. Egypt and Malaysia received financial rewards. It however cuts both ways into rewards and punishments as for Yemen, the consequence of opposing the Gulf War was the withdrawal of US aid and commitments. In 2003, the smaller non-permanent members of the Security Council such as Guinea, Angola, and Cameroon were courted extensively by both sides in divisive debates over Iraq, but due to the nature of the shifting fulcrum of debates/ loyalties, these States ended up getting no award, either positive or negative.

As regard the small and developing States, following observations are relevant:-

(a) **Considerable Clout**. By virtue of their absolute numbers, such States will continue to wield a tangible clout.

(b) **Game Plan**. Most of the time the game plan of these States would be to align themselves with that power block/stakeholder where gains/concessions are the maximum.

(c) **Known Alignments.** Otherwise, the small/developing States are likely to put their weight behind their traditional groupings like (NAM, EU, G-77 etc) and will lend their influence accordingly.

(d) **Relevance.** The cumulative weight of small and developing States is extremely relevant in the affairs/future of the UN. This influence may be in the form of lending weight/credence to respective side of decision makers or putting corrective pressure on the side forcing a unilateral/skewed decision on the UN.

Coalition, Blocks and Adhoc Groups

Formation Process and Influence. As the UN progressed into its years and decades of its existence, the developments on the World stage, viz, de-colonisation, cold war, emergence of small developing states etc led to the formation of many blocks of countries coming together on many grounds; geographical distribution (Western Europe, Eastern Europe, Africa, Latin America), common goals and agenda (NAM, G-77, G-20 etc), regional similarities (organisation of land locked countries, etc) or financial grouping (OPEC) etc. These groups exercise solid influence in the decision making process of UN. They shape common positions in issues and control a block of votes[27]. These also tend to act as 'single entity' in swaying world opinion in the name of 'common cause'. Like the G-20, which emerged in the WTO as the 'booming voice of the developing countries'[28] extorted its telling influence in the outcomes. In a similar fashion, various multilateral groups like G-77, ASEAN, NAM, OIC, Nordic Group, EU, etc, continue to represent the common interests of their blocks though, many a times it is difficult to forge group consensus due to differences among member countries. These groups exercise weight and influence in many important functional areas like selection of the non-permanent members of the UNSC, demand for NIEO, opinion on inclusion in P-5/extended P-10/15, or providing leadership position in UN (ECOSOC, UNHCR etc). Similarly, some informal groupings of transitional relevance like 'Contact Group on Namibia' in 'Friends of the Secretary General' on the latest UN Democracy Caucus exert their influence in forming opinion/decisions in the area/issue for which they are formed[29].

Vital Importance. All the various Blocks and Caucusing Groups are vital to shape the body politic of the United Nations and are the drivers which propel its functioning. After each of such groups have thrown in its weight/influence, the resulting balance of power and influence decides what the UN will actually do, or not do. Since all such Groups are based on very strong fundamental and existential foundations, these will continue to remain relevant into the future and will continue to guide the destiny of the UN in the future.

Secretary General and the Secretariat

The Second UN. While the member States which come in different shades and Groups as explained above, are called the 'First UN', the Secretary General (UNSG) and the UN Secretariat or 'the Secretariat' for short, are collectively referred to as 'Second UN'. This is so because, both individually and cumulatively, the UNSG and the Secreteriat have their independent identity much bigger than their official formatted brief. Both of these are central to the UN and its future in the 21st Century.

Secretary General. The Secretary General besides the UN Head is in fact, an 'International Civil Servant' having his own weight, clout, political identity and force of influence[30]. Here are some glimpses of his positional aura :-

(a) **Force of Influence**. This force often grows bigger than the position obtainable by the force of resolutions. There have been examples when the UNSGs have forged compliances and solutions for the States condemned by resolutions (Iraq Crises 2002-03). This force of influence allows the UNSG to maintain independent channels of communications capable of steering courses, exclusive of resolution position.

(b) **Great Achievements**. The UNSG over a period of time, have been great achievers. Daj Hammarskjold, the fourth UNSG, is credited with initiating the idea of UN Peacekeeping and Preventive Diplomacy, a major 'Tool of UN Influence' in the world today. UNSG Boutros Boutros Ghali elevated the UN as an independent information gathering and analytical body while Kofi Annan was a proponent of extensive budgetary and administrative reforms. This Nobel Laureate raised his voice of reason against various evils requiring world attention, HIV/Aids/Poverty and others. Also while Ban-ki-Moon's low profile and mishandling of Sri-Lankan crises has earned him much rebuke[31], his sphere of influence is much bigger than his official brief. Even after leaving office, UNSGs remain world figures. Kofi Annan trying to steer a torn

Syria to peace and democracy is a case in point.

The Secretariat. The UN body comprising of all Under and Assistance Secretary Generals, heads of various departments like peacekeeping, electoral assistance, UNDP, UNICEF, etc, is collectively known as 'UN Secretariat'. This component of the 'Second UN' wields tremendous influence and power. These are the 'humans' which staff the bodies and offices. Obviously therefore, their sense, understanding, comprehension, prioritisation and world view is the throughput of the bodies they head and hence is the 'throughput' of the UN. Like when Boutros Ghali saw the Rwandan crises only as a civil war, he did not press ahead for UN intervention since such interventions are prohibited in civil wars. The result was a full blown human disaster[32]. It is obvious to state that the perception of the world view (shaped by their own sense of priority) held by the Second UN will actually decide what the UN will do, or fail to do. They are the shapers and builders of UN Report Card.

Non State Actors : The Third UN

What Constitutes the Third UN? The NGOs, the academic and experts who serve the UN as consultants and the independent commissions of prominent individuals which interact with the first and second UN are collectively referred to as the Third UN. The Third UN is actually a balancing/ countervailing/shaping force that ultimately balances out and decides what the First and Second UN are able to do and achieve[33].

NGOs. NGOs are a great influencing force. These may be small NGOs or of International Statures (international NGOs or INGOs) or Govt NGO, (GONGOs) each has its own weight and steam in extracting UN action for the cause they represent. They may come together either to advocate a particular cause (human rights, peace, environment) or to provide a service (disaster relief, humanitarian and development assistance etc), they work up their agendas. Many of them have secured special privileges to participate as observers in Assembly Sessions. ECOSOC has the authority to grant consultative status to NGOs. Many times these bodies act as 'ombudsman' in many UN actions. They raise their claimed 'voices of reason' in international debates.

Academics and Experts. Right from its inception, the UN has always drawn upon the external wisdoms and wise counsel of experts and consultants external to the UN. Unfortunately, some of the contribution of these learned individuals have ended with their getting the Nobel. Needless to say that this treasure trove of expertise will continue to remain very relevant to UN.

Independent Caucus. Independent caucuses have been the fountainheads from where have emerged earth shaking reports, relevant to UN. Report on 'Our Global Neighbourhood' by Caucus on Global Government. 'A More Secure World; Our Shared Responsibility' by UNSG Kofi Annan's High Level Panel on Threats, Challenges and Change, come to mind straight away. This cumulative wisdom providing 'nourishing ideas' is going to empower the decision makers in taking the UN forward, in times to come.

The Millennium Project : From Words to Action

The Direction of Research. The research from here on, will turn from ideas to actions, in that, it will be the endeavour of the researcher to trace back various promises/goals/milestones which the UN decided for itself at a 'World Forum', check out their status on date and identify what course needs to be followed in the future if the promises have to be kept and the UN has to remain relevant (read successful) to the human race. We start with MDGs.

The MDG Strategy

The Goals and Targets. With the advent of the New Century and a New Millennium, the World Leaders at the historic UN Summit in New York in Sep 2000 (called the Millennium Summit) set eight targets to mobilise national and collative efforts on critical development issues to be achieved by 2015. There are eight main development goals and eighteen related targets. Each target has a specific time frame and aim and one or more indicators to be monitored to assess its movement towards achievement[34].

On Implementation of the Goals

> *"Working together, governments, the United Nations Family, the private sector and civil society can succeed in tackling greatest challenges. As 2015 deadline is fast approaching, we must be united and steadfast in our resolve to accelerate progress and achieve the MDG[35].*
>
> —UN Secy Gen Ban Ki-Moon

"The Millennium Development Goals have shown that we can make profound differences in peoples' lives. The journey we started in the year 2000 has seen us build a solid foundation for further progress"

—UN Secy Gen Ban Ki- Moon, MDG 2014

What is MDG Report 2014? The MDG Report 2014 is a UN document which is as latest as June 2014. This Report is based on a master set of data that has been compiled by an Inter-Agency and Expert Group on MDG Indicators led by the Department of Economic and Social Affairs of the United Nations Secretariat, in response to the wishes of the General Assembly for periodic assessment of progress towards MDGs. The Group comprises representatives of international organisations whose activities include the preparation of one or more of the series of statistical indicators which were identified as appropriate for monitoring the progress towards the MDGs. In addition, a number of national statisticians and outside advisers have also contributed towards the preparation of MDG Report 2014. There is no better way to gauge the progress on each Goal/Target than to relate it to the status as indicated in MDG 2014. The same has been attempted in the succeeding text.

Goal 1: Eradicate Extreme Poverty and Hunger

This Goal is divided into three targets:-

(a) **Target 1A.** Halve between 1990 and 2015, the proportion of people whose income is less than $1 per day.

(b) **Target 1B.** Achieve full and productive employment and decent work for all, including women and young people.

(c) **Target 1C.** Halve between 1990 and 2015, the proportion of people who suffer from hunger.

Status of Target 1A

The status of this target has been analysed in the light of MDG 2014.

Inputs as per MDG 2014

(a) **The World has Reduced Extreme Poverty by Half.** In 1990, almost half of the population in the developing regions lived on less than $ 1.25 per day. This rate has dropped to 22% by 2010, reducing the number of people living in extreme poverty by 700 million. This means, that the world has reached the MDG target of halving the proportion of people living in extreme poverty five years ahead of 2015 deadline.

(b) **Absolute Numbers**. In absolute numbers, people living in extreme poverty fell from 1.9 billion in 1990 to 1.2 billion in 2010.

(c) **Uneven Achievement**. Despite the above overall achievement, the progress in poverty reduction has been uneven. While, some regions such as Eastern Asia and South Eastern Asia have met the targets of halving the extreme poverty rate, others like Sub-Saharan Africa and Southern Asia, still lag behind. As per World Bank projections, Sub-Saharan Africa will be unlikely to meet the target by 2015.

(d) **Concentration of Extreme Poverty**. MDG 2014 has revealed that the majority of World's extreme poor live in few countries:-

(i) India - 32.9% (1.2 billion)

(ii) China - 12.8%

(iii) Nigeria - 8.9%

(iv) Bangladesh - 5.3%

(v) Congo - 4.6%

(vi) Other Countries - 35.5%

While the world poverty levels have indeed been on the wane, there have only been 'Islands of excellence' (China, India, Southern Asia) coupled with 'oceans of stagnation' (Sub-Saharan Africa). Various UN driven programmes on world poverty alleviation are bringing awareness and success to millions while sensitising the Nation States to address on priority, the associated factors related to poverty alleviation, such as good governance, economic stability, environmental protection and preservation of natural resources, et al. In sum, we are moving forward but there is a long way ahead. Some of the major obstacles to the international poverty alleviation efforts are as under:-

(a) **The Quantum**. While percentages are southward driven, the quantum to be alleviated continues to increase ceaselessly, thanks to inter and intra national conflicts, insurgencies, ethnic cleansing and many other crimes on hapless humans which increase the number of refugees, war scorn/displaced, internally displaced persons, etc.

(b) **Governance**. Deficit governance, failing States, failed States, atrocities perpetrated by States on their own citizens (Syria) continues to increase human misery and continues to depress thousands and millions to a life of poverty and depression. New hot - spots of misery and poverty are emerging as conflict rages relentlessly in many parts of the world (Iraq, Afghanistan, Palestine et al.).

(c) **Natural Resources**. Thanks to global warming trends, severe depletion of natural resource and other abuses, the fury of mother nature visits us frequently and unpredictably. Draughts, floods, cyclones, epidemic, pandemic... take their toll in crop failure, food shortages, human sufferings, diseases, poor health, making people poor to poorer.

Since all the above are global realities that are likely to continue well into our future, the efforts of the UN in poverty alleviation with all its goods and ills (corruption, mismanagement, sub-optimal expenditure etc) will continue to have effect but is likely to always trail behind the projected targets as has been the case till date.

Target 1B

This target related to employment and decent work has been analysed in the same manner as Target 1A.

Inputs as per MDG 2014.

(a) **Impact of Slow Economic Growth**. In 2013, global economic growth slowed to its lowest rate since 2009. The weak and uneven global economic recovery continued to take its toll in the global markets particularly in the developing world. This was reflected in limited progress in the reduction of low quality employment which has been widespread in most developing countries.

(b) **Vulnerable Employment Role**. This rate, defined as the percentage of own-account and unpaid family workers in total employment accounted for an estimated 56% of all employment in developing regions in 2013 as compared to 10% in developed region. The rate of decrease of this percentage over the years has reduced (2.8% reduction in 2008-13 compared to 4.0 % reduction in 2003-08), implying thereby that the world is slowing down in reducing the number of its vulnerable workers. This slow down was must pronounced in Western Asia (1.2% in 2008-13 from 8% in 2003-08). On the flip side, the vulnerable employment rate increased in Latin America and Caribbean.

(c) **Women vs Men**. Expectedly, the vulnerable employment rates in 2013 are higher for women (60%) as compared to men (54%).

(d) **On Gender Gap**. The largest gender gap (more than 10% points) was found in Northern Africa, sub-Saharari Africa, Western Asia and Oceania. The same is reducing is Latin Amernca and Caribbean.

(e) **Labour Productivity**. As a key measure of economic performance, labour productivity measures the amount of goods and services that a worker produces in a given amount of time. Annual average labour productivity growth rates slowed down markedly in most developing regions in the period 2008-13 as compared to the period 2003-08. On the whole the global productivity rate slowed down except in Oceania which experienced stronger productivity growth

Target 1C

Halve, between 1990 and 2015, the proportion of people who suffer from hunger.

Inputs as per MDG 2014. Salient points as to the state of thing in Jun 2014 is as under :-

(i) **Steady Progress**. The developing regions have shown a steady progress towards MDG hunger target. The overall proportion of undernourished population in these regions decreased from 23.6% in 1990-92 to 14.3% in 2011-13. If the trend continues, the prevalence of undernourishment under would barely exceed the target by about one percent.

(ii) **Uneven Progress.** The progress in reducing undernourishment is uneven across regions and countries, while significant progress in reduction has been recorded in South Eastern Asia,

Eastern Asia, Caucasus, Central Asia, Latin America and the Caribbean where the MDG target of halving has been almost achieved, Sub-Saharan Africa has shown limited progress remaining the region with the highest prevalence of undernourishment in the world.

It is the sense of the author that the overall picture of the global employment and global nutrition remains to be grim though percentages/ proportions may have shown an upturn in some figures. The debilitating global recession, Eurozone crisis, food security crisis, depleting environment under constant abuse are the major reasons. While all of these realities are going to remain challenges well into the 21st Century and beyond, the UN and MDGs will be very much in business to be the only international programme to address global issues with global solutions, no matter that many outcomes are only status quo, marginally positive or even negative.

Goal 2 : Achieve Universal Primary Education

Target. Ensure that by 2015, children everywhere, boys and girls alike will be able to complete a full course of primary schooling.

Status as per MDG Report 2014

(a) **Progress Slackening.** Despite impressive strides forward at the start of the decade, the progress in reducing the number of children out of school has slackened considerably in the recent times. While the net enrolment rate in the primary education increased by 7% points globally from 83% to 90% in the period 2000-2012, this rate of progress has since slackened with 58 million children worldwide still out of school in 2012.

(b) **Sub-Saharan Africa for a Change.** While in other targets this region might be at the bottom of the ladder, under this goal it has registered the greatest improvement with the net enrolment rate in primary education increasing by 18% points between 2000 and 2012. This despite its rapid population growth which has resulted in 35% more children in 2012 as compared to 2000 and despite negative experiences of armed conflicts, poverty etc.

(c) **Several Other Regimes Close to Target.** Under this target, the regions of Eastern Asia, South Eastern Asia, Caucasus, Central

Asia, Latin America and the Caribbean are close to achieving the target of universal primary education. Western Asia and Southern Asia have also closed the gap towards universal primary education.

(d) **Negative Impacts.** Children in conflict-affected areas constitute a larger percentage of out-of-school population. Take the case of Democratic Peoples Republic of Congo (DPRC) where almost one of the two children of primary school age has never been to school in 2010. The same number in Najaf (Iraq) is one in four. Almost 22% of the worlds primary-school-age population live in conflict ridden areas.

(e) **Poverty/Gender/Disabilities.** Abject poverty and gender biases against girls, especially, in the rural households has kept millions of children in the primary-school-age-group, out of schools. In addition, children with disabilities also constitute the disadvantaged group, a large percentage of which remains out of school, the world over.

(f) **Higher Rates of Dropouts.** Another impediment to achieving this target has been the persistent high dropout rates in primary education sector. While in Northern Africa, Eastern Asia and Caucasus close to 80% or more children who start at grade 1 reach the last grade of primary education, this percentage is just around 60% or there about, in Oceania, Sub-Saharan Africa and Southern Asia.

(g) **Global Number of Illiterates.** Despite remarkable progress in the youth literacy rates (15-24 yrs) which has jumped up to 89% from 83% in the period 1990-2012, the world illiteracy rates remain high. As of 2012, 781 million adults and 126 million youth worldwide, lacked basic reading and writing skills.

(h) **Donor Aid Declining.** Global donor aid to education, which had seen a steady rise from 2002-2010, has declined by 7% in the period 2010-2011. This has negatively impacted low-income countries, especially, in Sub-Saharan Africa. Even before the economic downturn, donor countries had not met their commitments made in Dakar in 2000, the current declining trend will make the situation worse.

Though some countries are almost there and many others are closing the gap, the world illiteracy remains a huge issue. Negative impacts due to armed conflict, gender biases and abject poverty are taking their toll in keeping children out of primary schools. High drop-out rates need to be arrested and the donors must not pull their hands off the low-income countries which badly need their support. All this and more will continue to engage the UN under this target much beyond 2015.

Goal 3 : Promote Gender Equality and Empower Women

Target: Eliminate gender disparity in primary and secondary education preferably by 2005 and in all levels of education no later than 2015.

Status As per MDG Report 2014.

(a) **Gender Parity Index (GPI).** The progress under the target is measured in terms of GPI which is defined as girls' gross school enrolment ratio divided by the corresponding ratio for boys. The MDG Report 2014 informs us, that GPI has shown important gains in all the developing regions at all levels of education (primary, secondary, tertiary). However gender disparities became more prevalent at higher levels of education.

(b) **Region-Wise Performance.** In 2012, all developing regions achieved or were close to achieving gender parity in primary education. The notable exceptions have been Afghanistan and Pakistan which were low on GPI index. On the flip side, in countries like Nepal and Bangladesh gender parity favoured the girls.

(c) **GPI in Secondary Education.** Gender Parity was larger in secondary education. In 2012, Latin America and the Caribbean were the only regions in the world where gender disparity favoured girls.

(d) **States of Tertiary Education.** The GPI reached 98 in developing world, indicating near parity. This achievement was led by high parity figures in Latin America, Caribbean, South Eastern Asia, Caucasus and Eastern Asia. It was revealed that girls from the poorest households face highest barriers in tertiary education.

The reasons are not far to seek, since tertiary education is costly. As regards the opportunities, equal access to the same between men and women remains a distant dream. Due to the obstacles to employment in the formal sector, women turn to informal non-farm jobs to run households. As regards women representation in governance, though women continue to be given representation in parliaments, the pace is slow.

(e) **Women's Status is Labour Markets.** Women's status in labour markets is improving. It has jumped from 35% in 1990 to 40% in 2012 as a global assessment. This notwithstanding, gender disparity still persists very visibly in this area in almost all countries.

At best, the goal of promoting gender equality and empowering women, remains a 'work-in-hand' where, though some progress has been achieved, a far more needs to be done. The special areas of emphasis being, the tertiary education for women, improving GPI figures for secondary education, equal job opportunities for women and a greater role for women in Parliaments of the world. The UN is likely to remain a vehicle of international awareness, initiative and assessment of results achieved in times to come.

Goal 4: Reduce Child Mortality

The Target. The target for this goal is to reduce by two-thirds between 1990 and 2015, the under-five mortality rates.

Status as per MDG Report 2014.

(a) **Substantial Progress But Still Short**. While substantial progress has been made in reducing the child mortality rates but the figures still fall short of MDG Targets. For example, the global rate for under-five mortality fell by 50% between 1990 and 2012 but the target of two-third reduction is still a distance away.

(b) **Region Wise Report**. With the exception of Sub-Saharan Africa and Oceania, all regions of the world have reduced child mortality by half. Interestingly, the world is currently reducing the under-five mortality rate faster than any other time in the past.

(c) **Causes.** Preventable diseases such as pneumonia, diarrhoea and malaria are the main causes of under five deaths almost half of which take place in the neonatal period.

(d) **Sub-Saharan Africa.** Globally, four out of every five death of children under the age of five occurs in Sub Saharan Africa and Southern Asia. It is thus critical to reduce the number of child deaths in these regions.

Despite substantial progress worldwide, the target is still far; however the same does not look impossible. Surely this target will slip in 2015 though by a small margin. The regions of the world requiring special focus are, Sub-Saharan Africa and Southern Asia. These regions for this target, as for several others, must remain on the UN focus.

Goal 5 : Improve Maternal Health

Target 6. The specific target to be achieved under this goal aims to reduce by three quarters between 1990 and 2015, the maternal mortality ratio.

Status As per MDG Report 2014

(a) **Much More Required**. While the global maternal mortality ratio dropped by 45% between 1990 and 2013 (380 to 210 deaths per 1000,000 live births), however the same is still well short of the MDG target of reducing martality by three quarters (75%) by 2015.

(b) **Region Report**. Sub-Saharan Africa had the highest material mortality ratio of developing nations (510 deaths per 100,000 live births) this was followed by Southern Asia, Oceania and Caribbean (190 deaths). In other developing nations maternal death has become a rare event.

(c) **Some Facts.** While Sierra Leone has the world's highest maternal mortality rate (1100 maternal deaths per 100,000 live births), Belarus has 1 death per 100,000 live births). One third of the entire percentage of deaths are concentrated in just two countries, namely India (17%) and Nigeria (14%).

While there has been a forward movement, but the target is still some distance away. Another disturbing fact is the wide disparities in the figures between countries. While there are countries that have dwarfed the problem to just 1 death per 100,000 live births, there are others which are on the wrong side of 1000 and what about the shame of nearly one third of all deaths in just two countries? This target will surely slip in 2015 but concerted global efforts must continue to address this challenge, simply because of the fact, that most maternal deaths are preventable.

Goal 6 : Combat HIV/AIDS Malaria and Other Diseases

- **Target 6.A.** Have halted by 2015 and begin to reverse the spread of HIV/AIDS.
- **Target 6.B.** Achieve by 2010, universal access to treatment for HIV/AIDS for all those who need it.
- **Target 6.C.** Have halted by 2015 and begin to reverse the incidence of malaria and other major diseases.

Status as per MDG Report 2014

(a) **HIV/AIDS.**

(i) **Menace Continues.** The menace continues as there are still too many new cases of HIV. Inspite of the fact, that globally the rate of HIV infections declined by 44% between 1990 and 2012, there were still 2.3 million cases of people of all ages newly infected with HIV and 5.6 million deaths from AIDS related cases.

(ii) **It is Sub-Saharan Africa.** Almost 70% (1.6 million) of the new HIV infections occurred in Sub-Saharan Africa where the proportion of women and men aged between 15-24 continued to engage in risky behaviour due to lack of knowledge about HIV/AIDS. Only 39% of men and 28% of women had comprehensive knowledge about AIDS.

(iii) **Children.** Though there was a rapid decline in AIDS related deaths in children. Nevertheless, about 210,000 children died in 2012 (as compared to 320,000 in 2005). This amounted to about 600 children dying every day due to AIDS in 2012.

(b) **Malaria and Other Diseases.**

(i) **World Moving Forward.** Between 2000-2012 the substantial expansion of malaria interventions led to 42% decline malaria mortality rates globally.

(ii) **Tuberculosis.** Another positive input in the MDG Report 2014 informs us that the number of new cases and deaths from tuberculosis is falling bringing the MDG target within reach.

Both in the field of control of AIDS and malaria, significant and steady progress has been registered. The unfortunate part is that in regions of Sub-Saharan Africa and in some other least developed countries like Northern Africa, Caucasus and Central Asia, the rate of progress in full control over AIDS/Malaria is slowing down. There is a need to keep up the momentum. Though it is certain, that achievement of this target will also default in 2015, we will be somewhere close to it as regards death due to malaria and tuberculosis.

Goal 7 : Ensure Environmental Stability

- **Target 7.A.** Integrate the principles of sustainable development into country policies and programme and reverse the loss of environmental resources.
- **Target 7.B.** Reduce biodiversity loss, achieving by 2010, a significant reduction in the rate of loss.
- **Target 7.C.** Halve by 2015, the proportion of the population people without sustainable access to safe drinking water and basic sanitation.
- **Target 7.D.** By 2020, achieve significant improvement in the lives of at least 100 million slum dwellers.

Details as Per MDG 2014 :-

(a) **Million of Hectares Being Lost.** There were 13 million hectares of forest lost worldwide each year from 2000 to 2010. However, the afforestation and natural expansion of forests have reduced the net loss of forests from an average of 8.3 million hectares in the 1990, to 5.2 million hectares between 2000-2010. This has been due - for the most part – to the measures taken by the various countries such as Brazil, Chile, China, Costa Rica, Rwanda and Vietnam to address de-forestation and manage their forests sustainably.

(b) **Green House Emissions.** Global emissions of carbon dioxide

(CO_2) have continued their upward trend increasing by 2.6% between 2010 and 2011. This has been due mostly to the fast growth in emissions from developing regions.

(c) **Ozone Depletion**. There is a positive input on this aspect as MDG 2014 Report states that the global consumption of ozone-depleting substances (ODS) decreased by over 98% between 1986 and 2013. It is estimated that the remaining ODS will be phased out gradually during the next two decades.

(d) **Renewable Water Resources.** Renewable water resources are becoming more and more scarce as the time goes by. In North Africa and the Arabian Peninsula, the withdrawal rates exceed 75% of the limit that is considered sustainable. This compares most unfavorably with the global withdrawal rate of 9%. Countries in West Asia, Caucasus and Central Asia and Southern Asia are hovering at withdrawal rates between 54-48%. 60% is the threshold which once crossed make water scarcity an issue.

(e) **Biodiversity**. It is estimated that protected areas around the globe are increasing thus helping to safeguard natural resources. The Convention on Biological Diversity, recognizing the importance of protected areas has set a protection target of 17% covering of global terrestrial areas and 10% coverage of coastal marine areas by 2020. Currently the protected areas cover only 14.6% of earth's land areas and 9.7 % of its coastal marine areas.

(f) **Extinction of Species**. The worldwide Red List Index (RLI) compiled by International Union for Conservation of Nature and its partners which measures the trends in the overall extinction risk of sets of species shows that overall the endangered species are declining. More needs to be done to reverse this trend, reduce extinction rates and hence safeguard our biodiversity heritage and the benefits which many of these species provide to the society.

(g) **Open Defecation**. While over a quarter of world's population has gained access to improved sanitation since 1990, yet a billion people worldwide still revert to open defecation. It is unfortunate to note that 82% of those one billion reside in two countries - India and Nigeria. In this context, the resolve of the Prime Minister of India, Shri Narendra Modi, from the ramparts of Lal Quila on the 15th of Aug 2014 that making of toilets (especially girl toilets) should be a high priority area the near future, could not have come at a better time.

(h) **Slum Dwellers.** Although the MDG target has been met, the number of people in slum conditions is growing. In that, while the percentages the quantum of slum dwellers worldwide has reduced from 40% in 2010 to 35% in 2012, owing to the sheer rise in population the numbers have jumped up for 650 million in 1990 to 863 million in 2012.

Under the broad head of environmental diversity, various indications show that while there is a definitive forward movement, there is a long road ahead. Most of these targets are likely to slip by 2015.

Goal 8 : Develop a Global Partnership For Development

This comprehensive goal was to be achieved through the implementation of following targets:-

(a) **Target 8.A.** Develop further an open, rule-based, predictable, non-discriminatory trading and financial system (includes a commitment to good governance, development, and poverty reduction-both nationally and internationally).

(b) **Target 8.B.** Address the special needs of the least developed countries (Includes tariff and quota-free access for LDC exports; enhanced program of debt relief for HIPC and cancellation of official bilateral debt; and more generous Official Development Assistance (ODA) for countries committed to poverty reduction).

(c) **Target 8.C.** Address the special needs of landlocked countries and small island developing states (through the Programmme of Action for the Sustainable Development of Small Island Developing States and the outcome of the Twenty-second Special Session of the General Assembly).

(d) **Target 8.D.** Deal comprehensively with the debt problems of developing countries through national and international measures in order to make debt sustainable in the long term.

(e) **Target 8.E.** In cooperation with developing countries, develop and implement strategies for decent and productive work for youth.

(f) **Target 8.F.** In cooperation with the private sector, make available the benefits of new technologies, especially information and communications.

Status as per MDG Report 2014

(a) **Status of Official Development Assistance (ODA).** The ODA is now at its highest level, reversing the decline of the previous two years. The same stood at $ 134.8 billion in 2013. This is 6.1% higher in real terms as compared to 2012. This amounts to 0.3% of Gross Natural Income (GNI) of all the developed countries.

(b) **Fund Flow.** About one third of the total donor aid flow has been in recent years to Least Developed Countries (LDCs).

(c) **Trade Liberalization.** Post the Uruguay Round of Multilateral laterals Trade Negotiations in 1995, the percentage of imports (less oil and arms) from developing countries that entered the developed countries increased by 2.5% in 2012, despite all the ongoing hurdles in the WTO (World Trade Organisation) negotiation.

(d) **Debt Burden.** The MDG Report intimates us that while the debt burden of the developing countries has come down significantly from about 12% in 2000 to about 3.1% in 2012, a pattern seems to have reached and the said burden is not declining any further.

At the end of a comprehensive evaluation on the implementation of 8 Goals and related targets set forth under the banner of MDG, if one sentence is to written, it would be, '*Good Going ... Miles to Go Before You Sleep*'. Thanks to the colossal efforts led by UN driven initiatives, the world is increasingly becoming aware as to, where we are? And where we need to go. The global economic crisis is taking its toll on various activities/programmes/aid giving and many regions of Sub-Saharan Africa continue to hang on the lowest rungs of the development ladder. Right through the 21st Century, this UN driven effort is likely to go on in full swing.

Beyond 2015? While it is very much visible that the world will default on many a MDG targets in 2015, the tangible forward movement in many areas is quite undeniable. In this context the question - 'What beyond 2015' becomes relevant. In the end it will be pertinent to quote the UNSG.

> *'Working together, governments, the United Nation Family, the private sector and civil society can succeed in tackling the greatest challenges. As 2015 deadline is fast approaching we must be united and steadfast in our resolve to accelerate progress and achieve the MDGs.'*
>
> —UN Secretary General

Looking Beyond the MDGs

UNDP Report[35]. According to a UNDP Report dated 27 Jan 2010 carrying a 'beyond midpoint' assessment of the implementation of MDG in its scheduled run time upto 2015, the implementation of MDG to a fair degree is only possible if the following four key facilities are addressed :-

(a) **Policy Choices and Programme Coherence**. The countries must adopt such national policies that promote the cause of MDG and are in coherence with the same. Also, it is important for the Nation States to stick to the chosen policy initiatives for a reasonable time, thereby allowing actions to return results.

(b) **Governance and Capacity Deficit**. Self explanatory.

(c) **Fiscal Space Constraints and Aid Effectiveness**. For any MDG initiative to show effect, the injected aid must be directed fully and holistically at the target group without leakage.

(d) **National Ownership, Political Will and Partnership**. MDG is not the UN baby, it is the baby of the Nation States which need to rear it up with ownership and adequate political will.

After MDG : What Next.[36] Hélène Gandois, a research scholar and a training associate at the UN Institute for Training and Research at New York has opined that 2015 deadline is fast approaching and the MDGs will not be met, so what next.

A Global Development Agenda Beyond 2015

What is it. A Global Development Agenda Beyond 2015, also referred to as Post-2015 Development Agenda refers to a process led by the UN to help define the future global development framework that will succeed the UN MDGs 2015.

Actions at a Glance. At the 2010 High Level Plenary Meeting of the UN General Assembly to review progress towards the MDG's, governments called for accelerating progress and for thinking on ways to advance the development agenda beyond 2015. After the 2010 High Level Plenary Meeting, the UN Secretary-General Ban Ki-Moon has taken several initiatives. He has established a UN System Task Team, launched a High Level Panel of Eminent Persons and appointed Amina J. Mohammed as his own Special Advisor on Post-2015 Development Planning. These processes are complemented by a set of eleven global thematic consultations and national consultations in 87 countries[37]. Some details about these actions are at succeeding paragraphs.

The UN Task Team. The UN System Task Team was established by the Secretary-General Ban Ki-Moon to support UN system-wide preparations for the Post-2015 UN Development Agenda. It comprises 60 UN agencies, as well as, the World Bank and the International Monetary Fund[38] In June 2012, it published the report "Realizing the Future We Want for All" which serves as an input to the work of the High Level Panel[39].

High Level Panel (HLP) of Eminent Persons

(a) **Composition**. On 31 Jul 12, Secretary General Ban Ki-Moon appointed a 27 member HLP consisting of persons from civil society, private sector and government leaders from all regions of the world to advise him on the Post 2015 Development Agenda[40]. The HLP is co-chaired by the Presidents of Indonesia and Liberia and the PM of UK. The Indian representation is by Professor Abhijit Banerjee, a Ford Foundation International Professor of Economics

(b) **Work of HLP**. The HLP's work is guided by 24 framing questions[41]. It held its first meeting on 25 September 2012 on the margins of the annual high level debate of the UN General Assembly and was to submit its recommendations on how to arrive at an agreement on the post-2015 agenda to the Secretary-General at the end of May 2013. One possible outcome of the panel could be the definition of broad parameters for the future framework rather than a set of new goals, similar to the MDG's. The terms of reference of the HLP include the consideration of the findings of the national and thematic consultations at regional and regional and national levels.

The HLP Report. On 30 May 2013, the High Level Panel on the Post -2015 Development Agenda released a Report, titled, 'A New Global Partnership: Eradicate Poverty and Transform Economies through Sustainable Development,[42]. This Report sets out a universal agenda to eradicate extreme poverty from the face of the earth by 2030, and deliver on the promise of sustainable development. The report calls upon the world to rally around a new Global Partnership that offers hope and a role to every person in the world. In the report, the Panel calls for the new post-2015 goals to drive the following five big transformative shifts :

(a) **Leave No One Behind.** After 2015, we should move from reducing to ending extreme poverty, in all its forms. We should ensure that no person-regardless of ethnicity, gender geography, disability, race or other status is denied basic economic opportunities and human rights.

(b) **Put Sustainable Development at the Core.** We have to integrate the social, economic and environmental dimensions of sustainability. We must act now to slow the alarming pace of climate change and environmental degradation, which pose unprecedented threats to humanity.

(c) **Transform Economies for Jobs and Inclusive Growth.** A profound economic transformation can end extreme poverty and improve livelihoods, by harnessing innovation, technology and the potential of business. More diversified economies, with equal opportunities for all, can drive social inclusion, especially for young people, and foster sustainable consumption and production patterns.

(d) **Build Peace and Effective, Open and Accountable Institutions for All.** Freedom from conflict and violence is the most fundamental human entitlement, and the essential foundation for building peaceful and prosperous societies. At the same time, people the world over, expect their governments to be honest, accountable, and responsive to their needs. We are calling for a fundamental shift-to recognize peace and good governance as a core element of wellbeing, not an optional extra.

(e) **Forge a New Global Partnership**. A new spirit of solidarity, cooperation, and mutual accountability must underpin the post-2015 agenda. This new partnership should be based on a common understanding of our shared humanity, based on mutual respect and mutual benefit. It should be centered around people, including those affected by poverty and exclusion women, youth, the aged, disabled persons and indigenous peoples, It should include civil society organizations, multilateral institutions, local and national governments, the scientific and academic community, businesses and private philanthropy.

Regional Consultations. Regional organizations are conducting consultations to formulate regional positions on the Post-2015 Development Agenda. Notably, the African Union has mandated the African Union Commission, the United Nations Economic Commission for Africa, the African Development Bank and UNDP Regional Bureau for Africa, to come up with an African Common Position on the Post 2015 Development Agenda. This Common Position will be a result of multiple sub-regional and regional consultations with African policy makers (national and regional), civil society organizations, academia, the private sector and other relevant stakeholders. In May 2014 the Planet Earth Institute hosted an event at the United Nations in New York where the panel (including Alvaro Sobrinho, Paul Boateng and Christopher Edwards) spoke on delivering the Post 2015 Applied Science and Skills Agenda for Africa: the Role of Business[43].

National Consultation. National consultations on the Post 2015 Development Agenda are designed to open to crowd sourcing the usually closed multilateral negotiation process. These consultations generated inputs into global policy making. The same went through in 87 countries through the process of meetings, conferences, on-line discussions and larger public debates. The consultations included different stakeholders to include civil society organisations, disadvantaged and minority groups, the private sector, academia, women organisations, youth and other constituencies according to a particular national context. The countries selected to participate are a representative sample across several dimensions; regional, country typology and different types of developmental challenges. Countries are determining how they want to take the consultations forward. The UNDG provided guidelines in support[44,45]. The objectives of the National Consultations are as under:-

(a) **Help countries build a national position**, which can later on facilitate the negotiation for the future framework.

(b) **Increase countries' empowerment of the future framework.** It took several years before the current MDGs, which were not designed in an inclusive way, were recognized by advanced developing countries.

(c) **Help build national and international consensus** on range of on a range of issues.

(d) Bring to the UN General Assembly an overall perspective of national and regional priorities on the post -2015 framework, thus facilitating the negotiation between the member states.

Global Thematic Consultations. Started in May 2012, the objective of the global thematic consultations is to organize formal and informal meetings with different stakeholders around current and emerging challenges. The consultations focus on eleven themes identified by UNDG: inequalities, health, education, growth and employment, environmental sustainability, governance, conflict and fragility, population dynamics, hunger, food and nutrition security, energy and water[46]. Several thematic meetings have already taken place. The first thematic meeting on growth, structural change and employment was held in Tokyo, Japan, on 15-16 May 2012[47].

Post-2015 Dialogue. Researchers have discussed that the Post-2015 dialogue is an opportunity to develop practical agenda to ensure that the principle 'leaving no one behind' translates into real changes to deliver essential services to those in poverty. They called for a potential agenda which must recognise that both institutional capacity and politics matter for the more equitable delivery of these services. They found not blueprint for this, but evidence from the Overseas Development Institute and others points to the need to adopt frameworks which are more flexible, grounded, and innovative service-delivery, which also require changes to donors' models[48].

"A Million Voices: The World We Want" Report from the Global Consultations[49]. This report by the United Nations Development Group (UNDG) collects the perspectives on the 'world we want' from over one million people around the globe. For almost one year, people have engaged energetically in 88 national consultations, 11 thematic dialogues, and through the 'My World' global survey. As member States consult on the shape and content of a successor framework to the MDGs beyond 2015, it is hoped that the opportunity to listen to these voices will contribute to reaching consensus on what is needed to move towards a common sustainable future.

Governance. Fragile and conflict affected States have been left behind and unchanged in the rapid decline in poverty since 2000 says a February 2013 paper[50] from the Overseas Development Institute. The researchers report that the outcome statement of the recent Monrovia meeting of the high level panel said- "Economic growth alone is not sufficient to ensure social justice, equity and sustained prosperity for all people...The protection an empowerment of people is crucial". They write that the global My World citizen survey also shows the extent that people see 'an honest and responsive government' as a top priority. This emerged as the second highest of a range of sixteen factors...second only to 'a good education' globally (and within the top five priorities for Low-Human Development Index countries). Researchers found that areas gaining traction in the post 2015 conversation include:-

(a) Building **accountability** for goals into the heart of a new framework.

(b) Ensuring there is **transparency** for how resources are used.

(c) Commitments on **civil and political freedoms**.

(d) Supporting effective **institutions of the State**.

They warn against the polarization of the debate around the strength of the post-2015 goals. They found that 'some political, governance and accountability features do seem to shape whether and how MDG commitments have been achieved (alongside important issues of resourcing, technical capacities and other)' and identified the following key factors:-

(a) **Credible political commitments** between politicians and citizens are essential.

(b) **More inclusive institutions matter**, as well as, the ability to work together. States effectiveness is a determinant of development progress, so State capacities and functions do need more attention.

(c) Their findings focus on **national level governance** 'because of the growing body of evidence relevant to development progress available at this level.'

Global governance is also important to the authors of the Report. They recognize a strong interest in bringing onboard, multilateral institutions, the private sector and non-governmental organisations in a future framework, based on the 'recognition that they can help or hinder future development outcomes'. They call for more work on global governance, and for the identification of viable options for doing so effectively, ambitious goals in the global consultation on governance and post 2015 goals and an open conversation and debate with new actors[51].

Global Web Platforms

(a) Launched in September 2012, the web platform, www.worldwewant2015.org, is a repository for both the thematic and the national consultations. It allows people from all over the world to participate in the global conversation on the issue they want to highlight in the post -2015 development debate.

(b) Moreover, the website (http:/www.myworld2015.org) hosts a complementary global survey, which asks people to submit their six priorities for a better world.

(c) In February 2014, the UN Special Envoy for Youth and the President of the General Assembly launched the Global Partnership for Youth in the Post-2015 Development Agenda, with a crowdsourcing platform to consolidate concrete language for youth priorities in the post-2015 goals.

Other Post-Millennium Development Goals Processes. At the UN Conference on Sustainable Development (Rio+20), held in Rio de Janeiro in June 2012, 192 UN member states agreed to establish an intergovernmental working group to design Sustainable Development Goals (SDGs) as a successor of the MDGs. The HLP's work will be closely coordinated with this working group in order to bring together the processes around the Post-2015 Development Agenda and the SDGs[52,53,54].

As can be seen from the foregoing, the UN and the world is thinking collectively and synergetically in multiple forums and along multiple dimensions on carrying forward the MDGs in their post 2015 avatar of Sustainable Development Goals. The MDGs are and will continue to be of great relevance in times to come. These also provide a degree of centrality to the UN System by placing it firmly at the fountainhead of the World Development Agenda.

Implementing the Recommendations of the High Level Panel on Threats, Challenges and Change

A Word About the Report. The Report of the Secretary General's High Level Panel on Threats, Challenges and Change under the title, 'A More Secure World – Our Shared Responsibility', is a work of a panel of sixteen eminent and experienced people drawn from different parts of the world who were tasked by the UN Secretary General Kofi A Annan in 2003, to assess the current threats to international peace and security and to evaluate how well our existing policies and institutions have done in addressing these threats and to recommend the ways of strengthening the United Nations to provide collective security for the 21st Century [55]. This report is considered to be an important base reference document in all aspects related to the reforming and strengthening of the UN.

Relevance of The Report. The Report of the High Level Panel (HLP) owes its overarching importance in comparison to the other UN Reform reports and proposals to a number of factors. It deals convincingly with question of both form and content of the fundamental UN reform in the peacekeeping sector. It links the outlook and the aims of 'North' and 'South' within the international community. It aims to take into consideration the position of the current US administration without yielding to it on central issues. It draws conclusions from the 'three years' post Sep 11 phase in world politics on the one hand, while also representing the conclusion of more than ten years of exhaustive discussion about institutional reforms of the United Nations and the Security Council on the other.

On Recommendations. The Report has laid out its recommendations in four parts as under :-

(a) **Part 1 : Towards New Security Consensus.**

(i) Different Worlds : 1945 – 2005.

(ii) The case for comprehensive collective security.

(b) **Part 2 : Collective Security and Challenges of Prevention.**

(i) Poverty, infectious disease and environmental degradation.

(ii) Conflict between and within states.

(iii) Nuclear radiological, chemical and biological weapons.

(iv) Terrorism.

(v) Transnational organised crime.

(vi) Role of sanctions.

(c) **Part 3 : Collective Security and Use of Force.**

(i) Using Force : rules and guidelines.

(ii) Peace enforcement and peacekeeping capability.

(iii) Post conflict peace building.

(iv) Protecting civilians.

(d) **Part 4 : A More Effective United Nation for the 21st Century.**

(i) The General Assembly.

(ii) The Security Council.

(iii) A Peace Building Commission.

(iv) Regional Organisations.

(v) The Economic and Social Council (ECOSOC).

(vi) The Commission on Human Rights.

(vii) The Secretariat.

(viii) The Charter of the United Nations.

Why This Report is Relevant? The aforesaid report is a cardinal document which is, not only, widely accepted and respected, but also, many of its recommendations are under various stages of consideration/ debate/ implementation. Much of the activities (and thus the future) of the UN in the coming years and decades will be consumed in debating the subject content and implementing the recommendations of the report. Hence the importance of bringing in focus, certain salient points related to the report in this thesis.

A Comprehensive Report that Defies Its Initial Criticism. Keeping in mind the average age of the panellists (70 yrs) and its US Canadian Centric leadership, the panel was initially ridiculed as Alzheimer's Commission, 'Relics trying to reform a relic' and a cross between déjà vu and amnesia[56]. However when they came out with their report, it was found to be comprehensive, coherent and presenting a total of 101 recommendations. The Report provides a brief survey of the sixty year history of the UN, a useful analysis of challenges confronting it today and a set of broad specific proposals to improve its performance and relevance. The report's four major conceptual-cum-normative advances are as under :-

(a) **Inter connectedness** of today's threats.

(b) **Legitimacy criteria** for the use of military force.

(c) An agreed **definition of terrorism**.

(d) Need to extend **normative constraints to non-state actors**.

Major Threats. The report identifies the major threats as war and violence among and within States, use and proliferation of weapons of mass destruction, terrorism, transnational organised crime, poverty, infectious diseases and environmental degradation. The threats can come from State or non-state actors and endanger human, as well as, national security. Collective security is necessary because today's threats cannot be contained within national boundaries, are inter connected and have to be addressed simultaneously at all levels. The report however does not address the real challenges of how to institute and operationalise a workable collective security system. According to the Panel, the primary challenge to the international community is to ensure that imminent threats do not materialise and distant threats do not become imminent. This requires early decisive and collective action against all threats before they can cause worst devastation. The panel endorses UN-authorised, not-unilateral preventive action.

Salient Aspects of HLP

Viable Recommendations. Though the Committee has made a total of 101 recommendations as stated, some vital issues touched by the panel are discussed in perspective at the succeeding paras. These have a long term bearing on the future of the UN in the 21st Century.

Poverty, Infectious Diseases and Environmental Degradation

Many Viable Recommendations. Under this broad head, the HLP has made many a viable recommendations. It has urged the Nation States to work towards eradicating poverty and achieving sustained economic growth. Has asked the defaulting States to reach their (0.7% of GNP) ODA targets. WTO to conclude its multi-lateral trade negotiations (target was by 2006, still going on). More assistance to poor and indebted countries. Greater funding awareness and action for prevention of AIDS. Requirement of new global initiatives (WHO driven) to re-build national public health systems. Requirements for further development of renewal resources and the need for the early finalization of the Kyoto protocol.

Additional Points

(a) **Linkages with MDG**. In fact the MDG with its 8 Goals and 18 Targets not only pre-dates the HLP by four years, but also, provides a much bigger canvas. Also, since MDG is an ongoing and a live activity with a much longer run-time (2000 – 2015), as also, subjected to Yearly Implementation Report, it is a more viable and a live-tool to check on various development goals which more than overlap the HLP recommendations, barring a few which could be discussed separately. Since the implementation Report 2012 on MDG has been discussed in the previous paragraphs only linkages need to be drawn.

(b) **On Poverty**. As regards the broad status of the recommendations above, it is essentially a work in progress at this stage. It has been reported for the first time that extreme poverty is falling in every region including Sub-Saharan Africa. The percentage of people living on $ 1.25 per day has declined from 47% in 1990 to 24% in 2008. That said, the work is far from over as large proportions of people in absolute numbers are still living in abject poverty. By the current rate of progress estimates, about one billion people will still be living on $1.25 per day in 2015[57]. As regards donor countries meeting up then ODA assistance targets or doling out more assistance to the poor and indebted nation States, hardly any progress can be reported thanks to the global economic crises, debilitating world-wide recession and EU Zone crises.

(c) **On AIDS.** As regard AIDs prevention, while the MDG report has stated that at the end of 2010 an estimated 34 million of the humanity was living with AIDS. This is up 17% from 2001 figures. Surprisingly the number of people dying of AIDS related causes fell to 1.8 million in 2010 down from a peak of 2.2 million in mid 2000s. This shows that while the life-saving antiretroviral therapy is having its effect, it has been more than outdone by the influx of new AIDs cases. In fact, in the 30 years since the HIV/ AIDS was first discovered, the disease has become a devastating pandemic having taken the lives of 30 million people around the world[58,59].

(d) **Doha Round.** As regards the call to complete the Doha Round of world multilateral trade negotiations, the negotiations still remain in progress though the HLP envisaged their completion and finalization by 2006. The Doha Development Agenda has established a Global Trust Fund and developing countries around the world are making contributions into it (Sweden - CHF 4.6 million on 26 Jul 2012). This assistance is meant to build the capacity of developing countries and least developed countries, help them negotiate effectively within the WTO and help them facilitate the flow of goods across nationalborders[60]. And finally, as regards the gap between the promise of the Kyoto Protocol and its performance, there is a need to re-engage on the problem of global warming and begin new negotiations to produce a long term strategy for reducing global warming beyond the period covered by the Protocol. As on today, experts opine that the Kyoto Protocol has failed to produce any discernable real world reductions in emission of green-house gases in the fifteen years gone by (1997-2012). This failure has opened an opportunity for a re-orientation towards a climate policy based on human dignity instead of human sinfulness[61]. It is felt that a climate policy based on human dignity will encompass ensuring energy access for all aiding in the creation of energy in a manner that would not undermine the global ecosystem and would equip the societies with the tools to withstand the risks radical climate poses on them. So essentially, Kyoto is a series of negotiations after negotiations (Copenhagen, Denmark 2009, Cancun Mexico 2010, South Africa 2011, Qatar 2012) which though has achieved 83 signatories and 191 ratifiers, the promises of Kyoto upto the commitment period of 31 Dec 2012 are unlikely to be met. It however cannot be over-emphasised that the negotiation have to be kept alive and the gap between the promises and actions on ground need to be closed[62].

Conflict Between and Within States

Essence of Recommendations. Another very viable set of recommendations have been offered by the HLP under the broad head of 'Conflict Between and Within States'. It has asked the UNSC to be ready to use the authority under Roman Statute and to refer the cases of suspected war crimes and crimes against humanity to the International Court of Justice (ICC). Private sectors to develop norms governing the management of local resources for countries emerging from risk of conflict. Democratically elected Governments should be protected against unconstitutional overthrow. Illicit transfer and brokering of small arms and light weapons be brought into legally binding frameworks. UN must have a field oriented dedicated mediation support capacity, comprised of small team of professionals, with relevant direct experience and expertise, as well as, the essentiality of incorporating important voices of civil societies in peace process and constructive use of deployment of peacekeepers.

On Status. The recommendations in this section cover a very vast domain. Each recommendation is a Chapter by itself. For example, while the ICC is slowly finding its feet and has produced convictions against international crimes like genocide, crimes against humanity and war crimes etc, the conviction and the follow up on the punishments awarded remains an issue. Article 94 establishes the duty of UN members to comply with decisions of the court involving them. If the parties do not comply, the issue may be taken before the UNSC for enforcement action. Another problem in this is that if the decision is against one of the P-5, its enforcement will invariably be vetoed[63,64]. Also, as related to conflict within States, there are numerous issues of peacekeeping, peace building, peace enforcement, right to protect and mediation support. All these issues have been dealt in detail in a separate chapter. In fact, in today's world, peacekeeping and variations thereof are one of the strongest foot prints justifying the continued relevance of UN.

Nuclear, Radiological, Chemical and Biological Weapons

Essence of Recommendations. Under this generic head the HLP has made some very viable recommendations. At the onset, it has asked the nuclear weapon States to restart disarmament. Nuclear weapon States must commit to practical measures to reduce the risk of accidental nuclear event. UNSC must pledge to take collective action in response to a nuclear attack or a threat of such an attack against a non-nuclear weapon State. It has suggested the route of negotiation to resolve regional conflicts which should include confidence building measures and a move towards disarmament. It has asked all chemical weapon States to expedite the scheduled destruction of all existing chemical weapon stockpiles by the agreed target date of 2012. Also, the States that are parties to Biological and Toxin Weapon Convention must negotiate for a credible verification protocol inviting the active participation of the biotechnology industry. IAEA must take all necessary actions towards stemming the nuclear proliferation among member States and act as a guarantor for the supply of fissile material for civilian nuclear users. It has urged the UN to ensure that all States be encouraged to join the Proliferation Security Initiative (PSI) voluntarily. States parties to Biological and Toxin Weapon Generation should negotiate new bio-security protocols. Conference on Disarmament should negotiate Verifiable Fissile Material Cut off treaty at the earliest and the WHO should put necessary procedures in place to deal with the overwhelming outbreak of infectious diseases.

The recommendations under this broad head cover a very wide agenda essentially aimed at making the planet a safer place to live despite the reality of nuclear weapons, reign in the devastating effects of nuclear, biological and chemical weapon proliferation or use (sic) through a regime of treaties and protocols and finally, to rid the world from the curse of the out break of epidemics, pandemics and infectious diseases. Work on none of the above issues can be claimed as finished though forward movement on each and every count is a verifiable reality. The role of the UN in pushing various agendas under the broad head of recommendations and pursuing with each recommendation in detail will remain critical and central in the 21st Century and beyond.

Some Action Points[65]

(a) **Additional Model Protocol.** While the desired end-state of total nuclear disarmament will remain an utopian dream, action by IAEA under Model Additional Protocol is capable of putting into place, stringent vindication norms. In this context, the UNSC must be prepared to act in case of deliberate non compliance. IAEA keeps reporting the compliance status of various additional protocols. This agenda needs to be kept alive.

(b) **NPT**. UN through NPT must continue to urge member States to voluntarily institute a time limited moratorium for the construction of any further enrichment of re-processing facilities. Besides, there is a long standing requirement to get all Nation States to be included under the NPT regime[66].

(c) **PSI**. There is also a need for the UN to strengthen and support the PSI in its efforts to interdict the illicit and clandestine trade in fissile material besides calling upon the member States to join the initiative voluntarily.

(d) **Other Actions**. State parties to BTWC should negotiate a new bio-security protocol to classify dangerous biological agents and establish binding international standards for export of such maternal. On disarmament, UN must move without delay in implementation of the disarmament process.

Terrorism

Action Points on Recommendations. In the context of terrorism, the HLP has made viable recommendations which can be translated into the following action points :-

(a) **Recognition**. The first step towards countering terrorism is for the world body to become a party to the issue by signing and satisfying all the international conventions on terrorism and eight special recommendations against money laundering.

(b) **Giving Teeth**. There is a requirement to strengthen the UN Counter Terrorism Committee (UNCTC). In keeping with its role to provide technical assistance to the States in fighting terrorism, the Committee must have adequate legal, administrative and police tools to provide the requisite assistance. This is also a requirement for 'capacity building' of the UNCTC through requisite funding support.

(c) **Need For Global Centralization**. There is a need for building global centrality in the fight against terrorism. This includes maintaining a central pool of relevant data, seamless sharing of intelligence and synergizing legal, police, administrative and preventive force support among member States. UNCTC must provide such a centrality.

Definition of Terrorism. Most importantly, there is an urgent need for the member States to adopt a universally accepted definition of terrorism. This is very important, since adoption of a definition will imply recognition and acceptance of the range and depth of the threat. The commitment to counter it can only follow thereafter. The definition suggested by the HLP is comprehensive and needs to be adopted by the UNSC by removing all fears of the member States about its misuse and misinterpretation[67]. It is a pity that even after 11 years of 9/11, UN still struggles with a universal definition of terrorism. This definitional impasse has prevented the adoption of a comprehensive convention on International Terrorism. Even in the immediate aftermath of 9/11, UN failed to adopt the convention and the deadlock continues till this day. The prime reason for the stand off is that the Organisation of the Islamic Conference (OIC), The Arab Terrorism Convention and the Terrorism Convention of the Organisation of Islamic Conference, define terrorism to exclude armed struggle for librations and self determination. This claim purports to exclude blaming up certain civilians from the reach of international laws and organisation. It is central to interpreting every proclamation by the States which have ratified these Conventions in any UN forum purporting to combat terrorism. As per OIC, there is a need to make a distinction, between terrorism and the struggle for the rights of self determination by people under foreign occupation. For the first time in 14 years, the UNGA decided in the fall of 2011, not to convene a spring session for the Adhoc Committee on measures to eliminate international terrorism. The stalemate simply continues. The researcher had only hoped that in the UNGA Session in Sep/Oct 12, some headway is made on this impasse.

Global Counter Terrorism Strategy. Once the globally accepted definition of terrorism comes into being, steps need to be taken to provide teeth to the Global Counter Terrorism Strategy covering the four dimensions of prevention, protection, prosecution and response[68].

Transnational Organised Crime

The Essence of Recommendations. The HLP urges all member nations to sign and ratify the 2000 United Nations Convention Against Transnational Organised Crime. It asks the member States to establish a central authority to facilitate the exchange of evidence among national judicial authorities. It asks for a comprehensive international convention on money laundering that addresses the issue of bank secrecy and the development of financial heavens. It also asks the member States to sign and ratify the protocol to prevent, suppress and punish trafficking, especially in women and children, and finally, it asks the UN to establish a robust capacity building mechanism for rule-of-law assistance.

Observations on the State of Affairs[69,70,71] Like with several other recommendations of the HLP, these ones also remain largely on paper. Transnational Organized Crime is one of the ten threat's warned by the HLP. The entire gamut of transnational organized crime is very vast. It includes money laundering, human smuggling, cyber crime, trafficking of humans, drugs, weapons, endangered species, body parts and nuclear material. Since, its scope is so large, a number of conventions and laws have been in force to stem the menace of Transnational Organised Crime. The United Nations Office on Drugs and Crimes (UNODC) developed a model law against Trafficking in Persons in Vienna in 2009. This law is to assist the States in implementing the UN Convention on Transnational Organised Crime. Then there is a United Nations Protocol to Prevent, Suppress and Punish Trafficking in Persons, especially women and children. This protocol has entered into force on 25 Dec 2003. This has been followed by the United Nations Global Plan of Action Against Trafficking in Persons adopted by UNGA on 30 Jul 2010. This Plan includes concrete actions to prevent trafficking in persons, protect and assist victims, prosecute related crimes and strengthen partnership among Govt, civil society organisations, private sector and media. There are a plethora of other conventions. UN convention on Rights of the Child, Sale of Children, Child Prostitution and Child Pornography, Convention on the Elimination of All Forms of Discrimination Against Women, Convention on Prevention of Child Labour, Forced Labour Convention, Convention on Abolition of Slavery and Slave Trading.

State of Things. It is an unfortunate story that in spite of a large number of conventions, laws, protocols armed to stem the various forms of Transnational Organized Crimes, the same thrive at full pace. The National Human Trafficking Research Centre (NHTRC) reports that Human Trafficking is a modern day slavery and has become the fastest growing criminal industry in the world today[72]. On the flip side, there are hundreds of NGOs and foundations that are involved in the heroic task of spreading awareness and reporting abusive practices of sale and trafficking of girls. Many are spreading education as the best bet prevention[73]. In the end, it still remains only a drop of good against an ocean of crime. Similarly, the World Money Laundering Report Aug 2012 gives vivid details of this crime growing at a fast pace in the world having long acquired the status of a flourishing criminal industry, much bigger in volume than the total economies of many nations[74]. Unfortunately, the report produced by the United Nations International Narcotics Control Board (INCB) states that with the increased influence of internet the production of the so called 'designer drugs' is soaring out of control throughout much of the world. In the Americas, the Central American Region and the Caribbeans remain the major trade points, with US having the dubious distinction of world's main destination for illicit drug shipment. Abuse of cocaine is spreading in Western Europe, which is also world's largest market for heroine. In Africa, cocaine smuggling is on the rise. East Africa is the main transit route for Asia. The manufacture, trafficking and use of synthetic drugs has significantly increased in Asia. While the annual prevalence of cannabis (drug) abuse in New Zealand (Australia) is among the highest worldwide[75].

With the plethora of conventions and protocols on one end and the flourishing Transnational Organised Crime on the other, it becomes very clear that the former is having a very little effect on stemming the later. Each side appears to have its own compulsions. In the domain of conventions and protocols the culprit is the toothlessness of UN to get its conventions enforced, because of the lack of strict enforcement tools and the inadequate interest/capacity/will of Nation States to enforce rule of law. On the other side, it is the alternate way of quickly making illicit dollars pitched in the face of worldwide economic recession, shrinking employment and government jobs that are putting more and more people to seek alternate avenues to generate huge money even if it is though the route of one or more of many Transnational Organised Crime. For many, it is roaring business. For others a job avenue for survival (labour, supply chain, managers, transitions). In sum, while the UN will keep raising the voice of law and reason, its effect on the stemming of crime is likely to be minimal unless the member States can bounce back with strict laws against various crimes. Why the crimes in some states like Saudi Arabia, UAE are less than in other countries speaks for itself.

The Role of Sanctions

Essence of Recommendation. The HLP makes a point that whenever the sanctions are imposed by UNSC against a member State(s) it must be effectively implemented and enforced. For this, there is a requirement to establish monitoring mechanisms and provide them with necessary capacity and authority to carry out high quality in-depth investigation. Besides, the adequate budgetary, provisions must be made to implement these mechanisms. In case chronic violations are reported to UNSC by the above mechanism, secondary sanctions must be imposed by the UNSC. In addition to an investigation mechanism, there should also be a system of regular audit. Sanction committee should improve procedures for providing humanitarian exemptions and routinely conduct assessment of the humanitarian impact of the sanctions. The UNSC must continue to strive to mitigate the humanitarian consequences of the sanction.

Sanctions have always been a sore point on many counts. Firstly, the mechanism of imposition and audit has been suboptimal, due to which the impact of sanctions becomes less than full, and secondly, there have been avenues of get away, either through loopholes in sanction resolutions or through un-ethical methods. Ironically, much to the dissatisfaction of UNSC and contrary to its ideals, the impact of sanctions has been severe in accentuating the humanitarian sufferings. Richard Becker, writing on the role of sanctions in respect of Yugoslavia observes, (quote) "Yugoslavia's economy was demolished by sanctions" (unquote). Sanction is a word with a deceptively mild ring to it. But the sanctions imposed by the UNSC on Yugoslavia, a country of 10 million people, has cut off the country's economic life blood. The once prosperous country with a GDP of $ 24 billion and per capita of $ 3000 with every person having the right to housing, education, quality health care, a job, an income has been reduced to a rubble with the GDP of $10 billion and per capita of $700[76](as of Dec 2011)(unquote). In an other informed article by UN scholars Enrico Carisch and Loraina Rickard – Martin, have opined the following[77] :-

(a) **Viability and Effectiveness.** The credible use of sanctions is firmly established as the primary disincentive in the international community's conflict resolution strategy.

(b) **Humanitarian Input.** There is a (yet unsatiated) need for ensuring continued minimisation of humanitarian impact of sanctions that combine the targeted measures with broader short-term measures as may be increasingly required by realities on ground.

(c) **Not a Panacea.** Targeted sanctions are not a panacea. Effective sanctions require coherence with other measures and are difficult to implement and maintain.

(d) **Operations.** Sanction regimes can operate efficiently only when all the actors, including non-state stakeholders such as the private sector fulfil their responsibilities in international peace and security.

It is felt that the regime of imposition of sanctions (albeit with all its shortcomings), is likely to continue in its present avatar well into the 21st Century. However, efforts are likely to be made by the UN to address its many deficits. On the other hand, the voice of reason/innocence from the 'victimized for no fault of theirs' will continue to be raised from various quarters of the world, as if to keep the UN alive of this 'less than perfect' tool.

On Collective Security and Use of Force

Essence of Recommendations. Under this important subject, the HLP has made some very vital recommendations. It has endorsed the emerging norm that there is a collective international responsibility to protect, exercisable by the Security Council authorising military intervention as a last resort, in the event of genocide and other large scale killing, ethnic cleansing or serious violation of humanitarian law which sovereign Governments have proved powerless or unwilling to prevent.

The R2P. The above vital recommendation favourably referred to as R2P has not only generated a great amount of debate/accolades/criticism, but also, and more importantly, has ended up saving millions of human lives otherwise condemned to the apathy, indifference or mercilessness of their respective Governments/rulers/dictators etc (sic).

Additional Observations

(a) **The Eternal Debate**. In the context of R2P, the debate on intervention vs sovereignty has raged for years. On one side of the debate are the critics who cite Article 2 (7) which prohibits the UN to intervene in matters which are essentially within the domestic jurisdiction of any State claiming that the sovereignty of a State is inviolable and humanitarian intervention has no place in the International Law[78]. The contrary school of thought opines that the sovereignty of a nation cannot be considered absolute or inviolable[79] and the UN (on behalf of the humanity) has the 'responsibility to protect' innocent loss of life if the member State is unable or unwilling to do so[80]. Member States, especially the developing nations, have expressed the same apprehensions regarding the said, 'responsibility to protect'.

(b) **What is UN's Position**? It is felt that in general UN must avoid interference in the matters that lie within the domestic jurisdiction of any member State. However, in case of humanitarian disasters and man-made catastrophies like mass murder, rape, ethnic cleansing, forcible exploitation, terror or genocide etc, which either befall upon a peoples of a member State or are inflicted by the State itself, the question before the UN must not be right (or absence of it) of intervention, it must be of the 'responsibility to protect' the lives of innocent people, especially when the State is unable and/or unwilling to do so[81].

(c) **Sovereignty**. In the contemporary world, the concept of State sovereignty must not be considered absolute or inviolable and the UN must fulfil its responsibility to protect civilians from man-made catastrophies[82].

(d) **In the Context of HR Violations**. The above said 'responsibility to protect' is also to be seen as complementary to UN's responsibility to protect Human Rights. This spirit was stated clearly in UNSC resolution 688 of Apr 91 which stipulated that in case of massive human rights violations, it is the legal responsibility of the Security Council to intervene[83].

Use of Force by UNSC

Article Position. Chapter VII of the Charter allows the UNSC to approve any coercive action including military action against a State which poses a threat to other States, people outside its borders and to international order[84]. In various debates on this subject at the UN World Outcome Summit, following apprehensions have been expressed against this provision:-

(a) Lack of Guidelines. There must be specific guidelines at the disposal of the UNSC to decide that a member State is indeed posing a viable threat and such other aspects as to the legality and consequences of the use of force.

(b) Unjust Tool in the Hand of Powerful. Many nations have felt that it will become a tool in the hands of the high and mighty to launch aggression on that member State.

Guidelines. The HLP has correctly recommended that there must be a basic criteria in deciding about the legal aspects of the 'use of force'. In essence, this criteria must include an assessment of the seriousnessbased on the threat, deciding on the exact purpose for the use of force, ascertaining before usage, that all non-military options for meeting the threat have been explored and use of force is indeed a 'recourse of the last resort', ensuring it to be minimum necessary and ascertaining before usage, that the proposed use has a fair chance of success.

Recommendations. Following recommendations are offered :-

(a) To Use or Not. With the type of threats that we face in the 21st Century (terrorism, WMD, ethnic cleansing, genocide etc), it is not an option whether the UNSC may/may not use force to maintain international order, it will become a necessity.

(b) Legality. The criterion given by the HLP if followed in the right spirit will indeed ensure that the provision is not misused. The big question is whether it is followed?

(c) Apprehension. The apprehension of the member States is very genuine. There is no magic wand to remove it. It can only be removed in the bigger framework of the overall UN reform agendas of UNGA and UNSC. The first requirement in this context will be an attitudinal change wherein, the member States do not perceive UN as a hostage of US and secondly a wider representation of the contemporary world order is demanded on the 'high table' where the larger world body takes conscientious majority decisions for the good of the world without being 'bitten by the viper of the partisan veto'. It is to be hoped that such an end-state is reached.

Peace Enforcement and Peacekeeping Capability

Essence of HLP Recommendations. The HLP has recommended that the developed States should do more to transform their existing force capacities into suitable contingents for peace operations. Member States should strongly support the efforts of the Dept of Peacekeeping Operations to improve its use of strategic deployment stockpiles, stand by arrangements, trust funds and other mechanisms in order to meet the tighter guidelines necessary for effective deployment. It has also urged the States with advanced military capacities to establish standby, high readiness, self sufficient battalions (up to brigade level) that can re-inforce United Nation Missions and should place them at the disposal of the United Nations. In addition, a small corps of senior police officers and managers has been recommended who could undertake mission assessments and organise the start-up of police components of peace operations.

It is sad to write that most of the recommendations related to capacity building and placing such capacities at the disposal of the UN have largely been on paper. Most of the developed nations have not lived upto the proposal of creating exclusive capacities in the name of UN Peacekeeping assets. While most of the countries, by and large are gearing up to provide the manpower required for UN peacekeeping missions, there are many defaulters and/or under subscription. Some specific reforms needed are as under :-

(a) **Mandate Inadequacies.** Mandate inadequacies have been the cause of failure in many missions. Mandates must be clearly and adequality defined. The same must have the required teeth and inbuilt flexibility to adapt to dynamic changes that may be reasonably believed to occur in the course of a mandated mission.

(b) **Status of Mission Agreement (SOMA) and Rules of Engagement (ROE).** The SOMA and the ROE must be insisted ab-initio with the host Govt unlike in Rwanda where the UN mission was in place from Jul 1994 but SOMA was not signed till late 1995[85]. This may however not be possible when the Government in power is to be ousted (Haiti 1995). The ROE must contain the procedures forgraduated response escalation and must set the limits for operations/actions by the peacekeepers.

(c) **Inordinate Delay**. Due to inordinate delay in putting the mission personnel actually on ground, success has been allowed to slip away in many cases. A composite force of modest dimensions inserted into the conflict zone quickly can achieve much more than a much larger force introduced months later[86]. One of the recommended measures to overcome this inadequacy is the earmarking of 'stand by forces' pledged by member States to UN.

(d) **Stand-By - Force -Yet a Dream**. Though the above concept of stand-by-force sounds so very appropriate, its realization on ground has largely been a dream not yet realised, basically owing to the deficit in support of commitments by member States. Though way back in Nov 2000, based on a Danish led initiative, a Stand By High Readiness Brigade (SHIRBRID) was created with about 4000 – 5000 troops pledged by eleven countries (Argentina, Austria, Canada, Denmark, Finland, Italy, Netherlands, Norway, Poland, Romania and Spain), the same has not been followed up really, for example when the UNMEE was formed out of SHIRBRID, Argentina and Romania opted out for financial reasons. Over time, there have been clarion calls to various member States to create stand by force but the deficit remains and is likely to remain into the foreseeable future[87].

(e) **Case for Standing UN Rapid Deployment Force (RDF).** In order to further enhance the time response of peacekeeping forces and get a capability of deployment within a matter of days, the HLP had recommended a Standby UN RDF. This proposal was not accepted in the Outcome Summit due to fears and apprehensions of the majority of member States of its misuse by the powerful States using the vehicle of a hijacked or a hostaged UN. If somehow the genuine apprehension of the member States are addressed, the concept could stand on its legs.

Future of Peace Keeping in the 21st Century. While a separate Chapter has been dedicated to the aspect of UN Peacekeeping, it would be essential to mention in context here, that the UN peacekeeping operations have evolved enormously since the 1990's bringing with them new challenges as also, new strengths and confidence in UN structures and contributions to peace and security. Most member States share a common opinion while addressing the role of UN peacekeeping forces, also, the international community has drawn lessons from the past operations and its successes/ failures. As new challenges are bound to appear in the future; it is important not to discourage ourselves and to view these challenges as positive obstacles for further strengthening the international community's response to crises[88].

Post Conflict Peace Building

The HLP has emphasized the role of UN in post conflict peace building. For this, it has recommended a standing fund at the level of at least US $ 250 Million that can be used to finance the recurrent expenditures of a nascent Govt, as well as, critical agency programmes in the areas of rehabilitation and re-integration.

Peace Building Commission(PBC). The recommendation of HLP to constitute a Peace Building Commission (PBC) stands approved by the UN[89]. What needs to be done now is to realize the administrative and support infrastructures required to operationalise the PBC.

Protecting the Civilians

Essence of HLP Recommendations. In the context of protecting the civilians, HLP has recommended that all combatants must abide by Geneva Conventions (a tall order indeed!). All member States should sign, ratify and act on all the treaties relating to the protection of civilians such as Genocide Convention, the Geneva Convention, the Rome Statute of the International Criminal Court and Refugee Convention. The UNSC must fully implement its resolution No 1265(1999) on the protection of civilians in the armed conflict and its Resolution 1325 (2000) on women peace and security. Member States should support and fully fund the proposed Directorate of Security and accord high priority to assisting the Secretary General in implementing the new staff security system.

While all the above sounds ideal and utopian, it is essentially a 'desired end state' where full and final achievement is still far from complete.

For a More Effective UN for 21st Century

Essence of Recommendations. In part IV of its recommendations, the HLP has given recommendations related to the structural and organizational reforms in the body of the UN. In that, it has dealt with the reforms of the General Assembly, Security Council, the Economic and Social Council, the Commission on Human Rights, Regional Organizations, the Secretariat of the UN, the Charter of the UN itself and has recommended the establishment of a 'Peace Building Commission'.

Observations on most of the above issues in the context of failings and remedies of various structures and organisations of the UN are at succeeding paras.

UNGA

The Critics. The critics of the UNGA have opined that UNGA has lost its vitality and often fails to focus effectively on most compelling issues of the day. Major failings and remedies are as under :-

(a) **Automatic Majority**. A stable and a long lasting coalition of member States strong in its belief of forging a majority at any time, tend to ignore the opinions and interest of the other States. The arrangement brings discomfiture at the international level because the sense of common human identity remains weak. There is no way to remedy this except through a realization by the member States themselves to vote and act on the call of their conscience rather than taking positions on their regional perception of groupings.

(b) **An Ineffectual Talk Shop**. The UNGA has been labelled as an ineffectual talk shop which only talks/debates/discusses endlessly. The formal agendas have grown seamlessly. Also, the increased number of Member States demand increased time and space. Experts believe that this challenge could be addressed by further promoting the already existing system of regional groupings and caucuses of like-minded delegations eliminating the need of individual reference to each Nation. Agendas need to be shortened through prioritization and the practice of informal consultations to identify critical issues for discussion.

(c) **Amplifier of Noxious Ideas**. US and its allies (read neo-conservatives) have tended to regard the UNGA as a source of toxic ideas, which if acted would worsen rather than improve the world. These neo-conservationists need to realize that unilateralism is no way to make a representative democratic institution function. Harry Truman said, "We all have to recognize-no matter how great is our strength-that we must deny ourselves the license to do always as we please".

(d) **Democratic Deficit.** This deficit in the UNGA does not refer to the substance of its resolutions but to the lack of connection between it and the people of the member States. The focus is not on 'We the Peoples' but on 'Governments'. While the latter are supposed to represent the will of the people it is not always so. In many cases, it is the civil societies in general and NGOs in particular, who generally represent and voice peoples perspectives and aspirations. As recommended by the Panel of Eminent Persons on UN Civil Society Relations, UNGA must establish better mechanism to enable systematic engagement with civil societies, NGOs and the like[90].

Specific Reforms. The need of the hour is to make the UNGA more functional, more democratic and more representative of 'We the People'. It should be revitalised as a universal forum by streamlining its agenda and proceedings[91]. The plenary session should be shortened from its current three months to six weeks to bring objectivity. Time limit be placed on proceedings, resolutions dealing with slightly different part of the same topic should be collapsed into a single resolution and the right of morality on a given question in the UNGA should be better protected.

UNSC

'Only a basic change in attitude by member States can turn the Security Council from a 'debating society' into a 'Keepers of Peace'.

In Essence. In essence, the reforms call for a wider representation at the UNSC in consonance with the current world order and the just aspirations of the majority world (developing) in having a say in the decision making organ of the UN. In this, certain permutations and combinations of membership options have been put forward by the experts. As rightly pointed out by Mr Hardip Singh Puri, India's permanent representative to the UN, that without a wider representation at the UNSC representing the current world reality, UNSC is an ineffective organization. He says, that keeping in mind the present pecking order in the world some of the permanent representatives will find it hard to justify their position on the high table[92].

On Proportional Representation. There is also a strong voice to suggest that those who contribute most to the UN financially, militarily and diplomatically should have a proportional representation in its decision - making organ. Strong views have been expressed in the anarchic and undemocratic nature of the veto and the damage it has done to stymie many an appropriate 'urgently called for' and 'majority endorsed' decisions of the UN. Knowing the hard reality that the veto cannot be wished away in totality, suggestions have been put forward to dilute its sting by limiting its application. Recommendations also included the provision for indicative voting to get the 'sense of the house' (UNGA) and for widening the jurisdiction of the UNSC to include the threats, we face in the 21st Century.

Regional Organisations

Status. Either as a function of Cold War legacy, or to project a collective identity or simply to ensure regional or sub-regional security in the face of perceived threats, regional organizations are a reality and a force to reckon with. Most of these have the necessary wherewithal, quantum representative (voting) power and hence, the clout to sway a decision in majority vote, one way or the other.

Requirement of Synergy. Regional organisations can play a very big role in taking on a UNSC mandated action all by their own or 'Standing in' till the UN forces under the UNDPKO can be made effective. For this to happen, the concept has to first get acceptance by allaying the apprehensions of member States against a possible misuse. Also, in working under the UN Mandate and not independently and respecting all associated constraints, the stated regional organisations, would have to give up portion of their individual character including their exclusivity in regional dominance. This will require a change in the mindset. Unfortunately many of such organisations in the past have acted out of their perception of the failure of the UN (NATO-Kosovo1999, US-Rwanda ...?). In sum, it is still a tall order calling for subjugating individual supremacy to the requirement of total coherence and synergy for the cause of global good. In order to provide adequate teeth to the weak regional organisation, UN may have to provide equipment and finance. Once enabled these organisations could actually contribute to the standing capacities towards the UN 'Stand by Forces' or UN RDF.

Finance

Relevance and Current Crises. HLP has opined that one of the fundamental issues relating to the future of the UN is to resolve the issue of mobilising adequate resources for the functioning of the UN. Currently the UN finds itself in a strait jacket partly because of the accumulation of huge arrears of payments and partly, because of the late payment by host of member States.

Voluntary Contributions. The researcher feels that the practice of voluntary contributions is fundamentally incorrect. It has introduced uncertainty and unpredictability in the work of the UN, since donor States try to extract maximum out of the voluntary contributions towards their own agenda. Voluntary contributions introduces a donor-recipient relationship which dilutes the basic UN principle of 'Sovereign Equality of all Member States'. Rapid increase in voluntary contribution actually amounts to economic hostaging of UN by the contributors.

Regular Budget. It is the sense of the researcher that instead of this undemocratic and unhealthy practice of voluntary contributions fillip should be provided to raising regular UN budgets through contribution by each Member State, as decided by the UNSC and made universally applicable. The Researcher understands that it is indeed a difficult proposition, but that is the only way, a democratic process of equality and dignity with a capacity driven sharing of responsibility can be put into effect, freeing the UN of the economic hegemony of a few States. To put this thought into action, a fresh exercise of assessment of ODA liabilities be undertaken by the UNSC based on current realities and payment capabilities. Interest should be charged on late payments except for a few very low income countries in genuine difficulties. Arrears from this group could be liquidated by one time proportional increase in the assessment of other member States. Deliberate non payment should attract sanctions. The present excessively high ceiling of 25% by any single member State should be reduced to 10-12.5%. The cost of ending this single state dominance should be shared by middle order economic powers based on their economic prowess as assessed by the UNSC.

Actions by the UN. The UN systems and organisations should re-assess and re-align their priorities and learn to manage their finances within the regular budgets. If the rampant corruption, huge wastages and gross over-spending and spending on non-essentials can be controlled, this will be possible.

Autonomous Sources. An expert group should examine various proposals for providing to the UN access to autonomous/alternate sources of financing. In fact, many practical financing options have been forward by experts. These could include taxes in currency speculations (Tobin Tax) taxes on international arms sale, global carbon tax on sale of fossil fuels. UN tax on premium air travellers on certain international sectors, tax on trade, marine ocean transport and use of outer space etc. Lastly, UNSG's recommendations of clearing of the peacekeeping budget through a single set of accounts should be implemented. In particular, his proposal to establish a reserve fund for pre assessment start up of peacekeeping operations should be accepted and urgently acted upon. In essence, the peacekeeping activities must not be starved of funds[93].

Implementation of The Secretary General's Report on 'In Larger Freedom'

Putting the Report in the Perspective

As a Part of UN Reform Agenda. The UNSG's Report 'In Larger Freedom: Towards Development, Security and Human Rights for All' can be best put in the perspective as a string in the overall UN Reform Chronology. In this chronology basically covering the period from 1945-2012 there have been some milestone developments in the reform agenda of which, the report 'In Larger Freedom' forms a part. Basically these developments can be condensed as under[94]:-

(a) **1945-49.** In the initial years the first decisive change was the **development of peacekeeping measures** to oversee implementation of cease-fire agreements (Middle East-1949, Kashmir-1950).

(b) **1950.** Soviet Union led reform of **replacing the post of the Secy General with a troika** to contain independence of secretariat.

(c) **1950 - 1965. Decolonization** and many new member States joining the UN system. Membership climbing to 118 in 1965. Development agenda being very strong.

(d) **1965. Establishment of UNDP** and start of Negotiations on NIEO.

(e) **1970s. North/South conflict.**

(f) **1980s. Financial crises,** retreat of the US triggering reforms of the budgetary process and downsizing of organisations.

(g) **1990s. Rediscovery and renaissance of UN with the end** of Cold War. Major expansion of the organisation and the reforms associated with the Agenda for Peace launched by Secy Gen Boutros Boutros Ghali. Interest started growing in the reform of UNSC, better coherence of UN and better humanitarian structures. New awareness on AIDS, re-vamping of peace keeping missions following Brahimi Report.

(h) **2000.** Millennium flavour gripping the member States. **Launch of the MDGs** at the Millennium Summit.

(j) **2003.** A milestone initiative by the Secretary Gen Kofi Annan to task a panel of 16 eminent and experienced experts to assess the current threats to the international peace and security and to evaluate how well our existing policies and institutions have done in addressing these threats and to recommend ways to strengthen the United Nations. The result was a seminal document called the '**Report of the High Level Panel on Threats, Challenges and Change**', now under implementation at various levels.

(k) **2005.** Another ground breaking work by the Secretary Gen Kofi Annan in bringing out the Report '**In Larger Freedom – Towards Development Security and Human Rights for All**' in the Millennium + 5 Summit or World Summit (Discussed later).

(l) **2007.** Secretary **Gen Ban-Ki-Moon continuing with the reform agenda** covering oversight, integrity and ethics and approving a number of loosely related reform initiatives.

(m) **2011.** UN Secretary Gen appointing Atul Khare of India to spearhead efforts to implement a reform agenda assessed at streamlining and improving efficiency in the world body[95,96]. Khare has been tasked to lead the **Change Management Team (CMT)** at the UN working with both departments and offices within the Secretariat and with other bodies in the UN System and 193 member States. The CMT is tasked with guiding the implementation of a reform agenda at the UN that starts with the devising of a wide ranging plan to streamline activities, increase accountability and ensure that the organisation is more effective and efficient in delivering its many mandates[97].

And the story continues...

Relevance of 'In Larger Freedom' Report. From the above chronology, it would be evident that apart from the MDG and HLP, the 'In Larger Freedom Report' is another important milestone in shaping the history, outcomes and future of the UN in the 21st Century. In fact the "In Larger Freedom" Report is a sequential development in time order, as also, a stock taker and more, of the implementation of the MDG on a check milestone of five years after its inception (2000-2005). While this research has already analysed the MDG and HLP, it will now be in order to dialate upon the 'In Larger Freedom Report'.

Report–'In Larger Freedom'

Anchor Thoughts. The anchor thought in the report is its triple aim of 'Development, Security And Human Rights For All'. These thoughts have been expressed as specific aims to work for, like 'Freedom from Want, Freedom from Fear, Freedom to Live in Dignity and Strengthening the United Nations'. In essence therefore, the Report encapsulates all the aspirations, all the fears, all the dreams and all the takeaways, which the member States in general and the peoples of the world in particular, could ever think of getting from the UN. It also takes into its sweep, the sum-total of all the various reforms and agendas that have ever been put forward by one and all in the six decades plus existence of the world body. In sum therefore, it is a complete and comprehensive report which says it all at one place. If the implementation of the points mentioned in the report is completed, the world would have 'done it all' as regards the UN and its future in the 21st Century.

Freedom From Want

A Sombre Note. The statement of this freedom starts on a sombre note – (quote) 'The last 25 years have seen the most dramatic reduction in extreme poverty, yet dozens of countries have became poorer, more than a billion people live on less than are dollar a day, each year, three million people die of HIV/AIDS and 11 million children die before their fifth birthday...' (unquote). The requirement therefore is to free the entire human race from 'WANT'.

Priority Areas For Action. In the broad head of 'Freedom From Want', certain priority areas for action have been identified. These are summarized below :-

(a) **National Development Strategies.** It calls for each member State in extreme poverty to formulate and implement a National Development Strategy, bold enough to meet the MDG target for 2015. This strategy must encompass the full spectrum of activities to include public investments, policies, gender equality, environment, rural development, urban development, health system, education, science and technology and innovations.

(b) **Financing For Development.** The report calls upon the member States to double the Global Development Assistance mostly by donor countries meeting the pledges already made (0.7 % of GDP). The Global Fund to fight HIV/AIDS/TB/Malaria must be fully funded.

(c) **Trade.** As to the WTO, the report calls for the early finalisation of the Doha Round of negotiations. As a first step it urges the member States to provide duty and quota free market access for all exports from Least Developed Countries. Is it not a pity that seven years down the line, we are still struggling with Doha negotiations which many experts call it as a 'dead dialogue' that needs to be replaced by a new deal[98].

(d) **Debt Relief.** The report defines debt sustainability of a member State as the level of debt that allows a country to achieve the MDG by 2015 without increase in debt ratio. It also calls for environmental sustainability, need to develop new tools for climate change and to preserve biodiversity. It is however a pity to see that even in Dec 2012 Kyoto Protocol has reached nowhere. The Developing countries led by BRIC nations are pursuing a well intentioned crusade to extract a commitment from developed nations. Is it not a pity to see that in the UN's Annual Climate Change Conference just concluded in Doha on 08 Dec 2012 while 194 countries have agreed to an extension of the Kyoto Protocol through 2020, they still omitted the world's two biggest greenhouse gas emitters- China and USA[99].

Freedom From Fear

In Essence. Under this broad head, the UNSG embraced the vision of Collective Security. He recounted, that the threats to peace and security in the 21st Century are not only international wars and conflicts, terrorism, WMD, organised crime, civil violence, these also include poverty, deadly infectious diseases, environmental degradation and war. He stated that the UN must be transformed into an effective instrument of preventing conflict thus ushering the humanity into 'Freedom From Fear'.

Key Policy Issues. Very briefly, some of the issues identified as key policies and priority action areas are as under :-

(a) Preventing Catastrophic Terrorism. Reiterating the need for a clear definition, the report identified five pillars for an anti terrorism strategy. These include, dissuading people from resorting to terrorism or supporting it, denying terrorist access to funds and materials, deterring States from sponsoring terrorism, developing State capacities to defeat terrorism and defending human rights. It is a pity to see that the pillars notwithstanding, the spread of international terrorism is on the rise, over-shadowing the entire humanity under the cloud of fear.

(b) NBC Weapons. The report is based on the dual pillars of disarmament and non-proliferations. On disarmament, it calls for reducing arsenals pursuing arms control and upholding tests moratoriums. On non-proliferations, it calls for strengthening IAEA through universal adoption of Model Additional Protocol and FMCT ratification. Looking at the current realities today, most of these utopian dreams are far from fulfilment.

(c) Reducing the Prevalence and Risk of War. Besides the basic theme, the report emphasizes for a smooth transition from War to Peace through the UN efforts of 'Peace Building Commission'. It also calls for zero tolerance on sexual exploitation of minors and other vulnerable people. Other priorities include effective cooperation to control organised crime, prevent illicit trade in small arms and light weapons. It is difficult to see that much distance needs to be covered on the path of risk mitigation, as envisioned in this report. This has been analysed later in this research document.

Freedom to Live in Dignity

The Essence. Under this main head, the report calls for specific action on the following points :-

(a) **Rule of Law**. It urges the international community to embrace. R2P as the basis of collective action against genocide, ethnic cleansing and crimes against humanity. It states that all treaties relating to the protection of civilians should be ratified and implemented. Steps should be taken to strengthen cooperation with the International Criminal Court.

(b) **Human Rights**. It calls for strengthening of the office of the High Commissioner for Human Rights through more resources and staff. This office must play an active role in deliberation of the Security Council and of the proposed Peace Building Commission. Various treaties should be rendered more effective and responsive.

(c) **Democracy**. The report calls for a Democracy Fund to be created. No effort must be spared to promote democracy and strengthen the rule of law.

Strengthening the UN

Essence. In this concluding portion, the Report recognizes the critical need for the UN to adapt to the circumstances of the 21st Century. In that, it calls for the following specific actions:-

(a) **General Assembly**. The General Assembly should take bold measures to streamline its agenda and speed up deliberative process. It should concentrate on the major substantive issues of the day and establish mechanisms to engage fully and systematically with the civil society.

(b) **Security Council**. The Security Council should be broadly representative of the realities of power in today's world (see the loose fit in the grip of the sentence; this itself is the realisation of what can and what cannot be!). The recommendations of the HLP (Model A/B) are recommended for implementation.

(c) **Economic and Social Council**. The ECOSOC should be reformed so that it can effectively assess progress in UN's development agenda, serve as a high level development cooperation forum and provide direction for the efforts of various inter-governmental bodies in the economic and social arena throughout the UN system.

(d) **Proposed Human Rights Council.** The Commission on Human Rights suffers from declining credibility and professionalism and is in the need of major reforms. It should be replaced by a smaller Human Rights Council as a principal organ of the UN or subsidiary of General Assembly. Its members must be elected by the General Assembly by two-thirds majority of member present and voting.

(e) **The Secretariat.** The Secy Gen should take steps to realign the Secretariat's structure to match the priorities outlined in the Report and should create Cabinet style decision making mechanism. This is proposed to be achieved through a one time staff buyout and refresh exercise.

"It is for the world community to decide whether this moment of uncertainty presages wider conflict, depressing inequality and erosion of the rule of law or is used to review institutions for peace prosperity and human right".

—Secretary General

All Encompassing! The Report "In Larger Freedom; Towards Development Security and Human Rights for All" covers the entire spectrum of the 'desired end-state dream' for the UN of the 21st Century. This important document coming out on the heels of HLP, five years after the Millennium Summit and upon a third of the run-up of the MDG, is a very viable 'check milestone'. Freedom From Want, Freedom From Fear, Freedom to Live in Dignity combined with the ideas on strengthening the UN actually 'sums up all' that is required for the international community suffering from multiple sub-optimalities/deprivations and repression, as also, from a huge UN monolith warning to crumble down under the dead weight of its inefficiency over staffing, poor monitoring and redundant mechanisms.

So, What Next. If all or even 60-70% of the points mentioned in the Report would have seen the light of the day in the roll on period from 2005 till 2012, there was no need for this research as the desired end-state would have seen achieved/nearly achieved. The sad reality is that most of the action points in the Report have remained only on paper. The forward movement of the research will now be directed at identifying that with reference to the points given in the Report, where are we and where we need to go? This thought is contained in the next heads.

Steps to Achieve Freedom From Want and Freedom From Fear

In order to chart out the status of implementation of various action points contained in the report under four major heads, the research content has been divided into the following four areas :-

(a) Economic Development.

(b) Human Rights.

(c) Environmental and Health.

Economic Development

Establishment of UN Institutions Over Time. The provisions in the UN Charter for the economic and social development of the humanity are reflected in a liberal vision of building institutions and programmes to promote prosperity and peace through international co-operation and industrial change. The implementation of the broad agenda of economic and social developments of member State has had multiple institutions, routes and programmes and implementational methodologies. Starting in 1940 as a programme for providing technical assistance to less developed countries (Expanded Programme for Technical Assistant or EPTA) many international projects jointly funded by UN took shape like, WHO, FAO, UNESCO. In 1965 the UN approved a new UN Development Programme (UNDP) to enhance co-ordination of various types of technical assistance programmes within the UN system[100]. Much of the human development and poverty alleviation has been driven through by certain key institutions like the World Bank, IMF, GATT (now the WTO) which are historically referred to as Bretton Woods Institutions. Also in the forefront of economic and social development is the ECOSOC. All these institutions put together are taking forward the broad agenda of the economic and social development of member States.

The Results Thereof. As to the results, while many a development goals have been achieved, billions and billions of hungry mouths fed, destitute sheltered and countries/humanities lifted out of the cauldron of subsistence to human existence, like most other UN bodies, the development institutions have also suffered from the known UN ills of unreal assured goals, under performance at times, duplications, wastages, lack of funding, etc. Notwithstanding this, there is more good than bad as the huge monolith of the Economic and Social Development Agenda has indeed survived. As already discussed in the research document there have been two major goal-setting exercises, one at the Millennium Summit (MDGs) and the other at Millennium plus phase (In Larger Freedom) besides numerous reform Reports like the HLP, Brahimi and others.

Evolving Ideas About Development

Economic Liberalism. Most of the institutions discussed above have pushed forward their economic and social agendas on the development thought of the Post WW II period which were anchored on the concept of economic liberalism. This concept is rooted in the Adam Smith's idea of human beings being rationale and acquisitive seeking their optimal development expeditiously, and for that to happen, the need and essentiality for separation of economics from State politics and free flow of the former. It calls for free flow of trade and economic intercourse, puts faith in the multinational co-operations in the private sector domain to be the engines for growth and an emphasis for basic skills of education, health, hygiene and national administrative services to sustain development.

Challenges. The economic development of member States through the route of economic liberalization and free market economy was challenged by the world economists belonging to the Marxist School of thought that propounded the 'dependency theory'. According to this, the free market route divided the nations of the world in rich and poor; the former at the core and later at the periphery, where though the drive of economies the rich became richer while the poor remained/or became poorer due to their permanent dependency on the rich and a perennial unfavourable trade balance between the export of core materials from them and import of manufactured goods from the rich. Such system was also believed to produce permanent economic inequalities, promote colonisation and eternal dependence. Due to this thought, the economic liberalization route did not have a free run and was ungirded on many of its initiatives.

New Turn to Economic Development, NIEO and its Status.

(a) **New Turn**. The G-77 along with the OPEC countries, bolstered by their overwhelming strength in forcing majority decisions, turned the direction of economic liberalization towards a call for establishment of a NIEO. This basically aimed at reducing the economic and trade disadvantages suffered by the developing nations vis-a-vis developed nations; something which the dependency theory postulated. The concessions demanded including the fixing of the costs of raw materials exported by developing countries in reference to the finished goods imported from the developed nations, greater authority of developing nations over their natural resources, increased foreign investment in developing nations, preferential treatment of exports from developing nations and improved means of technology transfer to make it cheaper and more appropriate for the local needs. In a sense NIEO, was a clarion call of the developing South to take on the developed North in a one-on-one challenge; this is famously referred to as the North-South divide.

(b) **Sense of the Author**. The G-77 along with the other countries of the developing South must be credited to firmly anchor in the concept of NIEO. Ever since its adoption by the UNGA in May 1974, it has had numerous successes and many failures; the fight/ the voice raising/need for recognition continue unabated. The poor nations on the vehicle of NIEO achieved several successes at the GATT to get a preferential treatment in their exports to developing world. One example is the waiving of tariff and entry taxes on more than 97% of their exported goods to the developed North. All the above notwithstanding, the appetite of the North is now getting satiated to stomach more of the NIEO related demands in international politico-economic system. One of reasons is their creaking economies and rising unemployment at home, and secondly, the shortening of divide that once separated them for the South on the high table being propelled by the rising costs of raw material imports, shrinking natural resources and steady development of many developing nations. In the ODA, the 'donor fatigue' is setting in as calls for re-structuring ODA contribution to UN get louder. The NIEO flavoured fight continues. We saw that in the US nominee Jim Yong Kini winning over the Nigerian (Ngozi OkonzoIweata) and the Colombian (Jose Antanio Ocampo) in the race to lead the World Bank (North Win)[101]. However the developing nations could forge a Doha 2012 resolution of Kyoto

Protocol extension upto 2012 by getting much of their demands included in the text including the new commitment period under the Kyoto protocol for a Universal Climate Agreement by 2015. It is felt that the NIEO as a vehicle of voice/resistance/raising awareness/protest and for fielding new demands of the South is here to stay in pushing forward the agendas of the developing nations although the comprehensive transformation, as was envisaged through the NIEO route is not likely in the foreseeable future.

Debt Relief. While most of the key elements under the NIEO have not been accepted by the developed North, another success area in the field of international economic development and poverty alleviation is the Debt Relief. In that, the poor nations have been raising their voices that their debt repayment is so crushing that there are no funds to commit for health, education, disease eradication, poverty alleviation etc. Their demand for debt relief was raised by a coalition of NGOs and Church groups. In an another achievement in the field of debt relief/reduction, IMF and World Bank in 1996 undertook a major policy shift called the Heavily Indebted Poor Countries Initiative (HIPC), an institution that was accelerated in 1999 and 2005 permitting 100% debt relief from IMF and World Bank for some extremely poor countries at the brink of failure/economic disaster etc.

Views on NIEO

(a) **A Great Institute.** NIEO has been a game-changer thought propounded way back in the seventies that has brought visible changes in the field of poverty reduction/debt relief etc. Riding on the vehicle of economic liberalism and rising from the ashes of dependency theory, it has been a major platform of North-South divide and many a poor and developing countries have benefitted from it. Since its mammoth and expansive end-state of reaching the other end of the tunnel in putting the member State out of the clutches of poverty and debt are far from over, this initiative will continue to be relevant all through in the 21st Century.

(b) **Counter Voices.** Like in all human endeavours related to UN the report card of NIEO driven movement has been at best of 'mixed success'. Sure enough, there are counter-voices calling for the modification of the economic liberalism policy based on its perceived failure of eliminating poverty, hunger, literacy and growing income equality. There are calls for the re-distribution of income to the poorest nations that have been left out of the development process. The researcher however feels that while the counter voices may have some meat (as the inevitable other side of the coin) much has happened and will continue to happen under the banner of NIEO, riding on the vehicle of economic liberalism.

Women and Development

Action Over Time. Right from the early days of the formation of ECOSOC, the development of women (and children) was considered an agenda for action. Predictably therefore, the Commission on the Status of Women was one of the six main constituents of ECOSOC. Over a period of time, many a new initiatives have been taken, commissions formed and resolutions passed. Women in Development (WID), International Decade for Women, UN Women's Conferences in 1975, 1980, 1985, 1990, 2000, 2005 (Beijing plus five), 2010 (Beijing Plus 10), approval of the convention on Elimination of All Forms of Declaration Against Women (CEDAW) in 1979, establishment of International Research and Training Institute for Advancement of Women (INSTRAW), establishment of UN Development Fund for Women (UNIFEM) all show that the UN in particular and the world at large is alive to the fact that one half (and more) of the humanity needs to be taken along the other on the path of development[102].

The Main Agendas. All the above and more are raising voices and taking actions on common agendas which is based on the empowerment of women through education and economic opportunities. It is raising its voices to give women the control over their lives by promoting education for girls, bringing in gender quality, improving maternal health and ensuring women, equal access to economic resources including land credit, science and technology, vocational training, information, communication and markets[103]. Need of the above call and action points had a deep reflection in the formation of Goals for the MDGs Initiative[104] as discussed earlier.

A Major Initiative. Finally a milestone initiative came in 2010, when the UN established an entity for Gender Equality and Empowerment of Women also known as UN Women. It became operational in Jan 2011 with the former President of Chile, Michelle Bachelet as its inaugural Executive Director[105]. UN Women has been supporting Inter- Governmental Bodies such as the 'Commission on the Status of Women' in formulation of policies global standards and norms. It is helping member States in empowerment of women, implementation of women friendly policies and is working to promote gender equality.

Multiple Action in Progress. A careful look at the world developments reveals a lot of 'voice-raising' and 'awareness spreading' that is taking place under the banner of UN Women. This organisation is telling the world that many facts about women which deserve to be heard/acted upon. For example, the global financial and economic crises has hit the women harder than men in the global job market as about 13 million jobs for women have been lost (ILO Report). On 13 Dec 2012 Policy makers and survivors convened at UN HQ on a two day forum to build consensus and identify common strategies on ending pandemic of violence against women and girls[106]. Post the gunning down of the Provincial head of women's affairs in Afghanistan, the UN Women in its Report 'A Long Way to Go' drew attention of the world to the fact that while reporting of crimes against women has increased, most women still suffer in silence in Afghanistan[107]. Strengthening and implementing laws to control violence against women and persuading more countries to adopt them will be the key goal in the 2013 Commission on the State of Women[108].

While all the above reads like a song; unfortunately, it is a dream song, since the realities of the world are different. More than half of 40 million people living with AIDS are women. In Africa, more than 75% of all AIDs victims are young women between the age of 15-24[109]. According to a report on the net by a US based NGO, one in every four women has experienced violence by a spouse/boy friend and on an average, 500 women are raped or sexually assaulted in the US each day![110] Rape has been historically used as a weapon of war. Take the case of Bosnian War where some 50,000-60,000 women were raped while only 12 cases have been presented[111]. These days, the frequent cases of gang rape have triggered State-wide protests in India. Unfortunately in India, the crime against women and children is on the rise. Besides the unsafe capital, the IT hub of the country has moved up from position three to position two in the crime graph of the country. As per a report published in the Hindu on 25 Dec 2012, Bangalore reported 1890 crimes against women in 2011 as compared to 1570 in 2011[112].

It can be said in sum that while the initiatives and agencies provided by the world body are laudable and are providing a platform for exposing the issues of women/development and crime, there is indeed a very long way to go.

MDGs - A Milestone in the History of UN

Role of NGOs. In the role of executing the women and development agenda, as also, raising prominent voices for the cause of preserving human rights, the NGOs have been playing a great role. Fighting for a voice and funding, way back in the eighties, today the NGOs are an integral part of delivering mechanism for various development related agendas whether it is WHO or UNHCR or Save the Children, or CARE or World Vision and more, the NGOs visibility and their positive work footprint has only grown with time[113].

Crystal Gazing. So what lies ahead for the UN in the indomitable task of bringing about economic development and sustainability? This is a complex question which has no straight answers, for there lie ahead huge challenges.

In Continued Centrality of UN. Is UN the sole voice on the world stage? Clearly no. With fast pace of globalisation, the phenomenal growth of MNCs, emergence of global markets, specially in the third world, the rise of NGOs as major players and the dynamic progress by the Bretton Woods Institutions, UN has become 'just another player' in executing the agenda of world economic development and sustenance. That said, it is also true that notwithstanding 'Just another player', UN still is the 'most important player' or more appropriately, the player on the most forefront of all the different agencies. It is still the UN that provides the 'world stage' for setting agendas, bringing the comity of nations on one floor, initiate world debates/summits/forums from what emerge all the major policies. Notwithstanding any other development in any area/forum, this centrality of UN is likely to remain undiminished right through the 21st Century.

Lessons From Past. In the sixty plus years of dishing out the policies and initiating actions, some important lessons have emerged for the UN. The foremost is the need to understand that the aid requirement of each country is specific and focussed and there is no broad-brush approach. If some country requires a breather from continued killing/atrocities/ethnic cleansing, the other may require technical assistance in standing on its own feet in emerging areas of self sufficiency. Co-ordination is another area to reduce wasteful expenditures, cut out duplication and put money to optimal use. The concept of sustainability has shown that the development dose has to be holistic. Poverty cannot also be reduced by pumping dollars, the problem of civil wars, ethnic conflicts and organised crime need to be tackled to crush poverty and violence traps.

Challenges. Huge challenges lie ahead the ever growing circle of economic and social development needs of the world community. These actually challenge the limited and finite capability of the UN to address the issue. There is just that much which the donors are wishing to put on the plate in these hard times of economic recession. Also, executing the aid programmes often meets the hurdle of state sovereignty when the State Governments resist interference by donor agencies/ countries to interfere with their State policies. So when the aid giving World Bank or IMF desires change in domestic economic policies or wants to crush out corruption of State level offices there are problems. Lastly, the New International Economic Order NIEO is showing the world reality to all, that it is no longer a US driven world. In the parlance of economic prowess, there are many other emerging tigers which call the shots today; BRICS, G-20, G-7 and so on. These realities are likely to persist well into the 21st Century.

Human Rights

> बडे भाग मानुस तन पावा, सुर दुर्लभ सद्ग्रन्थन गावा ।
> साधन धाम मोक्ष करि द्वारा, पाए न जेहि परलोक सवाँरा ॥
>
> —राम चरित मानस

> *"A soul gets a human body only through great good fortune. Even Gods pray to the Almighty for it".*
>
> —*Ram Charita Manas*

So Fundamental. As enshrined in the immortal verse of Sri Ram Charit Manas, 'being born as a human' is in itself the biggest bliss and one of the bliss of being a human is one's natural and inalienable inheritance of the human rights as something fundamental to life itself[114].

Badly Abused. It is however so ironic to state that the most fundamental is 'most abused'. Today, our whole country is hanging its head in shame to see the mauling of human rights of a 23 year old women whose modesty was outraged so brutally by some savages. Where are human rights?

Gaining Prominence. While the abuse of human rights is in existence from times immortal, these have really shot into prominence soon after World War II when the whole world, was mauled by the gigantic scale of human atrocities; mass killings, millions of war casualties, atrocities of NAZI Germany on Jews and more. Much in the latter half of the 20th Century and into the 21st Century as well, the human abuse is only on the rise; ethnic cleansing, chemical attacks, State's indifference to social deprivation of peoples and their pitiable existence-all are various states of human rights violation.

UN's Role. The UN has played an important role in the process of bringing in a global awareness on human rights, the end of apartheid, recognition of women's rights as human rights, spread of democracy, emerging norms of human interventions, R2P etc provide evidence to this trend.

Human Rights Related to Charter and Organisation. One of the primary purposes of the UN as set forth in Chapter 1, Article 1, is international co-operation in solving various international problems including those of 'humanitarian character' and 'in promoting and encouraging respect for human rights and for the fundamental freedom for all' without distinction as to race, sex, language and religion. Similarly, the General Assembly's broad mandate is to discuss any issue within the scope of UN charter and raise specific issues related to human rights violation. In 2006, the UNGA overwhelmingly approved the creation of a new 47 member Human Rights Council to regularly report to the Assembly on all aspects related to human rights. On the other hand, though the Security Council has definitely embraced human rights, it has had a mixed record in responding to the complex humanitarian emergencies since the end of Cold War. Its actions in crises from Haiti to Bosnia, Somalia, the DRC, East Timor, Darfur, Libya, and now Syria have been a mixed bag of successes and failures. This itself draws us to the conclusion that organization, agencies and intentions notwithstanding, the all important aspect of Human Rights and its preservation against all odds is a huge issue which needs to be taken head-on.

Some Other Organisation. One another important addition to the UN organisational structure relating to human rights, is the Office of the High Commissioner for Human Rights (OHCHR) established in 1993. It provides a visible international advocate for human rights in the same way that the UN High Commissioner for Refugees focuses international attention on that problem. Increasingly, OHCHR has assumed an operational role providing technical assistance to countries in the form of training courses for judges and prime officials, electoral assistance and advisory series on constitutional/legislative reforms etc[115].

Articulation of Human Right at UN. For UN, the international articulation of human rights started with the unanimous approval of the Universal Declaration of Human Rights on Dec 9, 1948. It is a pity however, that even in Dec 2012; 64 years down the line, the adherence to the Universal Declaration is only a mixed bag with hundreds of cases of gross violation to the tenets of the Declaration in letter, spirit and misdeeds.

On Monitoring. One of the basic tool for ensuring the adherence to human rights lies in putting in place, an effective monitoring mechanism. While the ILO and OHCHR are the two fundamental UN agencies for monitoring, the actual watch is being kept by a host of active NGOs/IGOs and interest groups representing traumatised communities. In essence, while the UN human rights monitoring has improved over the years, it has also remained limited on its measurable impact.

Trends. In relation to Human Rights maintenance, a few major trends are visible. Firstly, there has been an effort by the OHCHR at main streaming the Human Rights issue. One indicator towards this cause is the linking up of Human Rights issue with the Human Development Agenda. The spirit of this thought lies in the belief that basic human needs like food, water, shelter, clothing elementary health care etc, as tenets of human development index must be seen as inalienable Human Rights of all individuals. Similarly, towards the cause of providing basic safety to life against a host of natural/ man made disasters as enshrined in the still evolving concept of R2P is also to be seen as yet another dimension of human right.

Enforcement. Another facet of ensuring human rights observance and adherence is the act of 'enforcement'. Since 1990, a series of enforcement actions have been authorized under Chapter VII of the Charter to deal with humanitarian emergencies in Northern Iraq after Gulf War, Somalia, Bosnia, Rwanda, Sierra Leonne, East Timor and Haiti. In select cases, the Security Council has explicitly linked egregious human rights violation that result in large scale humanitarian crises to security threats and authorized enforcement action without the consent of State concerned. From a human rights point of view, these action represented a substantial step beyond the kind of humanitarian relief UN has long provided for refugees through the

UNHCR and Relief Works Agency for Palestine Refugees in the Near East. These humanitarian interventions have employed UN Peacekeeping forces in the 'Coalition of the willing to protect relief workers, guard', medical and food supplies, run convoys and shield civilians from further violence and sufferings in so called safe areas that often were far from safe due to inadequate number of UN troops and unwillingness to employ armed forces.

Resistance to Enforcement. Many Governments are suspicious of strengthening the UN's power to intervene in what they may still regard as their domestic jurisdiction. Still, with the evolution of complex peace building missions and the debate over R2P, some of humanitarian intervention have set important precedents for the UN enforcement actions in the field of human rights.

The Role of NGOs. The NGO's have been a major player in the entire game of reporting human rights violation and ensuring/implementing activities dedicated to providing human rights. NGOs provide much of the information to the UN Treaty bodies since many State Reports are self-serving and rarely disclose treaty violations. NGOs evaluate such reports, gather additional information, push States for compliance and publicise abuse. The best known international human rights NGO is Amnesty International founded in 1961. Other key human rights NGOs include Human Rights Watch and International Commission of Jurists.

Milestone Activities of UN in Preserving/Enforcing Human Rights

General. UN has been the most visible and viable platform which has projected the human rights issue as an international agenda highlighting the need for promoting human rights, enforcing human rights and in setting and monitoring standards.

Major/International Issues in Human Rights.

(a) **Anti Apartheid Campaign**. Out of its many milestone achievements the successful culmination of the apartheid campaign in South Africa indeed stands out. Both the General Assembly, as well as, the Security Council went beyond the regime of sanctions and kept up the tempo of sustained criticism of South Africa for almost 40 years. In a testimony to UN's key role in delegitimising and defeating apartheid, Nelson Mandela made one of his earliest public speech after being freed to the UN General Assembly, thanking members for the support.

(b) **Women's Rights as Human Rights**. Another major development in the UN system has been the recognition of women's rights as human rights. Before this, the Women's rights were considered separate and different from human rights even though the Universal Declaration of Human Rights states "rights and freedoms set forth in this Declaration must be given without distinction to race, colour, sex or language". In this context, the seminal work done by many NGOs working under the provisions of Conventions on the Elimination of All Forms of Discrimination Against Woman (CEDAW) must also be acknowledged. The four successive UN sponsored World Conference on Women in Mexico City (1975), Copenhagen (1980), Nairobi (1985), Beijing (1995) also raised huge awareness on Rights of Woman. The formation of UN Woman has provided an institutional home for woman's activities in economic development and human rights.

(c) **Human Trafficking and Slave Like Practice**. Another major gross human rights violation area is the continuing menace of human trafficking or condemning humans to slave like practices of forced labour. According to an open source report, as of 2012, approximately 12-27 million people have been enslaved and put into forced labour. About a quarter of these have been trafficked. The UN has come out with the Convention Against Transnational Organised Crime with an additional protocol for trafficking in persons. As of 2011, 143 countries have been a party to this protocol. The UN Global Initiative to fight Human Trafficking, better known as UN GIFT was established in 2007 by ILO, UNHCHR, UNICEF and UNODC. One of the things that is striking about trafficking is absence of a single dominant NGO in this field. Essentially, it is a work in progress with the menace growing at one end and the UN trying to mitigate the same at the other. This trend is likely to play out on similar lines much into the 21st Century.

(d) **Genocide; Crimes Against Humanity; War Crimes**. Another major slur on the face of human rights is the curse of genocide.

The infamous holocaust bringing about the death of some 6 million Jews, gypsyies and others an 'undesirables' under Nazi Germany is a blood-curdling event. As early as 1948, the General Assembly unanimously adopted the convention on Prevention and Punishment of Genocide.

In Retrospect. Despite the convention and its universal acceptance, cases of genocide are shaming the humanity with unflinching regulatory. The so called 'ethnic cleansing' (sic) by Croatia and Bosnian Serbs in the Yugoslavia's civil war is actually a heinous war crime which is very much equivalent to a genocide. In fact, the Security Council members lacked the political will to stop killings in Bosnia. Another failure of the UN system was in Rwanda in 1994, when the evidence of genocide was much clearer. In fact, as the evidence mounted of the systematic slaughtering of minority Tutsis by Hutu extremists, the P-5 ignored the evidence and never used the word genocide[116]. Despite affirmations of 'never again' the UN response has been too little and too late for the 300,000 victims of genocide in the Western region of Darfur. Another two cases of genocide which illustrate the political insensitivity to the crime and dilute UN's stand include Sri Lankan Civil War of 2009 where a large number of civilian casualties were committed by Govt troops and the Gaza war of 2008-09 highlighting war crimes both by Israel and Hamas. And now, what is happening in Syria? The way the Syrian authorities are causing mass civilian casualties is no less than a heinous war crime. The history will condemn them for their acts of commission and omission.

The UN Efforts. In sum, the UN has been central to the efforts to codify standards relating to genocides, crimes against humanity and war crimes. It has also been instrumental in most recent efforts to apply these standards in preventing these egregious crimes and to establish judicial bodies to try those accused of committing them. Despite all this and more, the human rights record, the world over has only been a mixed bag.

Amnesty International Report on the State of World Human Rights

Why This Evaluation? With all the human rights organisations, agencies, policies and arrangement in place, let us see how their cumulative action has manifested on the world human rights scene. To evaluate this aspect, what better way than to pick up the Amnesty International (or World Human Rights Watch) report on the Status of Human Rights in the World

2012. The researcher has had a detailed look at the Amnesty's Report. Some salient points are at succeeding paras.

What was 2011? 2011 was truly a tumultuous year when millions of people took to the streets to demand freedom, justice and dignity. 'Change', 'courage' and 'conflict' all characterised 2011 when people rose up in protest against governments/dictators. They protested against the abuse of power, lack of accountability, growing inequality, deepening poverty, mounting unemployment and the absence of leadership at every level of Govt. The UNSC seemed tired, out of step and increasingly unfit as people took the revolution in their hands and drove it through their blood, guts and sheer frustration. Successful uprisings in Tunisia (Arab Spring) and Egypt ignited protests across the regions in the world starting from Moscow, London, Athens in Europe to Dakar and Kampala in Africa to New York, La Paz and Cuernavaca in Americas.

Peoples Uprising. Inspired by these events people elsewhere in Africa also risked reprisals by protesting against their desperate social and economic conditions expressing their desires for political freedoms. In Europe and Central Asia, as well as, in Asia Pacific Region people repeatedly challenged injustice and violation of human rights. Many autocratic regimes tried to strengthen their grip by crushing protests, arresting leaders and silencing dissenting voices.

Sparks Everywhere. The demand for human rights also resounded across America, both on the streets, as well as, in national courts. Calls for justice from individuals civil societies and indigenous peoples gained strength. Many forms of discrimination deprivation and social inequalities sparked protests across the globe. It became repeatedly clear that opportunistic alliances and financial interests have trumped human rights as global powers jockeyed for influence in various parts of the world. The language of human rights was adopted only when it served the political and corporate agendas.

UN's Role. What about the UN? In this climate of peoples uprising against various forms of injustices, oppressors and tyranny, the UN system has by and large behaved as a passive by-stander. Its failure to intervene in Sri-Lanka in 2009, when large number of civilian casualties were caused by security forces and its nearly toothless stand against Syria, one of Russia's main customer for arms, leaves the UNSC looking redundant as the guardian of global peace. Though there is a clear compelling case for the situation in Syria to be referred to the International Criminal Court for investigation of crimes against humanity, the same is unlikely to happen. The determination of some members in the P-5 to shield Syria, leaves accountability for those crimes as elusive. This actually amounts to a betrayal of Syrian people.

From a deep study of the world scene, the following points are relevant :-

(a) **Atrocities Continue.** While there is an increased awareness in the world community on the aspect of human rights of the peoples, the injustice/oppression/ atrocities continue on the hapless populations trapped deeply in the black hole of deeping poverty rising unemployment and worsening food security.

(b) **Peoples-Driven-Revolution.** A new-found awakening in the 'Peoples-Driven-Revolutions' have shown that autocratic regimes, unrelenting dictators, tyrannical anarchies and corrupt Governments can be shaken from their foundations. Unfortunately, at the same time, it has also been shown that though peoples-driven-change is possible, it is not enough, since the successive corrupt processes in selecting alternative leaders or putting systems in place may squander away limited gains. Opportunists among the residual systems, quite divorced from the peoples revolution (like military) may rise again and usurp power.

(c) **A Weak UN.** The autocratic and oppressive regimes have shown very scant regard for the initiatives of UN mediations/Peace process/Resolutions/Sanctions et al. This was shown clearly by the futility and ineffectiveness of UN's initiatives in Syria and elsewhere. It has brought out clearly that the UN's monitoring and enforcement mechanisms are weak, because it offends the States which are its constituents.

(d) **Wheel within Wheels.** Events have shown once again, how vested national interests could influence world decisions. How the arms-sale interests of Russia do not allow Syrian autocratic regime to be brought to the book for all its atrocities and mass killing of its unarmed civilian population. The frustrating reality of P-5 is out in the street again.

(e) **UN Stymied.** Another reason which makes the UN a bystander, is the continuing stance of many nations to block UN actions under the garb of non-interference and state sovereignty. China for example, is a strong proponent of the sovereignty argument. Rwanda's attempt to keep the report of its atrocities hidden and Israel's vehement defence of its record in the light of Goldstone Report, confirm that state sovereignty is not a dead issue. Similarly, the US pressurising UN to eliminate the position of its human rights investigation in Afghanistan following a report of critical human rights abuse by US Military is a grim reminder of the reality of Super Power hegemony. The unfortunate reality is that something will move only when it either coincides with cumulative (and individual) interest of P-5, or, escapes the faux-paus of US – UN duo.

(f) **US-ICC**. Historically, no major power has played any leading role in promotion of human rights. US resistance to ICC is a formidable blank in advancement of international criminal law.

The Residual World Scene. Such is the world scene on human rights- dynamic and in flux. Such is the ineffective and impotent stand of the UN, battered by the whims/fancies (read national interests) of the P-5. Such is the new awakening in the peoples driven 'revolutions of frustration' against their repression/continuing atrocities/mass killings/dictators/autocratic regimes/lack of governance/absence of leadership/craving for democracies and more. The crying need for 'teething' the UN to silence autocratic voices, rogue regimes though a strong hand of enforcement remains a dream, a distant dream[117,118].

On Environment And Health

Conventional Wisdom and Change Over Time. The conventional understanding of international peace and security has generally meant the State security and the defence of States from external threats. This was the focus of the world and thus the raison-d' être for the establishment of the UN post World War II with the sordid memory of Leagues' failure to prevent a 'World War'! Beyond the confines of its war time orientation, the ideas of international or State security has since expanded to include 'human security' in a method to conceptualise a variety of threats that effect States, vulnerable groups such as women and children – threats that go beyond physical violence. In 2000, for example, the MDGs set the goal of 'Freedom from Fear' and 'Freedom from Want' for all people. In 2004 the High Level panel on Threats, Challenges and Change incorporated many ideas related to human security in its report.

An Expanded View. As per the above seminal documents, the threat to human security were identified from poverty, infectious disease and environmental degradation in addition to such traditional threats as conflict, civilian genocide, nuclear weapon, terrorism and transnational agressed crimes[119].

The Genesis. The UN Conference on the Human Environment, 1972, commonly referred to as **Stockholm Conference** put the environmental issues on UN and global agenda. It initiated a process that has led to the piecemeal constitution of international environmental institutions, expansion of global environmental agendas, increasing acceptance by States of international environmental standards and monitoring regimes and extensive involvement of both NGOs and scientific and technical groups in policy making efforts. Pulling environmental issues on UN agenda was as important to development as peacekeeping was to UN's role in monitoring international peace and security.

Further Progress. The ideas generated at Stockholm continued to be challenged in the next two decades. The UN General Assembly in 1983 established the Brundtl and Commission whose report, 'Our Common Future' introduced the concept of sustainable development by making a link between economic development and the necessity of balancing economic concerns. The Commission's Report was adopted in 1987.

The Milestone - Earth Summit. The 1992 UN Conference on Environmental and Development (UNCED) or the Earth Summit at Rio de Janeiro was a milestone conference that took forward the Stockholm process and the debate over sustainable development and the necessity of balancing economic growth with preserving environment. However, over the years, moving from promises and commitments to implementing sustainable development proved difficult. Rio Plus 10, convened in 2002 in South Africa produced nothing beyond promises.

UNEP. The UN Environment Programme which was the product of Stockholm Conference became the central organisation championing the cause of environment and its preservations. UNEP today plays a key role in the field of environmental preservation and its linkages to external development[120].

IPCC and Kyoto Process. In 1988 another major development took place with the formation of UN's Intergovernmental Panel on Climate change, or IPCC. This independent network of scientists have championed the cause of 'global warming'. Over the years, the key European States have provided leadership on climate change while the US has either been absent or obstructionist. The IPCC efforts were substantiated by the Kyoto Protocol which aimed to stabilize the concentration of green house gases. It asked the developed countries to reduce their overall greenhouse gas emissions by at least 5%, below 1990 levels by 2010 and 8% below 1990 levels by 2020.

Kyoto 2020. While the UN's climate conference in Doha in Dec 2012 has adopted the plan to extend the Kyoto Protocol till 2020, it has many flaws. Firstly the new agreement only covers the developed nations whose total share of world green house emission is less than 15%. It excludes major developing polluters like China and India besides US which refuses to ratify it. The Conference Chairman Abdullah bin Harmed al Alliyah who 'begged' the countries to offer something out of the Conference termed the Deal as 'Doha Climate Gateway'. The Climate Action Network (CAN) a group of 700 NGOs from around the world said that the Doha talks had failed to deliver increased cuts to carbon pollution[121].

What Have We Got Out of Kyoto? Experts feel that 15 years after its painful birth in Kyoto (Japan) the first legally binding agreement to lower emission of greenhouse gases that ended its conference in Doha, Qatar in Dec 2012 actually produced nothing. The biggest flaw is that the protocol applied only to the rich industrialized nations which actually ended up cutting their greenhouse gas emissions by 16% below 1990 levels in 2012 as compared to only 4.7% promised in the conference. Since most of their economics collapsed, this had to happen anyway. Ironically, in the same period the global emissions have risen by 50%, thanks to the rapid industrialization of nations like China, (not covered in the original deal)! Worse still, most of the rich industrial nations have actually achieved their targets by moving their carbon-intensive industries such as steel and aluminium manufacturing to offshore nations not covered by the protocol. Also, most new manufacturing nations are both highly inefficient users of energy and power, their manufacturing processes use dirtiest of all fuel, ie coal resulting in higher emissions. Expert opines that in all this jugglery the Kyoto process may actually have resulted in a substantial increase in the global emission! In any case, with Russia, Japan, New zealand and Canada pulling out, US refusing to ratify it and be a party in future talks, the whimper of Kyoto seems to be on the ebb as a redundant unproductive and ineffectual talk shop[122].

Dilemmas in Human Security

Need For Governance Vs the UN Weakness. A great amount of awareness and visibility now exists in the context of human rights. Also, these are more widely accepted as a permanent part of UN's agenda though it has only been around 1990, since when the framing of environmental degradation and health as human security issues, has actually happened. Institutionalization, however has tended to be piecemeal and adhoc with little thought given on how the co-ordination had to occur. There is also a perennial shortage of funds to tackle the governance challenge posed by human security issue. The big question is whether there should be a centralization of human security issues at UN or should it be decentralized? The sense of the researcher is that while UN must remain in the centre stage for monitoring and pushing these initiatives, all duplications and redundancies in its agendas and organisation need to be ruthlessly cut down. There must not be overlapping mandates, too many meetings and competition for scarce resources[123].

The Old Debate on Sovereignty. Human security issues are all pervading and span across national borders. The old dilemma of 'interference in State sovereignty' is pitched against the international responsibility to mitigate the suffering of fellow humans, the famous R2P. Sometime national interests drive actions. For example, the US concern on Haiti in 1990 was prompted due to a flood of huge number of refugees to US shores. Quite obviously, the dictators and anarchic rules will understandably resist all effort of humanitarian interventions to their nefarious designs on the pretext of State sovereignty. Such offenders should in fact be brought to the ICC.

Need For Co-operation. For any issue/agenda/programme to get implemented at the international state, the collective will of the Nation States is needed. If that is not present, the programme/initiative will end in a whimper. Look what has happened to the climate issue and the joke of 'Doha Climate Gate way', USA not ratifying the Kyoto process, Japan, Russia and Canada and New zealand pulling out, India - China not covered though big major polluters, the Kyoto is a meaningless exercise. So will it be the case with any other humanitarian suffering alleviation exercise, if the world community's support is not forthcoming by way of a majority (read big players) consent.

What has actually been achieved in the field of environment and health is huge awareness and visibility at the world stage. Unfortunately, there are still a great amount of overlapping agendas in UN bodies dedicated to human development and security (UNEP, WHO, UNHCR etc). The IPCC initiative is reaching nowhere with the Kyoto process gasping for breath or is it a dead issue already! The years ahead in the 21st Century will unfold along similar lines. The human development agenda will be driven and measured on the yardstick of MDG implementation in 2015 and beyond. There will be repeated calls for taking up unfinished agendas called for in the Report 'In Larger Freedom'. The NGOs will continue to push their 'survival agendas' in coming forward with the proposals to implement human security programmes of UN. Great work will however continue to be executed by truly noble NGOs like Bill and Melinda Gates Foundation and its contemporaries. The suffering millions will not only get a voice, but also some succour in kind through the noble efforts of some UN programme correctly planned and some real help flowing through the well meaning NGOs. The UN, of course, will remain centre stage in the issue of human security through environment and health protection.

Towards Effective, Efficient and Equitable Security in The Emerging World Order

Raisond' être. The UN was created in 1945 above all else "to save the succeeding generations from the scourage of war"-to ensure that the horrors of the World Wars are never repeated. Maintaining international peace and security was therefore the main focus and raision d' être for the formation of UN. This portion of the research work will examine how the UN has faired in its main task over the years, how the concept of threat itself has undergone a metamorphosis, and what lies ahead in the future.

Changing Nature of Conflict. As recorded by the High Level Panel on Threats Challenges and Change, the nature of threat to international peace and security has been changing. The biggest security threats that we face now, or in the decades ahead, go far beyond States waging aggressive wars. The 21st century threats include poverty, inflectious diseases, environmental degradation, war and violence within States, the spread of possible use of nuclear, radiological, biological and chemical weapons international terrorism and transborder organised crimes. All these threats stand discussed at various portions of the foregoing research work.

The Conflicts in Recent Past. As stated, the natures of conflicts and war has changed signficanlty in the last sixty years. These has been a sharp decrease in the incidence of inter State wars. The number of inter-States (internal) armed conflicts resulting from the collapse of an already weak State such as Somalia, ethnic conflict as in formal Yugoslavia. Civil wars such as north-south civil war in Sudan (1983-2005) or civil war internationalised through intervention of other States or groups such as in the Democratic Republic of Congo (1996-2001) have more than doubled in the 1990s. Yet because there were nine wars terminated, there was a net decrease in the conflicts. This trend has however reversed since 2005. Although most new conflicts are relativity minor (i.e they kill fewer people), these are a result of three political changes, namely, end of colonitiasm, end of cold war and unipolar moment and a perceptable decrease in the superpower rivalry of the cold war era[124].

UN's Report Card in Maintaining International Peace and Security

Peaceful Settlements Through Preventive Diplomacy[125].While the traditional UN brick-batting can throw up many a supportive cases highlighting the failure of the world body to maintain international peace and security, there are quite a few success stories in the field of peaceful settlement of disputes through preventive diplomacy. Some examples which come to mind are the border disputes between Ethiopia and Eritrea (2002) ruled by the Permanent Court of Arbitration. UN's deployment of 1000 peacekeeping troops to Macedonia from late 1992 to 2001 at a cost of $ 0.3 billion as opposed to an estimated $ 15 billion, had the violence in the other regions of former Yugoslavia spread to Macedonia[126].

On Preventive Diplomacy. The essence of success of preventative diplomacy is timeliness. In the past record of UN, there have been many cases where opportunities have been missed due to nagging delays attributed to indecision and/or unwillingness to act. Preventive Diplomacy is therefore regarded as an area where a greater pro-active concern needs to be shown by the UN. The UN World Summit in 2005 stressed the importance of preventing armed conflict by promoting a 'culture of prevention' and developing a coherent and an integrated approach[127]. In 2008 the UN created a "Mediation Standby Team" as a mobile SWAT team for preventive diplomacy. The team consisted of six individuals from around the world with expertise on key issues like cease fires, transitional justice, constitution writing, security arrangements and power sharing.

With all the SWAT team notwithstanding, the UN's effort at mediation and preventing conflicts through diplomatic efforts have been a mixed bag of few success and several failures. The main reason is the scant regard given to the UN and its mandates/peace-proposals/ mediation efforts by the parties to the conflict. Take the latest case of Syria where the efforts of UN at mediation have had only a lukewarm effect. Firstly, it was the Kofi Anan's Six Point Peace Plan for Syria[128] launched in Feb 2012. Though the plan enforced a Cease Fire to take place across Syria since 10 Apr 2012, the Houla Massacre and the consequent Free Syrian Army's (FSA) ultimatum to the Syrian Govt periodically made the cease fire agreement redundant leading to its collapse in May 12. Kofi Anan himself resigned on 02 Aug 12 citing the intransigence of both the Assad Govt as well as the rebels to bring about any peaceful resolution of conflicts[129]. In Aug 2012 Lakdar Brahimi was appointed by the UN as a new peace envoy to Syria. Brahimi put forward his own peace plan which has also had very meagre effect, as both the rebels and Syrian Army have resumed large scale operations.

Why UN Mediation Efforts Fail. The above sequences of events described above have happened several times before wherein, the UN effort ends in a whimper or are largely ignored by parties to conflict. Why such a thing happens is probably due to the following reasons :-

(a) **An Ineffectual 'Talk Shop'**. Parties to the conflict largely regard the UN as an ineffectual 'talk shop' which dishes out toothless peace plans/proposals that lack one or all the following :-

   (i) **The collective resolve of the international community**.

   (ii) **Power to enforce its will.**

   (iii) **An unequal/irrational/one-sided/redundant end result scenario** which belies the 'revolution and the sacrifies made therein' and/or does not address the 'key issue' driving the conflict.

(b) **P-5 Politics**. Rarely ever a resolution or a peace proposal has the willing nod of the all the P-5. In most cases, one or more pulls in a different direction, probably to serve its own national agenda/ interest or extracting political mileage or showing loyality to one's allys. All this and more is showing its ugly face in the actions of

Russia and China in the Syrian Peace Process.

(c) **Toothless.** Since the firm resolve of the entire international community is seldom behind a UN initiative, there is no commitment/ collective will to push it through on the R2P route or otherwise lack of capability/will to enforce, results in only talk and no action. 'Take it if you please, leave it if you please' appears to be the UN stance/proposal on resolutions as perceived by the parties to the conflict.

UN's Role in Arab Spring - Lessons[130]

The Spring Perse. Arab Spring in general relates to a revolutionary wave of demonstrations, protests and wars occurring in the Arab world since 18 Dec 2010. The same is believed to have been instigated by dissatisfaction with the rule of local Governments, though some have speculated that wide gaps in income levels may have had a hand as well. Numerous factors have led to the protests including issues such as dictatorship, or absolute monarchies, human rights violations, government corruption, economic decline, unemployment, extreme poverty besides a number of demographic structural factors such as a large number of educated but dissatisfied youth within the population. These series of protests and demonstrations across Middle East and North Africa are also referred to as 'Arab Spring and Winter/Arab Awakening/Arab Uprisings'. It got sparked by the first protest that occurred in Tunisia on 18 Dec 2010 in Sidi Bouzid following Mohammad Bouaziza's self immolation in protest of police corruption and ill treatment. This struck Algeria, Jordan, Egypt and Yemen before spreading to Arab countries as a world phenomenon.

World Wide Impact. While in Tunisia, the initial sparks and violent protests ended up ousting of the long time President Zine El Abidine Ben Ali, it had tremendous and visible effects in countries where it spread; ousting of President Hosni Mubarak in Egypt, bringing to an end 42 year rule of the dictator Muammar Gaddafi in Libya, ushering of democracy in Yemen and the bloody war, unrest and civilian killings that is raging high in Syria today. All these are reminiscent of the fact that, time has come when the people will not accept unsolicited misery, tyranny and the crushing grind of dictators. They will rise against, governments, kings, presidents, dictators and the like, who abuse power. They would rise against lack of accountability and growing inequality deepening poverty, sky-rocketing unemployment, and above all, the 'failure of leadership' at every level of the

Govt. The sharp contrast between the courage of the protestors demanding their rights and the failure of the leadership to match that courage with concrete actions to build stronger societies based on respect of human rights, also come out very visibly[131].

The phenomenon of the Arabs Spring that erupted way back in Dec 2010 in Tunisia has indeed had a tremendous impact whose tremors have indeed been felt worldwide. One can see certain typical signatures of the revolution which are unprecedented. First of all, the entire revolution has been 'grass-roots upwards and people driven'. No formal conventional or Govt/anti-Govt machinery has been visible actually planning and executing the revolution, per se. It has been like the cumulation of many a simmering sparks of dissatisfaction, frustration and injustice that simply joined in out of the common chord of 'we also are in the same miserable (read sinking) boat – let's get the hell out of here and shake this bloody dictator/Government, since 'enough is enough'. The whole thing became an inferno. Another fact that has come out from such uprisings is the earth-shaking power of 'people' the unarmed civilians in brute force of togetherness for a cause. Of course, there are world players who would fund them/arm them and keep them alive for their specific national agendas. Interestingly, revolutions have done unprecedented things quite oblivious of the world power blocks (the UN, the US and the like). Even the world super power was not spared when in Oct 2011, global protests to occupy 'Wall Street' swept the US and the question being thrown at the US citizen was 'Are you ready for the Tahrir Moment?'. Another very distinct and very visible fact coming out of these revolutions has been the power and role of social media. While many an experts opine that social media was the main instigator of the uprising, others claim that it was merely a tool. Either way, the perception of the social media has changed. Its role in the uprising has demonstrated to the world its awesome power. 'The power of Facebook' to get the message across and get the people churned up for a cause was seen by the whole world. The power of 'collective intelligence' and a common binding thread of the social media to support a collective action in order to forment a political change was a 'new find' of the resolution that continues in various part of the world today and beyond.

Role of UN in Arab Spring

Far Reaching Implication. Having had a taste of the flavour of the Arab Spring, it will be relevant to connect it to the role of UN played/

not played in this significant international development. Foreign Secy of UK, William Hague has described the Arab Spring as the most significant event of the 21st Century, far more strategically important than the 9/11 in 2001 or the financial crises in 2008. Arab Spring can be seen as the third wave of democratisation following the Latin America in 1980 and Eastern Europe in 1999. Autocratic Leaders have lost power (Egypt, Libya, Tunisia, Yemen). The Syrian regime is under increasing pressure. There is a reform process under way in Morocco, Jordan, Algeria, Bahrain and other Gulf states. Even in Saudi Arabia, the decision to allow women some of their rights to vote is a direct result of Arab Spring.

On the other hand, experts opine that the upheaval in the region has led to new threats in the form of rise of political Islam. In Egypt, Tunisia and Morocco, the religions parties have come to the top. Above all, it is the expression of the wishes of the people against the corrupt and inefficient rule and the ruler. The expression of protest has emerged in its all pervading and all powerful avatar, riding high on the powerful vehicle of the social media. The courage shown by the protestors in the past 12 months has been matched by the failure of leadership that makes the UN Security Council seem tired and increasingly unfit for the purpose. Let's examine this aspect in greater detail.

Weak Prediction/Debate. Right at the onset, it is observed that the prediction of likely events related to Arab Spring protests was rather weak at the UN. Too much time has been spent at the UN on ritualistic details about Israel and Palestine and not on the fundamental issues raised by the lack of political and economic reforms in the Arab world or many other 'people issues' – inequality, lack of social justice, tyranny of the dictators raging unemployment, women security, financial downturn and the like, that are raging high in much of the civilised world, namely in Europe and the America.

Only Reports. The UNDP did produce a series of reports between 2001 and 2005 analysing the economic social and demographic strains in the Middle East and North African region. These accurately predicted that if the economic, social and political reform process is not accelerated there would be upheaval, protests and turmoil. This report expectedly did not result in any political action.

Some Positive Aspects. On the positive side, the UN has taken some positive steps and made some right noises. The UNSG has always called for the erring Govt to stop civilian atrocities and killings and respond to the just wishes of its peoples. Like it asked the Egyptian Govt to listen to the violent calls emanating from the Tahrir Square. It made some very correct and bold statements in Libya, Syria, Yemen and Bahrain. It has time and again raised up the cause of humanitarian intervention and the responsibility to protect (R2P).

Actions on Wider Canvas. On the wider institutional canvas, the Human Rights Council suspended Libya, established a Commission of Enquiry and effectively rejected Syria's candidature for the HRC. The General Assembly switched accreditations to the Libyan opposition and Human Rights Resolution on Syria in Dec 2011. More importantly, the UNSC referred Libya to the ICC and adopted wide ranging sanctions, imposed no fly zones, authorised force to protect civilian lives. Together these constituted the most wide-ranging resolutions passed by the Security Council in the last 20 years. The same laid the foundation of the five month military campaign conducted by NATO and coalition allies in Libya. Security Council also authorised military action by UN Peacekeepers in Cote d'Ivoire against President Gbagbo's attempt to remain in power, who finally was made to face trial in ICC.

Other Actions. UN has been active in other regions as well. UNDP is assisting the Egyptian and Tunisian authorities with elections and constitution writing. The UN Peacekeeping action in South Sudan is helping to ensure stability in the newest member of the UN system and above all, the UN has not yet given up on Syria[132].

Turning Phase of Arab Spring. Two years down the line, after the bubble first burst in Tunisia in Dec 2010, the mood of the Arab Spring is turning darker, forcing the world leaders at the UN to revisit the perilous outcome of this earth-shaking development. The weakness of post Gaddafi Govt in Libya was demonstrated when gunmen attacked US Consulate in Benghazi. A new wave of long suppressed Muslim Brotherhood now dominates Egyptian politics. What began in Syria as a non-violent uprising is already a towering inferno. Making their debut in the 193 member General assembly are the new leaders of the young Governments in the so called Arab Spring nations, who besides delivering economic results, must now address the Anti-Western sentiment triggered by anti-Islamic video. The UN must now address it further to stop the killing of civilians in Syria. Russia must search for accountability after its third and final veto on Syria[133].

The Syrian Imbroglio and UN. UN has responded to Syria in multiple ways. After the failed attempts of its first peace envoy Kofi Anan, the UN on 17 Aug 2012 announced the appointment of Lakhdar Brahimi as its joint special representative of Syria. Brahimi is holding wide ranging discussions with Syrian Govt, US, President of Russian Federation for Middle East and others to bring an end to the continuing bloodshed. He opines, that the Geneva Commission of 30 Jan 2012 will be the basis for reaching a political solution. The current status is still nebulous. How and when it will fructify into tangible action to stop the Syria bloodshed is yet to be seen[134].

Changing/Exciting Times. These are indeed changing and exciting times at the UN. Peoples revolutions starting from the grass roots and riding high on the all pervading powers of the social media are sweeping much of the Arab World and North Africa. People are showing their anger and frustration against corrupt Governments and erring dictators. The civilian unrest and casualties are on the rise pushing up the cardinal significance and relevance of issues like human intervention vis-a-vis State sovereignty and the responsibility to protect civilian loss of life even by authorisation of military force. The pressure of NIEO to shake the high table of P-5 for a wider world representation is raging with high momentum, though yet far from making any paradigm changes. Arab Spring in its journey back home after the upswing revolution is showing new ominous signs-Muslim brotherhood/ anti-western sentiments, continued mass civilian casualties/ weak emergent Governments not fully prepared to take the young liberated democracies forward. The UN has to re-align to these world realities, sooner than later.

Conclusion

This Chapter contains the major portion of the entire work. The foundation of the Chapter is laid on the foregoing work which basically covers two verticals. In the first vertical, its spells out the contours of the **emerging face of the 21st Century** complete with its challenges and threats in their multifarious dimensions. The second vertical draws out the **strengths and weaknesses of the UN**, aggregated in terms of its successes and failures over the past nearly seven decades of its existence.

Working on the interplay of the above two verticals, essentially throws up the very many ailments that affect the UN. This Chapter aims to suggest the cures. In doing that, it dwells on the invaluable and trailblazing work done in the past by various bodies of UN scholars, as well as, experts and analyses how the same can be implemented and taken to its logical and fruitful conclusion.

Endnotes

1 UN General Assembly Document No A/59/2005 available on http://www.un.org "Report Of The Secretary General In Larger Freedom". Accessed on 01 Jul 12.

2 http ://www.en-org/en/members.shtml. Accessed on 01 Jul 12.

3 http://www.un.org/en/membodies/Secretariat. Accessed on 01 Jul 12.

4 http://www. unchr.org/OHCHR/English/Your Human Rights/diary. Accessed on 01 Jul 12.

5 Thomas G. Weiss, Tatiana Carayann is and Richard Jolly. "The Third United Nations", Global Governance 15, No 1 (2009), page 123.

6 http://www.unhistory.org/brefing/3 Third UN.pdf. Accessed on 01 Jul 12.

7 26 (Chapter 1) ibid. 2 ibid page 350.

8 John Allphin Moore and Jr Jerry Pubantz, "The New United Nations : International Organisation in the 21 Century" (Upper Saddle River, New Jersey) 2006, page 53.

9 http://www.ibnlive.in.com, Jul 14, 2012. Accessed on 14 Jul 12.

10 Margaret P. Karn and Karan A. Mingst"The United States as Dead Beat ? US Policy and UN Financial Crises", Boulder : Lynne Rienner, 2002 pages 267-294.Accessed on 14 Jul12.

11 Jhon Washburn, UNAUSA "World Bulletin" March 3, 2010, www. unausa.org/world bulletin/030310 Accessed on 14 Jul 12.

12 Donald J.Puchala, "World Hegemony and United Nations", International Studies Review 7, No 4(2005):575.

13 Gideon Rachman, "Think Again, American Decline", Foreign Policy, Jan-Feb 2011, page 63.

14 Ken Mathews, "The Gulf Conflict and International Relations" London Rout ledge, 1993, page 81.

15 Michael Grossman, "Role theory and Foreign Policy Change : The Transformation of Russian Foreign Policy in the 1990s", International Politics, 42 Nos (2005), pages 334-35.

16 Dmitry Shlapertokh, "Outside View : Russian Troops in Iraq" Washington Time, 2004 http://www.washington times.uni/vp. – Breaking/2004. Accessed on 14 Jul12.

17 www.globalpolicy.org/UN..UN../member-states-assessed-share-of-un-budget. Accessed on 14 Jul 12.

18 AJR Groom and Paul Tailor "United Nations and United Kingdom" UN University Press, 1995, pages 376-409.

19 Elizabeth G. "Economy, The Game Changer Coping with China's Foreign Policy Resolutions" Foreign Affairs 89, No 6, 2010, page 143.

20 Ann Kent, "China International Socialization : The Role of International Organisations" Global Governance 8 No 3, 200, page 34.

21 Ann Kent, "Beyond Compliance China, International Organisation and Global Security" Stanford University Press 2007, page 63.

22 Sadako Ogata, "Japan's Policy Towards United Nations" ed. Alger, Lyons and Trent, pages 231-270.

23 Mary.N.Hampton, "Germany, In Politics of Peacekeeping in the Post Cold War Era", ed Sorenson and Wood, pages 43-49.

24 Hugh Smith, "Australia in Politics of peacekeeping in Post Cold War Era", Sorenson and Wood, pages 9-13.

25 Keith Krause, "Canada, United Nations and the Reforms of International Institutions "Alger, Lyons and Trent, page 171.

26 Sally Morphet, "Multilateralism and Non Aligned Movement" Global Governance, 10 No 4, 2004, page 553.

27 Courtney B. Smith, "Politics and Process at UN; The Global Dance", Boulder : Lynne Reinner 2006, Chapter 3.

28 Greg Hittand Scot Miller. 'Booming Voice for New Block' Wall Street Journal Dec 17-18, 2009

29 Teresa Whitfield, "Friends Indeed ? UN Group A Friends and Resolution of Conflict" Washington DC ; US Institute of Peace Press : 2007.

30 Oran R. Young, "The Intermediaries : Third Parties in International Crises". Princeton University Press, 1967, page 283.

31 "The Score at Half Time" Economist Jun 11, 2009 available at www. economist.com/ node/ 13825201/print.

32 Barnet and Fennemore, "Rules for the World, pages151-152.

33 Weiss, Carayannis and Jolly, "The Third UN", page 127.

34 ibid page 327.

35 "The Millennium Development Goals Report 2012", UN Document 12-24532 printed at the United Nations, New York Jun 2012 Sales No E.12.1.4, page 72. http//: www.content.undp.org/go/news/room/.../mdgs/beyond-the-midpoint. Accessed on 12 Aug 12.

36 HélèneGandois, "After Millennium Development Goals; What Next?" carried in Irwin Arieft (Ed), "A Global Agenda Issues Before the United Nations",2011-12 United Nations Association of USA, 2011, pages 134-136.

37 http://www.guardian.co.uk/media-network-blog/2013/may/07/united-nations-crowdsource-global-development. Accessed on 04 Feb 2013.

38 Member of the UN System Task Team (htt://www.un.org/en/development/desa/policy/untaskteam_undf/unit_members/pdf), United Nations Development Policy and Analysis Division. Accessed on 04 Feb 2013.

39 Realizing the Future We Want for All-Report to the Sectary –General(htt://www.un.org/millenniumgoals/pdf/Post_Posst_2015_UNTT report.pdf), United Nations Millennium Development Goals website. Accessed on 04 Feb 2013.

40 UN Secretary-General appoints high-level panel on post-2015 development agenda http://www.un.org/sg/management/pdf/PRpost2015.pdf), United Nations Press Release. Accessed on 04 Feb 2013.

41 Framing Questions(http://www.un.org/sg/management/pdf/HLP_Framing_Questions.pdf), United Nations. Accessed on 04 Feb 2013.

42 http://www.post 2015 htpp.org/featured/high-level-panel-releases –recommendations-for-worlds-next- development -agenda/).

43 http://planetearthinstitute.org.uk/events/africapost2015.

44 Post-2015 Development Agenda: Guidelines for National Consultations (htt://www.beyond 2015.org/sits/default/files /Post% 20ENG1.pdf) Beyond 2015. Accessed on 04 Feb 2013.

45 Post-2015 Agenda: Unprecedented global discussions about development priorities start in 100 countries(http://www.undp.org/content/undp/en/home/presscenter/articles/2013/01/15/posst-2015agenda-unprecedented-global-discussions-about-development-priorities-start-in-100-countries-/), United Development Programme. Accessed on 04 Feb 2013.

46 http://www.worldwewant2015.org/sitemap.

47 Setting the development agenda beyond 2015(http://www.oil.org/global/

meetings-and-events/ events/ setting- development-agenda-beyond-2015/ hang-en/index.htm), International Labour Organization. Accessed on 04 Feb 2013.

48 Leni Wild and Marta Foresti, 2013 Working with the politics-How to improve public services for the poor, http://www.odi. org.uk/ pulications/7864-politics-service-delivery-institutions-aid-agencies .

49 http://www/worldwewant 2015.org/million voices.

50 Leni Wild and Grina Bergh; Are we making progress with building Governance into the post 2015 http://www.org.uk/publications/7295-progress-governance-post-2015-millennium-development-goals-mdgs.

51 Leni Wild and Gina Bergh; Are we making progress with building governance into the post 2015 framework? Accessed on 04 Feb 2013 http://www.odi.org.uk/pulications/7295-progress-governance-post-2015-millennium-development-goals-mdgs.

52 Rio+20 Sustainable Development Summit (http://undp.org/content/undp/en/home/presscenter/events/2012/June/rio-20-sustainbale -development html), United Nations Development Programme. Accessed on 04 Feb 2013.

53 Sustainable development goals (http://sustainable development un.org/index.php ?menu=1300), United Nations Sustainable Development Knowledge Platform. Accessed on 04 Feb 2013.

54 Helen Clark: "Our World in 2050: More Equitable and Sustainable-or Less?" (http://www.undp.org/ content/undp/en /home/presscenter/speeches/2012/11/07/helen-clark-our-world-in2050-more-equitable-and -sustainable-or-less-/), United Nations Development Programme. Accessed on 04 Feb 2013.

55 24 (Chapter 2) ibid.

56 Brabare Crossette, 'Sixteen Wise People and the Future of UN', UN Wire, www.unwireorg , 01 Dec 2003. Accessed on 19 Aug 12.

57 http://www.one word.net/guides, "Learn About World Poverty". Accessed on 19Aug 12.

58 http://www.one.org/HIV-AIDS "World Wide AIDS Facts 2011- Treatment Prevention and Care". Accessed on 26 Aug 12.

59 http://www.Helpage.org/HIV Aids Statistics "HIV Aids Statistics". Accessed on 26 Aug 12.

60 http://www. wto.org/english/tratop-e/ada-e/ddd-e.htm, "WTO/The Doha Round". Accessed on 26 Aug 12.

61 Prises, Gwyu it.al, "The Hartwell Paper – A new direction for climate policy

after crash of 2009" London School of Economics May 2010 . Accessed on 26 Aug 12.

62 http: //www.en.wikipedia.org/wiki/Kyoto-Protocol . Accessed on 02 Sep 12.

63 http://www.ictg.org/international-crimes . Accessed on 02 Sep 12.

64 http://www.en.wikipedia.org/wiki/international-court_of_justice.Accessed on 02 Sep 12.

65 http://www.iaea.org>publications>factsheets . Accessed on 02 Sep 12.

66 http://www.iaea.org/publications/fact sheet/.../nptstatus-overview.html. Accessed on 02 Sep 12.

67 http://www.commentry magazine.com/2012/02/14 universal-definition-of-terrorism. Accessed on 02 Sep 12.

68 IgancioCarido 'The Fight Against InternationalTerrorism:Defence Aspect' EU5151 session Document A/1900' Report 14 Jun 2005 pages 162,168 . Accessed on 02 Sep 12.

69 http://www.en.wikipedia/wiki/transnational organized crime. Accessed on 02 Sep 12.

70 http://www.ec.europe.en>Together against trafficking in Human Beings. Accessed on 02 Sep 12.

71 http://www.un-documents.net/a 55 or 25 htm. Accessed on 02 Sep 12.

72 http://www.polarisproject.org . Accessed on 02 Sep 12.

73 http://www.not for sale campaign.org . Accessed on 02 Sep 12.

74 http://www.wm tro.com . Accessed on 02 Sep 12.

75 www.hugfintionpost.com/.../drug-trafficking-trends-around–the world. Accessed on 02 Sep 12.

76 http://www.lacenter .org/bosnia/becker.htm .Accessed on.02 Sep 12.

77 http://www.library.fes.de/pdf-files/1ez/08819 pdf, 'Global Threats and Role of United Nations Sanctions". Accessed on 02 Sep 12.

78 VS Mani, "Humanitarian Intervention and International Law", IJIL, Volume 33, 1993, pages 1-11.

79 Ferrando R Tesorn, "HumantarianIntervention : An Enquiry into Law and Morality" New York Press, 1998, page 3.

80 Jarat Chopra, "The Obsolescence of Intervention Under International Law" Miami, 1992, pages 1-129.

81 W Andrew Knight, "The Changing Human Rights Regime", State Sovereignty

and Article 2(7) in Post Cold" War Era, New York, 2005, pages 12-16.

82 Bijayalaxmi Mishra, "UN and the Security Council in the New Millennium", New Delhi Kilao Books, 2004, pages 23-69.

83 UNSC Resolution 688: "A Reappraisal in the Light of Changing World", America University Journal of International Law and Policy, Volume 7 (1993), page 383.

84 Robert. E. Osgord, Woodrow Wilson, "Collective Security and Lessons of History" and Dhirendra Diwedi, ed. "Collective Security Under UN : Retrospect and Prospect", page 41.

85 Anthony Parsons, "From Cold War to Hot Peace", Penguin Books, 1995, page73.

86 SatishNambiar, "Robust Peacekeeping Operations, Rapid Deployment Capability for the UN : An Indian Perspective", USI Journal, Oct – Dec 2006 , page 257.

87 http:/www. en.wikipedia.org/wiki/standby-High-Readiness-Brigade. Accessed on 14 Nov 12.

88 http://www.unac.org/. Accessed on 02 Sep 12.

89 Joseph Nye, "Does the UN Still Matter?"Financial Express (US) 02 Sep 12.

90 UN Document Number A/58/817,UN Deptt of Public Information.

91 Report of the Commission on Global Governance, "A Call to Action" 1995, page 15.

92 Times of India, Bhubaneswar Edition, 05 Nov 12.

93 Gupta KR, "Reform of the United Nations" (Volume 1 and Volume 2), Atlantic Publishers and Distributors (P) Ltd, New Delhi 2006, page 43.

94 http://en.wikipedia.org/wiki/reform_of_the_united_nations. Accessed on 09 Sep 12.

95 "Ban Appoints Experienced UN Official to lead Change Management Team" http://www.un.org/apps/news/story.asp?News ID = 38563. Accessed on 29 Nov 12.

96 "UN Secretary General Ban appoints AtulKhare of India to be the Leader of his Change Management Team" http://www.un.org/ News/Press/Docs/2011/ Sqa/295.doc.htm. Accessed on 29 Nov 12.

97 "UN Change Management Team" Spearheaded by AtulKhare, http://www. decanherald.com/contact/165568/Indian-lead-un-change-mangement.html) Deccan Herald 11 Jun 11. Accessed on 29 Nov 12.

98 http://www.economist.com/topics/doha -development - round. . Accessed on 09 Sep 12.

99 Environment News Services, "Dec 08 2012 Doha Outcome : Kyoto Protocol Lives", Global Climate Deal by 2015.

100 Mark Malloch Brown, "United Nations and Changing World Policies", page 285.

101 http://www.blogs.hbr.org/cs/2012/04/the-new-international-economic-order-Vinod K Aggarwal. Html. Accessed on 09 Sep 12.

102 Esther Boserup, "Women's Role in Economic Development" London : George Allen and Unwin, 1970. Accessed on 09 Sep 12.

103 "Platform for Action", An Agenda For Women's Empowerment : Report of the Fourth World Conference on Women; The Beijing Declaration. UN Document A/Conf/177/20. Accessed on 09 Sep 12.

104 Devaki Jain, "Women Development and UN; A Sixty Year Quest for Equality and Justice". Indiana University Press, Bloomington, 2005, page 157.

105 http://www en.wikipedia/wiki/un-women. Accessed on 09 Sep 12.

106 Sun.Star Magazine 16 Dec 2012 and http://www.womens agenda.com.in. Accessed on 09 Sep 12.

107 http://www.un.org/apps/news/strong.asp. Accessed on 18 Dec 12. http://www.stripes.com/news/un-women-have -a-long-way-to-go-in-Afghanistan. Accessed on 09 Sep 12.

108 http://www.trust.org/trust law/news/un-forum-goals-challenges and strategies for-CSW-2013.Accessed on 09 Sep 12.

109 http://www. english – online. at/geography/world/status of women.htm. Accessed on 09 Sep 12.

110 http://www.futures withoutviolence.org/fact – State domestic – violence. Accessed on 09 Sep 12.

111 http://www.icly.org/x/file/about . Accessed on 09 Sep 12.

112 http ://www.the hindu-com/news/cities/Bangalore/crime-against-women-children- in- the- rise/article 4237645.ece. Accessed on 09 Sep 12.

113 http://www.social.development.in, 'Women Development'. Accessed on 26 Dec 12.

114 Cudad Colon 'Human Rights Reference Handbook' (3rdEdition.rev.ed), Costa Rica : University of Peace, ISBN 9977-925-18-6.

115 Julie Mertus, "The United Nations and Human Rights : A Guide for a New

Era", 2 ed, New York, Rout ledge Chapter 2.

116 Michael Barnett, "Eyewitness to a Genocide; the United Nations and Rwanda" ,Ithaca: Cornwell University Press, 2002 .

117 http://www.files.amnesty.org/air12/air- 2012/amnesty-international-report-2012-the- state of- world- human-rights. Accessed on 14 Sep 12.

118 http://www.hrw.org/world-report- 2012-human-rights-world. Accessed on 14 Sep 12.

119 Richard Jolly and others, "The Power of UN Ideas : Lessons from the First 60 Years" New York, UN Intellectual History Project, 2005, page 34.

120 Elizabeth R. De Sombre 'Global Environmental Institutions', London Routeledge, 2006, pages 14-20.

121 http://www.zee news.india.com/lags/kyoto-protocol-html. Accessed on 14 Sep 12.

122 http://www.newsscientist.com/.../dn 23041/has_the_kyoto_protocol_ donemore_harm_than_good.Accessed on 05 Jan 13.

123 Frank Biermann, "The Care for a World Environment Organisation". Environment 42 No 9 (2000), pages 22-31.

124 "The Human Security Report" 2009/10, New York, Oxford University Press www.hrsgroup.info.Accessed on 14 Sep 12.

125 Timothy D. Sisk, "Introduction; the SRSGs and the Management of Civil Wars", Global Governance 16 No (2) 2010, pages 237-242 .

126 UN "World Summit Outcome?" Document No A/60/L.1 sec, 81, 82.

127 Kofi Anan's 'Six Point Plan For Syria' Al Zazeea, 27 Mar 2012.

128 op cit. Accessed on 14 Sep 12.

129 Press Conference by Kofi Anan, Joint Special Envoy to Syria, UN HQ Geneva .

130 http://www. en.wikipedia.org/wiki/Arab Spring. Accessed on 14 Sep 12.

131 http://www.amnesty.org/en/annual - report/2012/forward / leadingforthestreets. Accessed on 14 Sep 12.

132 http://www. ukun.fco.gov.uk/en/news/?views .Accessed on 14 Sep 12.

133 http://www.online.wsg.com/…/so/world.leaders-gather-at-unasarabspring turns perilious. Accessed on 22 Jan 13.

134 http://www.un.org/new/forces/syria .Accessed on 22 Jan 13.

5

Role of United Nations in Global Peace

Challenges of UN Peacekeeping in The 21st Century

> *"In the 21st Century, I believe the mission of the United Nations will be defined by a new, more profound awareness of the sanctity and dignity of every human life, regardless of race or religion. More than ever before in human history, we share a common destiny. We can master it only if we face it together"[1].*
>
> —Kofi Annan

International Peace – Central to Charter. Fresh on the heels of the bloody aftermath of the Second World War, the founding fathers of the United Nations focussed on the centrality of their wartime orientation, which implied that the reason d'être for the foundation of the United Nations was to save the succeeding generations from the scourage of war and to ensure that the horrors of World Wars were never repeated.

Changing Times. While maintaining international peace and security has remained the primary purpose of the UN, but how the UN undertakes this task has changed over time in ways never envisaged by its founders. Many provisions of the Charter that lay largely unused during the forty years of the Cold War have seen far more use since 1989. Over time, UN has also created new ways of addressing security threats and seeking to secure peace, demonstrating the flexibility of UN Charter.

Charter Position. The UN Charter in Article 2, obligates all members to settle disputes by peaceful means, to refrain from the threats or use of force and to co-operate with UN sponsored actions. This normative prohibition was a direct outgrowth of the Kellogg-Briand Pact concluded in 1928. The use of force for territorial annexation is now widely accepted as illegitimate. This was witnessed in the broad condemnation +of Iraq's invasion of Kuwait in 1990 and the large number of States that contributed to the US led multilateral effort to reverse the occupation. The use of force in self defence against an armed attack is accepted and was the basis of Security Council's authorization of US military action after Sep 2011 terrorist attacks. A large majority of States accept the legitimacy of using force to promote self determination, replace illegitimate regimes and correct past injustices. The UNSC refused in 2003, the authorization for use of force against Iraq leading US to form an adhoc coalition to remove Saddam from power. In 2011 however, the Council authorized 'all necessary means' to stop the Libyan Govt from using force against its citizens. The response of UNSC has therefore been different on different occasions depending on the circumstances under which such use of force has been asked for.

Other Rule Position. Chapter VI specifies the way in which the Security Council can promote peaceful settlement of disputes. Chapter VII is the 'teeth' of the Charter. It specifies actions the UN can take with respect to peace, breaches of peace, and acts of aggressions. Chapter VII has been invoked on many occasions to authorise the use of force and various types of sanctions either by the UN or by a regional organization or by the 'coalition of the willing' led by a particular country, like the US (Haiti), Australia (East Timor) and Great Britain (Sierra Leone). It is common for most UN peace operations to have a mandate under Chapter VII.

The UN Report Card

Having seen the rule position and Charter provisions, a brief examination of the implementations of the same in various situations over time will reveal how the UN has been able to deliver or otherwise in converting words to action.

On Preventing Wars. On many occasions, the UN actions in the form of sanctions/enforcement actions/authorisation of force to prevent wars/ genocides/ethnic cleansing/acts of atrocities by States on its own citizens have been 'too little' and/or 'too late' to prevent sufferings of atrocities of many types. Take the case of Kurd genocide in Mar 1988. The UN stood by as the genocide occurred with the infamous 'Chemical Ali' slaughtering some 100,000 – 200,000 Kurds (sic) in bloody chemical attack[2]. The UNSC did not adopt a resolution condemning chemical attack till as late as Aug 1988. In Liberia and Sierra Leone, a civil war forced more than 800,000 people into exile in the neighbouring countries in the period 1990-1995. UN remained a passive by-stander, eternally debating the issue of intervention vs sovereignty. It was only by 2000, that it could finally send a peacekeeping force. It was 'too little and too late'.

Other Examples

Rwanda. There is perhaps no more damaging indictment of UN than its failure to prevent genocide in Rwanda. When thousands upon thousands of Rwandans were being slaughtered in the Hutu – Tutsi clashes, UNAMIR stood by, taking shelter under their mandate that their mission was only to monitor the implementation of Arusha Accords, i.e to make the Rwandan capital a weapon – secure area. The impotency of the mission in trying to maintain the so called neutrality and impartiality ended up in the massacre of 1074017 Rwandans by Feb 2002 out of which 94% were Tutsis. In some cases, the UN Forces failed to give shelter to the threatened Tutsi tribe on the pretext of maintaining neutrality[3]. Worse still, the UN forces actually colluded with those engaging in mass murder further disgracing the UN record. Also, the UN ignored the warning for an impending massacre given by Commander of UNAMIR. Thus by refusing to address the crimes in Rwanda when it had the opportunity, UN set off a devastating chain of events that fuelled further chaos in Africa. The next to be engulfed was Congo. The conflict pitched the forces of Rwanda and Uganda against those of Zimbabwe, Namibia and Angola. In all, some 800,000 (sic) people were massacred.

Srebrenica. In the terrible genocide and massacre of Bosnian muslims at the hand of Serbs in 1992 another dimension of the failure of UN came out. Not only the massacre took place in the so declared 'UN Safe Areas', the Dutch Peacekeeping force was grossly undermanned. The peacekeepers put up no fight to save the Bosnian muslims. Worse still, the UN forces got no support from the NATO forces based in Italy. UNPROFOR remained a by-stander as scenes of unimaginable savagery unfolded[4]. The UN's failure in Srebrenica spread chaos in former Yugoslavia. Another UN safe area came under assault as Sarajevo was shelled by Serbian Artillery and Kosovo and Croatia were subjected to ethnic cleansing[5].

Failure in Iraq 2001. In the aftermath of liberation of Kuwait when the Iraqi Army launched genocidal operations to crush the Kurdish rebellion in northern Iraq and Shia uprising in southern Iraq, UN failed to prevent the disaster through the use of force. It adopted resolution after resolutions which were simply ignored by Iraq.

Self Contradiction. In the wake of Sep 11, UN adopted resolution 1373 which unambiguously denounced international terrorism. Within a weak the UNGA overwhelmingly elected Syria to sit on the UNSC knowing fully well that Syria was a known sponsor of terrorism for more than 20 years.

Impartiality and Neutrality. In many cases UN forces under the myth of monitoring impartiality and neutrality have corrosively ended up equating the aggressor and victims. In 1995-96 in Afghanistan, the UN forces betrayed domestic opponents of Taliban by maintaining neutrality towards Taliban despite their brutalities and the aid it was getting from Pakistan[6].

Somalia. The long story of suffering and gross human rights violations and mass casualties in the famine struck Somalia is a standing testimony of how an intervention can be rendered impotent and can result in a failed mission when the interests of a sole super power determines the course of events. The failure of UN operations in Somalia (UNOSOM), intervention and atrocities by Ethiopian forces finally", de-generating into a US led offensive against Al Qaeda, all point towards a terrible growth of events over time and increasing ineffectiveness and exploitation of UN[7].

Biggest Marginalisation. 2003 was to witness the unprecedented marginalisation of UN when USA and UK unilaterally invaded Iraq without any UN authorization. The events that followed is history.

Of Successes and Positive Actions in Global Peace. Beside many an incidence of failure to maintain global peace, genocides, mass killings, human rights violations and more, there are many positive contributions of UN in monitoring global peace. Some examples :-

A World Without Global War. The defining sentence of the UN Charter reads, "To save the succeeding generations from the scourage of war and to ensure that the horrors of the World War were never repeated". **The experiment has been successful since over the subsequent 60 years and more, there has not been a catastrophe like a world war (sic)**. Many portions of the world have enjoyed unparalleled peace and prosperity and the world has been spared the horrors of another conventional global war.

Inter State Wars. There have been fewer inter state wars in the latter half of the 20th Century, as compared to the first half. This is in spite of the fact that the number of States has grown almost four fold.

PeaceKeeping. Notwithstanding its many imperfections, the **UN deserves great credit for its ingenuity in inventing peacekeeping**. Initially not included in the Charter, peacekeeping was conceived as a UN response to conflicts within States. Former Secretary General Dag Hammarskjold described it as **Chapter VI ½ of the Charter**, ie. Actions between peaceful techniques of moderation and fact-finding (Chapter VI) and more robust tools such as intervention (Chapter VII)[8].

Peacekeeping: Cold War Era. As Hammarskjold saw it, UN peacekeepers were a buffer between warring factions[9]. The objective has been to defeat aggression but prevent fighting, keep order and monitor violation of cease fire agreements, **quite a few success can be counted.** UN Emergency Force (UNEF) in end 1950 restrained Britain, France and Israel to invade Egypt. UN organisation in Congo (ONUC) prevented fragmentation of a newly independent African country. Sanctions against Southern Kurdistan ended minority rule, and against South Africa, put tremendous pressure on the country to end its social policy of Apartheid[10]. Swift intervention actions within hours of Iraqi invasion of Kuwait in 1991 is another success story.

A Mixed Report Card. It can be deduced from the above that while the UN's report card in monitoring global peace has been a mixed one, what is there to be carried forward into the 21st Century are two of its most significant functions, namely, peacekeeping and R2P. It is these two functions which will define for the UN, its successes or failures, in time to come. Therefore in the context of the Future of the UN in the 21st Century, the above two aspects need to be analysed in greater detail.

On Peacekeeping

A UN Invention. As already stated, peacekeeping was not originally a part of UN Charter. It was a UN invention to respond to the global requirement of keeping peace amidst various complex situations of conflict between one or more member States.

A Major Role. Since the UN Peacekeeping has evolved into such an important and a critical function of the UN. The same has actually evolved over the years and is likely to be a major factor in deciding and shaping in what UN will do or fail to do in maintaining Global peace in the tumultuous times we live in. It therefore becomes imperative to examine this aspect in greater detail. The same has been attempted by the researcher under the following heads :-

(a) **History and evolution** of US Peacekeeping over the decades.

(b) **The Peacekeeping Report Card**. Emergence of many shades of peacekeeping over the years.

(c) **Challenges of Peacekeeping** in the 21st Century.

(d) **Recommendations.**

History

"The United Nations is our world's greatest mechanism for making peace"[11]

—Gillian Sorensen

The Early Years. UN Peacekeeping was born at a time when Cold War rivalries frequently paralyzed the Security Council. Peacekeeping was primarily limited to maintaining ceasefires and stabilizing situations on the ground, providing crucial support for political efforts to resolve conflict by peaceful means[12]. Peacekeeping missions of this time primarily consisted of unarmed military observers and lightly armed troops with mandates limited to monitoring, reporting and confidence-building roles. The first two peacekeeping operations deployed by the UN were the UN Truce Supervision Organization (UNTSO) and the UN Military Observer Group in India and Pakistan (UNMOGIP). Both of these missions, which continue operating to this day, exemplified the observation and monitoring type of operation and had authorised strengths in the low hundreds. The military observers were unarmed. The earliest armed peacekeeping operation was the First UN Emergency Force (UNEF I) deployed successfully in 1956 to address the Suez Crisis. The UN Operation in the Congo (ONUC), launched in 1960, was the first large scale mission having nearly 20,000 military personnel at its peak. ONUC demonstrated the risks involved in trying to bring stability to war-torn regions. 250 UN personnel died while serving on that mission. In the 1960s and 1970s, the UN established short-term missions in the Dominican Republic-Mission of the Representative of the Secretary-General in the Dominican Republic (DOMREP), West New Guinea (West Irian) – UN Security Force in West New Guinea (UNSF), and Yemen – UN Yemen Observation Mission (UNYOM). It also started longer term deployments in Cyprus – UN Peacekeeping Force in Cyprus (UNFICYP) and the Middle East – UN Emergency Force II (UNEF II), UN Disengagement Observer Force (UNDOF) and UN Interim Force in Lebanon (UNIFIL). In 1988, UN peacekeepers were awarded the Nobel Peace Prize. At that time, the Nobel Committee cited "the Peacekeeping

Forces through their efforts have made important contributions towards the realization of one of the fundamental tenets of the United Nations. Thus, the world organisation has come to play a more central part in world affairs and has been invested with "increasing trust".

Post Cold-War-Surge. With the end of the Cold War, the strategic context for UN Peacekeeping changed dramatically[13]. The UN shifted and expanded its field operations from 'traditional' missions involving generally observational tasks performed by military personnel to complex 'multidimensional' missions. These missions were designed to ensure the implementation of comprehensive peace agreements and assist in laying the foundations for sustainable peace. The nature of conflicts also changed over the years. UN Peacekeeping, which originally developed as a means of dealing with inter-State conflict, was increasingly being applied to intra-State conflicts and civil wars. UN Peacekeepers were now increasingly asked to undertake a wide variety of complex tasks, from helping to build sustainable institutions of governance, to human rights monitoring, to security sector reforms to the disarmament, demobilization and reintegration of former combatants.

Period 1989 – 1994. After the Cold War ended, there was a rapid increase in the number of peacekeeping operations. With a new consensus and a common sense of purpose, the Security Council authorized a total of 20 new operations between 1989 and 1994, raising the number of peacekeepers from 11,000 to 75,000. Peacekeeping operations established in such countries as Angola – UN Angola Verification Mission I (UNAVEM I) and UN Angola Verification Mission II (UNAVEM II), Cambodia – UN Transitional Authority in Cambodia (UNTAC), EI Salvador – UN Observer Mission in EI Salvador (ONUSAL), Mozambique – UN Operation in Mozambique (ONUMOZ) and Namibia – UN Transition Assistance Group (UNTAG), were all deployed to help implement complex peace agreements; stabilize the security situation; re-organize military and police; help in electing new Governments; and subsequently build democratic institutions to bring in good governance for continued peace and stability.

The Mid-1990s: A Period of Reassessment. The general success of earlier missions raised expectations for UN Peacekeeping beyond its capacity to deliver. This was especially true in the mid 1990's in situations when the Security Council was not able to authorize sufficiently robust mandates or provide adequate resources. Missions were established in situations where the guns had not yet fallen silent, in areas such as the former Yugoslavia - UN Protection Force (UNPROFOR), Rwanda - UN Assistance Mission for Rwanda (UNAMIR) and Somalia - UN Operation in Somalia II (UNOSOM II), where there was no peace to keep. These three high-profile peacekeeping operations came under criticism as peacekeepers faced situations where warring parties failed to adhere to peace agreements, or where the peacekeepers themselves were not provided adequate resources or political support. As civilian casualties rose and hostilities continued, the reputation of UN Peacekeeping suffered. The setbacks of the early and mid-1990s led the Security Council to limit the number of new peacekeeping missions and begin a process of self-reflection to prevent such failures from happening again.

Closer to Millennium. With continuing crises in a number of countries and regions, the essential role of UN Peacekeeping was soon emphatically reaffirmed. In the second half of the 1990s, the Council authorized new UN operations in Angola - UN Angola Verification Mission III (UNAVEM III) and UN Observer Mission in Angola (MONUA), Bosnia and Herzegovina - UN Mission in Bosnia and Herzegovina (UNMIBH), Croatia - UN Confidence Restoration Operation in Croatia (UNCRO), UN Transitional Administration for Eastern Slavonia, Baranja and Western Sirmium (UNTAES) and UN Civilian Police Support Group (UNPSG), the former Yugoslav Republic of Macedonia - UN Preventive Deployment Force (UNPREDEP), Guatemala - UN Verification Mission in Guatemala (MINUGUA), Haiti - UN Support Mission in Haiti (UNSMIH), UN Transition Mission in Haiti (UNTMIH) and UN Civilian Police Mission in Haiti (MIPONUH)[14].

Reflections on the Early History. The early years of UN Peacekeeping operations and their journey from infancy to adolescence throws up following significant points :-

- **(a) Slow Evolution**. The Peacekeeping has actually evolved over the years. Starting from the low visibility observation missions to 'keeping' and 'enforcing' missions over time.
- **(b) Response to the Need of the Hour**. Peacekeeping actually evolved as a response to the changing geopolitical and geostrategic scenario in the world. In that, as the years rolled by, the incidence and the threat of large-scale conventional wars involving multiple nations receded in the oblivion. What came to the fore were many inter-

state conflicts, human crises due to lack of governance, genocides, ethnic cleansing, stark poverty, deprivations and inequalities, food crises, famine, drought, epidemics, pandemics and the like. Peacekeeping tried to metamorphosize itself to peace enforcement which largely did not work, essentially due to 'lack of teeth' and mandate deficits (will be analysed later). It then changed gears to sustain human (citizen) life, or protect it from being mauled by the State.

(c) **Post Cold War**. In the short afterglow of the unipolar moment immediately post the Cold War, the Peacekeeping operations flourished in the absence of the debilitating force of UNSC vetos.

(d) **Of Success and Failure**. Why some missions succeeded while the other did not will be analysed later.

The Peacekeeping Report Card

The Charter Position of Peacekeeping. The UN traditionally defined peacekeeping as, "an operation involving military personnel, but without enforcement powers, undertaken by the United Nations to help maintain or restore international peace and security in areas of conflict"[15]. Since there is no Charter provisions for peacekeeping, it lies in the 'grey zone', between the 'Peaceful Settlement' provision of chapter VI and 'Military Enforcement' provisions of Chapter VII. Peacekeeping is therefore sometime referred to as Chapter VI ½, as stated earlier.

Evolution of Many Shades of Peacekeeping. Peacekeeping has evolved from a primarily military model of observing ceasefires and separation of forces after inter-state wars to incorporate a complex model of many elements - military, police and civilians working together to lay the foundations for sustainable peace[16]. Over time, two states of peacekeeping are easily identifiable, viz, Traditional Peacekeeping and Multi dimensional Peacekeeping.

Traditional Peacekeeping

(a) **Limits to Performance**. All of the conflicts where traditional peacekeeping has been used, have been between States. Peacekeepers' purpose was to contain fighting and monitor a cease-fire agreement until negotiations could produce a lasting peace agreement. The peacekeepers were either unarmed or lightly armed and often stationed between hostile forces to monitor truces and troop withdrawals, provide a buffer zone, and report violations. Such peacekeepers were authorized to use force only in self-defence. Their size and limited capacity meant that they could not stop a party determined to mount an offensive, as Israel has repeatedly shown in attacking Lebanon despite the presence of the United Nations Interim Force in Lebanon (UNIFIL).

(b) **Example: Traditional Peacekeeping**. Kashmir and Cyprus provide two examples of longstanding traditional peacekeeping missions. In Kashmir, UN observers have monitored a cease-fire line between Indian and Pakistani forces in the disputed area of Kashmir since 1948 with little movement toward a settlement. The United Nations Force in Cyprus (UNFICYP) was established in 1964 to monitor a cease-fire between local Greek and Turkish Cypriot forces. UNFICYP remained in place even during the Turkish invasion in 1974 and continues to patrol a buffer zone between the two communities today. The presence of UN peacekeepers and a variety of diplomatic initiatives have failed, however, to produce a settlement of the Cyprus conflict.

(c) **Traditional Peacekeeping in Action**. In the late 1980s, traditional peacekeepers facilitated the withdrawal of Soviet troops from Afghanistan and supervised the cease-fire in the eight-year war between Iran and Iraq. These actions resulted from changes in Soviet foreign policy initiated by General Secretary Mikhail Gorbachev and also quiet diplomacy by Secretary-General P'erez de Cue'llar. The Nobel Peace Prize for 1988 was awarded to UN peacekeeping forces in recognition of their "decisive contribution toward the initiation of actual peace negotiations". Traditional peacekeeping is still important in the Middle East where UN forces remain in place in Lebanon and on the Syrian-Israeli border. It was used to monitor cease-fires along the Iraq-Kuwait border after the Gulf War in 1991 and between Ethiopia and Eritrea (2000-2008). Traditional peacekeeping is primarily useful in inter State conflicts where there is a cease-fire or peace agreement and a limited mandate. Most peacekeeping operations since the Cold War's end, however, have been complex ones with broader mandates, often with Chapter VII authorization to use "all necessary means." and a variety of tasks intended to lay the foundations for a long-term stability in internal or civil conflicts. The guiding principles of peacekeeping – consent, impartiality, and limited use of force – still hold.

Distinction From Peace Enforcement.

(a) **Traditional Peacekeeping.** Traditional Peacekeeping is quite distinct from Peace Enforcement and Peace Building. The key distinction between Peacekeeping and peace enforcement lies in three principles. These are :-

(i) **There is a consent of the parties** to conflict, for the UN to intervene and keep the peace between them.

(ii) Irrespective of the genesis, rationale or the nature of the conflict, **UN Peacekeepers are impartial to the parties** to the conflict.

(iii) Military force is to be used by UN personnel as a **last resort and in self defence only**.

(b) **Enforcement.** On the other hand peace enforcement, as the name implies demands 'enforcement of peace' between the warring nations. Traditionally therefore, to start with, there is neither any peace to keep (as happened in Somalia, Yugoslavia and Congo), nor the consent of parties to the conflict for the UN Forces. Enforcement missions have to 'build peace' and thereafter enforce it. This requires 'muscular missions' with adequate teeth of mandate provisions. If the above two imperatives are deficit, the peace enforcement missions will fail (Yugoslavia, DRC etc).

(c) **Advantages of Peacekeeping.** In principle, **peacekeeping has numerous advantages over enforcement.** First, no aggressor need to be identified. So no one party is blamed for the conflict. This makes it easier to get an approval for an operation. This also helps and facilitates the UN peacekeepers to remain neutral and impartial to the parties to the conflict. Secondly, in peacekeeping there is at least a nominal consent of the parties to co-operate with the peacekeepers. This consent is however problematic when various armed rebels and militia operate quite independently as happened in DRC. On the point of impartiality, if the peacekeepers are seen (or even perceived) to favour one of the parties to the conflict they become targets themselves for the other groups (This is what happened in Somalia, Bosnia and Cote d' Ivoire. Another advantage of peacekeeping operation is that these require much lesser boots-on-ground than peace enforcement. In monitoring/ observer missions, their numbers could be as less as below 100 to just over a thousand. This compares favourably with huge missions of 20,000 peacekeepers as were deployed in Cambodia, Somalia and Bosnia.

Complex, Multi-dimensional Peacekeeping.

(a) **Evolution**. In the brief unipolar moment pursuant to Cold War, **the UN achieved quite a success in number of peacekeeping missions.** This led to increase in world's enthusiasm to apply peacekeepers in more missions. The success of Peace Missions ending conflicts in Central America, Southern Africa and South East Asia called for new types of missions. Weak State institutions, the rise in civil wars and complex humanitarian emergencies in the former Yugoslavia, Angola, Mozambique, Somalia, Rwanda, Congo and Sierra-Leone demanded larger, more muscular and more complex operations with challenges to link and network with multiple agencies like NGOs, UNHCR, UNICEF and UNDP etc.

(b) **Peacebuilding**. Most of the above operation actually boiled down to post conflict 'peace building' which can be defined as '**external interventions' that are intended to reduce the risk that a State will erupt into or return to war**[17]. Of the 51 peacekeeping operations UN has undertaken since 1988, the majority have involved Peace-building task. The events urged the HLP to recommend the institution of a 'Peace-building Commission'.

(c) **Another Challenge**. Another challenge which the UN Peacekeepers face is in the States **where there is no peace to keep**. For example in the UN missions in Somalia, Yugoslavia and DRC there was no peace between the complex warring factions which the deployed peacekeepers could be tasked to preserve.

Evaluation of Success and Failure in Peacekeeping/ Peace Building Missions

The Concept of Success. The word success in a typical peacekeeping/ peace building missions may mean different end-states to different groups of people/member States. For the world at large, success will mean, end of fighting or the emergence and acceptance of a political situation in the form of a peace agreement, return to democracy, elections and more. For local population, it could be return to homes. For member States, it could be recall of peacekeepers home. For the UN it may mean an overall stability and security in a region.

Successes. Basically success has embraced those UN Peacekeeping missions where one or more of the following prevailed:-

(a) **There was some peace among the parties to keep** which the peacekeepers were expected to preserve.

(b) **There was a consent** (and hence co-operation from) the parties to the conflict for the peacekeepers to intervene and do their job.

(c) **The missions were less complex** and multi-dimensional involving identifiable parties to the conflict.

(d) A political (acceptable) **solution** to the conflict was possible and where the parties to the conflict **agreed on a framework** of a solution to end conflict and return to peace.

(e) The vast majority of the victimised/oppressed saw the '**Blue Helmets' as rescuers** and co-operated with them.

(f) Where the **world opinion** was overwhelmingly with the peacekeepers and there was negligible or non-existant superpower rivalry (clash of interest).

Many success examples come to mind. UNEF that restrained Britain, France and Israel from invading Egypt; ONUC, which prevented the fragmentation of a newly independent African country; sanctions against Southern Rwandan to end minority rule; the cease fire in Croatia in 1992; and the maintenance of peace through 14,000 peacekeepers under UNPROFOR. Many other missions like El Salvador, Angola, Mozambique, Cambodia, Namibia etc had mixed bag of successes and failures.

Failures. Talking of failures, it is the sense of the researcher that the missions have failed where one or more of the following prevailed:-

(a) There was a **mandate deficit.** The deficit can take many forms :-

(i) Mission sent for peacekeeping, but there is **no peace to keep.**

(ii) The **task involved peace enforcement but the mandate only called for keeping peace** following the principle of non-intervention, neutrality and impartiality.

(iii) The peacekeepers **fell short in members** (too less) or teeth (not properly armed with mandate provision) to enforce peace.

(iv) **Rules of engagement (ROE) not clearly defined/agreed upon** by parties to conflict.

(b) Mandate getting stuck between the eternal debate of sovereignty vs intervention leading to UN not getting involved while huge human tragedies occur (between 1991 – 96 in Sierra Leone 50,000 people died and about half the country's population was displaced UN sent a mission only by 2000 – too little too late!).

(c) The impotency of the mission under the garb of maintaining 'neutrality' and 'impartiality' ended up in the massacre of 1074017 Rwandans by Feb 2002 out of which 94% were Tutsis. **UNAMIR failed miserably.**

(d) Mission undermanned and worse, getting no support from external forces resident in the area like NATO. This happened in Srebrenica. The Dutch peacekeeping force was grossly under manned. The peacekeepers put no fight to save the Bosnian Muslims. Worse still, no help came from NATO forces based in Italy.

(e) **Superpower interest (clash between two or pushing of interest by one).** The long story of suffering and gross human right violation and the mass casualties in the famine struck Somalia is a standing testimony of how an intervention can be rendered impotent and can result in a failed mission when the interest of a superpower determines the course of events.

(f) **Peacekeeping/enforcement missions also fail when the**

peacekeepers start showing a moral corrosive equivalence, in that they start equating an aggressor and a victim or worse still, start co-operating with one of the parties to the conflict against the other.

Evolution of Various Shades of Peacekeeping Over the Years

New Challenges. The United Nations peacekeeping today stands at a critical juncture. Although the UN has been striving to improve its capacity to support existing operations and plan for new ones, meeting the demand for peacekeeping operations has stretched the organization's capacity to the limits.[18] The traditional model of UN peacekeeping developed during the Cold War era as a means of resolving conflicts between States, involved the deployment of unarmed or lightly armed military personnel between belligerent parties. The rise in the number of intra-state conflicts has resulted in a shift towards multidimensional peacekeeping operations that are often mandated to support the implementation of a comprehensive peace agreement between parties to a civil war. This has, in turn, led to an expansion of the non-military component of peacekeeping operations whose success is increasingly dependent on the work of civilian experts in key areas such as the rule of law, human rights, gender, child protection, and elections[19]. The difficult experiences of the mid-1990's in countries such as Bosnia-Herzegovina and Rwanda prompted the UN to reassess its approach to peacekeeping.

Brahimi Report. In March 2000, a Panel on United Nations Peace Operations issued a report known as the 'Brahimi Report'. The report offered an in-depth critique of the conduct of UN peace operations and made specific recommendations for change. The report also underlined consent by the warring parties, a clear and specific mandate and adequate resources as minimum requirements for a successful UN mission. Consequently, the UN and Member States initiated a number of reforms aimed at improving UN peacekeeping, such as the establishment of a pre-mandate financing mechanism to ensure that adequate resources are available for new mission start-ups.

Several Shades of Peacekeeping. The UN shifted and expanded its field operations from 'traditional' missions involving generally observational tasks performed by military personnel to complex 'multidimensional' enterprises [20]. These multidimensional missions were designed to ensure the implementation of comprehensive peace agreements and assist in laying the foundations for sustainable peace. The nature of conflicts also changed over the years. UN Peacekeeping, originally developed as a means of dealing with inter-State conflict, was increasingly being applied to intra-State conflicts and civil wars. UN Peacekeepers were now increasingly asked to undertake a wide variety of complex tasks, from helping to build sustainable institutions of governance, to human rights monitoring, to security sector reform, to the disarmament, demobilisation and reintegration of former combatants. Although the military remained the backbone of most peacekeeping operations, there were now many faces to peacekeeping including administrators, economists, police officers, legal experts, de-miners, electoral observers, human rights monitors, civil affairs and governance specialists, humanitarian workers, communications and public information experts and the list goes on.

Towards the 21st Century : New Operations, New Challenges. At the turn of the Century, the UN undertook a major exercise to examine the challenges to peacekeeping in the 1990s and introducing reforms. The aim was to strengthen its capacity to effectively manage and sustain field operations. With a greater understanding of the limits – and potential – of UN Peacekeeping, the UN was asked to perform even more complex tasks. This started in 1999 when the UN served as the administrator of both Kosovo in the former Yugoslavia – UN Interim Administration Mission in Kosovo (UNMIK), and in East Timor (now Timor – Leste) – UN Transitional Administration in East Timor (UNTAET), which was in the process of gaining independence from Indonesia. In the following years, the Security Council also established large and complex peacekeeping operations in a number of African countries to include Burundi – UN Operation in Burundi (ONUB), Chad and the Central African Republic – UN Mission in the Central African Republic and Chad (MINURCAT), Cote d'lvoire – UN Operation in Cote d'lvoire (UNOCI), Democratic Republic of the Congo – UN Organization Mission in the Democratic Republic of the Congo (MONUC) and UN Organization Stabilization Mission in the Democratic Republic of the Congo (MONUSCO), Eritrea/Ethiopia – UN Mission in Ethiopia and Eritrea (UNMEE), Liberia – UN Mission in Liberia (UNMIL), Sierra Leone – UN Mission in Sierra Leone (UNAMSIL), Sudan – UN Mission in the Sudan (UNMIS) in the south of the country and African Union-UN Hybrid Operation in Darfur (UNAMID), UN Interim Security Force for Abyei (UNISFA) and UN

Mission in the Republic of South Sudan (UNMISS), to name a few.

Peacekeeping to Peacebuilding. Peacekeepers also returned to resume vital peacekeeping and peace building operations where fragile peace had frayed; in Haiti –UN Stabilization Mission in Haiti (MINUSTAH) and the newly independent Timor–Leste – UN Integrated Mission in Timor-Leste (UNMIT). Many of these operations have now completed their mandates, including the UN Mission in the Central African Republic and Chad (MINURCAT), UN Organization Mission in the Democratic Republic of the Congo (MONUC), UN Operation in Burundi (ONUB), UN Mission in Sierra Leone (UNAMSIL) and UN Mission in Ethiopia and Eritrea (UNMEE), UN Mission in the Sudan (UNMIS), and UN Integrated Mission in Timor–Leste (UNMIT). However, inspite of the expiry of the mission mandate, it is now a norm to extend the mandate or revise the mandate.

Peacekeeping Operations as they are Today. By May 2010, UN Peacekeeping operations had more than 124,000 military, police and civilian staff[21]. In its current state, UN Peacekeeping has entered a phase of consolidation. The numbers have, for the first time in a decade, started to decline slightly with the reduction of troops in UN Organization Stabilization Mission in the Democratic Republic of the Congo (MONUSCO) and the withdrawal of UN Mission in the Central African Republic and Chad (MINURCAT) at the end of 2010. The short peacekeeping operation in Syria-UN Supervision Mission in Syria (UNSMIS) which had to be withdrawn four months after its establishment in April 2012 and the morbidity of Arab Spring, all fall into the realms of what is desired out of United Nations.

In the first decade of the Century, UN Peacekeeping found itself stretched like never before and was increasingly called upon to deploy in remote, uncertain operating environments and into volatile political contexts. While the numbers of military peacekeepers may be decreasing, the demand for field missions is expected to remain high, and peacekeeping will continue to be one of the UN's most complex operational tasks. Moreover, the political complexity facing peacekeeping operations and the scope of their mandates, including on the civilian side, remain very broad. There are strong indications that certain specialised capabilities – including police – will be in high demand over the coming years. Today's multi-dimensional peacekeeping will continue to facilitate the political process, protect civilians, assist in the disarmament, demobilization and reintegration of former combatants; support the organization of elections, protect and promote human rights and assist in restoring the rule of law.

Challenges of Peacekeeping in the 21st Century

Defining Success?

What defines success in peacekeeping or peace building? As stated, this is neither sacrosanct nor definable. Different actors view the same differently with the perceptions of the success varying as under :-

(a) An **end to the fighting**?

(b) Or a **political solution** in the form of a peace agreement?

(c) Or a period of **sustained non fighting** or renewed violence and what length of period?

(d) Or establishing a **functioning government**?

(e) Or successful holding of **free elections**?

(f) Or setting up of a **democratic state**?

(g) Or **completion of a mandate**?

Of Challenges Today. Peacekeeping operates within a changing physical, social, economic and political environment. There is an urgent need to be flexible to address a changing set of issues[22]. Success is never guaranteed, because UN Peacekeeping, almost by definition, goes to the most physically and politically difficult environments. Recent changes in the international security system have moved Peace Operations from the margins of military-political affairs to the very centre stage[23]. There is a strong inverse relationship between peacekeeping deployment and war casualties - as peacekeeping goes up, casualties come down. With peacekeeping operations, the rate of success of peace agreements almost doubles. In purely economic cost-benefit terms (not counting the human cost) peacekeeping is one of the best possible investments. The latest surge in demand for complex peacekeeping operations has placed new strains on an already overstretched system. A robust military presence is considered essential during the initial stages of a peacekeeping operation in order to deter potential spoilers and establish the mission's credibility. Finding troops with the necessary training, equipment and logistical support to effectively undertake the complex and often dangerous tasks required of UN peacekeepers remains a key determinant of an operation's success. However, this is easier said than done, since the member States who possess such troops have often proven unwilling or unable to make them available for UN peacekeeping operations. Threats to the safety and security of UN field personnel have also become an issue of great concern[24]. Improvements are ongoing in this area and require further support by Member States. Restoring some semblance of a functioning State is an increasingly important aspect of complex peacekeeping operations. There is a growing consensus on the need to shore up basic State services, including the judiciary, civil administration and public utilities, in order for post-conflict societies to return to normalcy as quickly as possible. In this regard, the rule of law component has become a critical part of mission planning and considerable progress has been made in establishing capacity to support police, judicial and other re-build activities in post-conflict societies. Additionally, in recent years, it has become increasingly apparent that elections, which are often identified as the end point of post-conflict transitions, are not a quick fix and can only serve as an exit strategy for the UN if other conditions have been fulfilled. But UN peacekeeping paradigm of operations needs to change because of three major challenges to its effectiveness today viz overstretch;[25] the squeeze on member States' resources, and, the brittleness of the current international system.

These aspects have been deliberated below :-

(a) **Overstretch. The UN system is overloaded by the current surge of mission activity**. Although the UN Secretariat's capacity to manage Peace Operations has improved with quicker finance, rapid supply, better airlift and its expanded ability to do non-military functions like police, prisons, demobilization and disarmament etc, the system is struggling to meet the current growth in demand.

(b) **The 'Squeeze'**. The competing demand on member States resources is caused by shrinking defence budgets, increased demand, and armed forces structured inappropriately for new operational requirements. For the world's most capable armies (eg. US, UK) commitments are rising. NATO's commitments are rising, and many regional organisations are now engaged in peacekeeping operations for the first time. It is becoming harder and harder for the UN to find the troops (and police, etc) that it needs to meet increasing commitments.

(c) **The Brittleness of the International Security System**. The essentially bipolar system shaped by decades of Cold War is still evolving to meet the new challenges. It can no longer be assumed that the world's major powers will support the UN in crisis. The whole international security system is at risk of disintegration in the face of a major crisis enveloping the world and its continued vulnerabilities.

The real challenge that lies ahead is to find a way out of the multifarious challenges identified in this.

Challenges and Dilemmas of R2p

Sovereignty vs Intervention – The Eternal Debate. While the Charter precludes the UN from intervening in the matters of States' domestic jurisdiction the once rigid distinction between the domestic and international issues are getting weakened. This is so because in the horrific incidents of the past decades, millions of innocent civilian human lives have been maimed/butchered/slaughtered, either as a result of bloody wars or genocides or ethnic cleansing or famine or mass starvation or pandemics and more. The UN stands at a precipice, whether to intervene as a moral responsibility to save human lives or stand impotently behind the iron gate of State sovereignty and see possibly, the huge destruction of humanity. The HLP therefore has made a strong case for 'Responsibility to Protect or R2P' which must cut across the illusionary boundaries of the so called State Sovereignty. The same is only inviolable till the time the State stands up to protecting the lives of its innocent non combatant civilians, if it fails to do so, or worse still when it engages in destroying its very own civilian life itself, then its false and malice boundary of sovereignty must be breached by the international community which must move in to save the wanton loss of humanity. This is the entire essence of R2P.

The Dilemmas of R2P. Continuing the above thought, the R2P has been ridden with challenges. These challenges have actually shaped the success or failure of many a UN efforts at preserving human lives in challenging international scenarios. A brief deliberation follows :-

(a) **Selectivity**. The first challenge has been of 'Selectivity'. Why did UN authorize a humanitarian mission in Somalia but ignored the long running civil war in Sudan in early 1990? Why did the international community mobilize so rapidly in providing aid to tsunami victims but failed to respond promptly to humanitarian disaster in Darfur? Why Libya but why not Yemen, Bahrain or Syria. The question of selectivity either as a precipitate of the UN's sense on sovereignty vs intervention or as a result of Super power/ member State's interest has spelt doom in many parts of the world. R2P must not be applied selectively.

(b) **Timely Action**. What is that R2P that does not come in time. 'Too little and too late' has failed to save human lives in Somalia, Srebrenica, Rwanda, Sierra Leone, DRC, Darfur .... It is because of this reason that there are strong recommendations for some sort of a rapid reaction force available to the UN.

(c) **Political Will**. A big essential if human lives have to be saved. In cases where major powers have no strategic interest they are apt not to respond, also where the P-5 have conflicting interests, the response is either absent or it is too little too late. Case in point – Rwanda, Sudan, Libya.

(d) **Legality/Legitimacy**. The eternal debate continues. Too much debate on should we/ should we not, eliminates the golden opportunity of timely action where lives could have been saved.

In sum, following can be stated :-

(a) **Preserving Sovereignty**. Save otherwise as stated in sub para (b) below, the UN must avoid interference in matters that lie within the domestic jurisdiction of any member State.

(b) **Right to Protect**. In case of humanitarian disasters and man-made catastrophes like mass murder, rape, ethnic cleansing, forcible exploitation, terror-and genocide etc, which either befall upon a Peoples of a member State or are inflicted by the State itself, the question for the UN must not be right (or absence of it) of intervention, it must be of the 'responsibility to protect' the lives of innocent peoples especially when the State is unable and/or unwilling to do so[26].

(c) **Sovereignty**. In the contemporary world, the concept of State sovereignty must not to be considered absolute or inviolable and the UN must fulfil its responsibility to protect civilians from the man made catastrophes[27].

(d) In Context of the HR Violations. The above said 'responsibility to protect' is also to be seen as complimentary to UN's responsibility to protect Human Rights. This spirit was stated clearly in the UNSC resolution 688 of Apr 91 which stipulated that in case of massive human rights violations it is the legal responsibility of the Security Council to intervene[28].

(e) Guiding Rules for the Use of Force. The report of the HLP has recommended basic criteria in deciding about the legality aspects of the use of force. In essence, this criteria includes an assessment of the seriousness of the threat, deciding on the exact purpose for the use of force, ascertaining before usage, that all non military options for meeting the threat have been explored and use of force is indeed a recourse of the last resort, ensuring it to be minimum necessary, and ascertaining before usage that the proposed use has a fair chance of success.

Conclusion

This Chapter has dealt with the cardinal role of the UN in maintaining global peace. Starting with the fact that monitoring international peace and security in the world is central to the Charter, the Chapter highlights, how the same has been the raison d'être in the establishment of UN in the first place.

Against the backdrop of the above nodal role, the research work has examined how the UN has actually performed over time. Factual scenarios and outcomes have been quoted from around the globe where the UN has been operating. These include Rwanda, Srebrenica, Iraq and Somalia besides others.

In the light of the above Report Card, this Chapter has then highlighted in great detail, the entire phenomenon of peacekeeping, peace building and peace enforcement, giving due credit to the UN's ingenuity in not only inventing, but also, in successful implementation of the same across the globe. Tracing the baby steps of peacekeeping from the Cold War era, the research has worked through the early years and has covered a period from post Cold War to the contemporary times.

As an important end piece and highest in the hierarchy of relevance of the content, the Chapter has highlighted the challenges of peace keeping in the 21st Century. In this, the all important issues like sovereignty vs intervention, Right to Protect (R2P) and use of force etc, have been discussed.

Endnotes

1 http://www.brainyquotes.com/quotes/key and/United-nations-2.html. Accessed on 30 Sep 12.

2 David Mc Dowell "A Modern History of the Kurds" London : IB Tauris 1996, pages 357-363.

3 Human Rights Watch, "Leave None to Tell the Story" : Genocide in Rwanda 1999 at http://www.hrw.org/reports /1999/rwanda/geno/15-08-01. html pages 88-245. Accessed on 30 Sep 12.

4 UN General Assembly "Report of the Secretary General Pursuant to General Assembly Resolution 53/35 : The Fall of Srebrenica".

5 Richard Holbrooke, "To End a War", New York, Rwandan House 1998, page 99.

6 William Malley, "The UN and Afghanistan : Doing its Best for Failure of Russia", New York, NYU Press, 2001, page 195.

7 'UN Chronicle' Volume 13, No 1, March 1993, pages 13-16.

8 http://www.noble prize .org/noble-prizes/peace/laureates/1988/VII – history. html. Accessed on 07 Oct 12.

9 Bijaylaxmi Misra, "UN and Security Challenges in New Millennium" New Delhi, 2004, page 48.

10 MP Vorster, "UNSC Resolution 418 (1974)", South Africa Yearbook of International Law, 1978. Pretoria, pages 130-152.

11 http://www. betterworld.net/quotes/un-quotes.htm. Accessed on 13 Feb 13.

12 http://www.un.org/en/peacekeeping/operations/early.shtml . Accessed on 13 Feb 13.

13 http://www.un.org/en/peacekeeping/operations/surge.shtml . Accessed on 07 Oct 12.

14 13 op.cit.

15 United Nations, "The Blue Helmets : A Review of the United Nations Peacekeeping" 3rd Ed, New York, UN Deptt of Public Information. 1996.

16 United Nations "Peacekeeping Operation 'Principle and Guidelines", New York.UN Department of Peacekeeping Operations, 2008.

17 Michael Barnet et al. "Peace Building : What is in a Name" Global Governance 13, No (2007), page 37.

18 IDSA Publications – "United Nations Multilateralism and International Security", page 580.

19 http://www.unis.unvienna.org/pdf/60years_peacekeeping .pdf. Accessed on 28 Oct 12.

20 "Men, Militarism and Peacekeeping – A Gendered Analysis" by Sandra Whitworth , page 185.

21 http://www.un.org/en/peacekeeping/operations/present.html . Accessed on 11 Nov 12.

22 http://www.un.org/en/peacekeeping/issues. Accessed on 25 Nov 12.

23 http://www.challenges forum.org/cms/images/pdf/shrivenham_report.pdf. Accessed on 25 Nov 12.

24 http://www.ipinst.org/media/pdf/publications/epubmeetnote_being _a_ peacekeeper.pdf . Accessed on 25 Nov 12.

25 http://kutuphane.ieu.edu/wp-content/13challenges-to-peace-operations.pdf . Accessed on 25 Nov 12.

26 W Andrew Knight, "The Changing Human Rights Regime, State Sovereignty and Article 2(7) in Post Cold War Era", New York, 2005, pages.12-16.

27 Bijayalaxmi Mishra, "UN and Security Council in the New Millennium", New Delhi, Kilaso Books. 2004, pages 23-69.

28 UNSC Resolution 688: "A Reappraisal in the Light of Changing World". American University Journal of International Law and Policy, Volume 7 (1993), page.383.

6

Recommendations

"If United Nations is to survive, those who represent it must bolster it; those who advocate it must submit to it; and those who believe in it must fight for it."

—*Norman Cousins*

Where We Are And Where We Need To Go?

Where We Are. The chapters till now have shown that today the UN stands between the following two mutually opposite positions:-

One View. "*UN has been buried many times by critics, but it has survived... It has survived because the world does need a multilateral forum and a frame work of international rules to create order and asset security*"[1].

Counter View. "*It may not be a bad thing if the "UN fades into the sunset on the Manhattan's East River*", At least, we will not have a situation of having a world body based in a country whose administration has no time for the values it stands for.

—A UN Critic

Where We Need to Go. And as to the aspect of where we need to go from here, the author feels that if UN has to have any worthwhile future in the 21st Century, then the points given out at the succeeding paras need to be carefully considered and addressed. These points reflect the essence of what has been given earlier in the book.

Residual Belief at this Stage. At the end of a long study the following view point has emerged :-

(a) **Strongest Symbol**. The UN, as the heritage of mankind, is the strongest symbol of the hopes and aspirations of the humanity.

(b) **Despite All, It Will.** Despite all threats of repeated failures, non-funding/under-funding by many member States, calls for boycott, sub-optimalities in ICJ, trimable and 'wasteful fat' in terms of a maze of duplicated agencies/organizations/programmes; unwise and reducable expenditures and more, the UN, as a representative persona of the civilized world is here to stay for the for foreseeable future.

(c) **On Future Possibilities**. While the future of UN might be ridden with multiple challenges, there is a future, and it is firmly believed that it can be made much brighter and more secure than what it appears today.

(d) **A Crying Need**. Having said that, there is no denial or getting away from the hard truth that there is an urgent crisis of implementing the reforms in the body politic, organizational structures and the currently prevalent procedures for the conduct of business of the world body.

(e) **Inevitable Ills**. However bitterly we may criticise some existing ills and evils of UN, these will persist for a long time into the future. Some of these include :-

  (i) **The bickering/political push pull/skewed and irrational actions by P-5**, driven by narrow verticals of national interest of one's own or those of allies.

  (ii) The **institutional resistance** by the current players to open up the high table for new and more deserving members.

  (iii) **Institutional resistance** of P-5 to any permutations and combinations that tend to widen the current set up of non-permanent UNSC members.

(f) **Call for NIEO**. The calls for NIEO, as well as, a proportional and rightful representation of the current realities of the world (that is vastly different from the one that represents the victorious powers of World War II) will continue.

(g) **NGOs. The NGOs will grow in strength**, stature, clout, and relevance in times to come and will continue to perform a defining role in the affairs of the UN.

(h) **On Financial Crises.** While the UN's financial stability and anchorage will strike a new low in the current grim scenario of recession in global economy and impending crises of failed economies/bad debts/bankruptcies etc, this will also pass and the UN is likely to survive the storm.

(j) **Multipolarity.** After a brief unipolar moment post the Cold War, it will not be the erstwhile bipolar equation but multipolarity that will dominate the geopolitical and geo strategic landscape.

(k) **World Peace.** The world peace at large will remain a hostage of what the sole superpower does or does not do, in making friends or buying new enemies around the globe. The tremors of such nefarious activities like international terrorism, religious intolerance, transnational organised crimes and inter State wars will also play out their parts in shaping would peace/crises.

(l) **Poverty.** The poor/deprived/underprivileged/malnourished will continue to swell in numbers at one end while the World's (read UN's) effort to alleviate the curse of humanity (through MDG implementation or HLP recommendations or through hundreds of ongoing schemes/programmes/initiatives) will continue at the other. The sea-saw will continue to swing either way, more likely on the positive side.

(m) **Major Threats.** The major threats that stare us in the eye in the 21st Century include social and economic threats as a challenge to sustainable development, threats of infectious diseases, food insecurity, growing poverty and deprivation, threats of climate change and environmental degradation, threat of inter State and internal conflicts, threats of nuclear, biological and chemical weapons, the threat of international terrorism and the transnational organised crimes.

(n) **Bottom Line.** In sum, while there may be any crises to the UN and its relevance, it is likely to continue to exist as the last rung hope of humanity and a 'First Port of Call' for the civilised world.

Having made the above remarks as to the overall emerging view based on the study, a series of recommendations as extracted from the deliberations of the foregoing work are given below:-

(a) **Can/Cannot.** The fundamental question, 'Can the UN address the challenges of 21st Century?' has no easy answers, least of it in binary terms (yes/no). In fact it could be yes and no with the humanity craving for the former. For it to become an emphatic yes, the following must happen :-

(i) **Representation: Fundamental Issue**. The UNSC (read P-5) must budge a little and start showing some accommodation or acceptance to the NIEO and a proportional democratic representation of 21st Century on the high table. No earth-shaking changes are expected, only a move towards the idea is our best bet.

(ii) **Global Governance**. The current deficit in Global governance must be addressed by UN. How? New programmes? New initiatives? More funding? Better coordination with NGOs? More peacekeeping? No easy answers again. I think the key lies in the capacity and the willingness of the member States to commit themselves to international co-operation and for the UN to optimise its cumulative strength made up of member States.

(iii) **US Hegemony**. The US hegemony/dominance/lead role as a rational fall out of its world position notwithstanding, the UN deserves a little more respect and accommodation and far more funds from the Sole Superpower. Its act of bypassing the UN and reducing it to irrelevance needs to become history (A very tall order indeed!).

(iv) **Peacekeeping**. Huge challenges and enhanced future demands of peacekeeping/peace building/peace enforcement must be addressed through cooperation by member States in terms of funds and boots-on-ground while such unsurmountables, such as, R2P, sovereignty vs intervention must be taken head on and overwhelming opinion of the civilized worlds must be made to bear on the member States.

(b) **Correcting Representations, No Easy Answers**. Since one of the major deciding factor in keeping the UN effective and relevant in the 21st Century would be to correct the anomaly of an unrepresentative, undemocratic and a skewed UNSC, suggestions made at Chapter 2 regarding the restructuring, re-formatting, structural adjustment and veto re-visit etc must be addressed on priority. The author is deeply (and painfully) aware that there are no easy answers (Ramesh Thakur – when 16 distinguished world citizens acting as individual cannot choose between Model A and Model B can 191 separate Governments do so?).

On UN Financing

(a) **An Existential Crises.** As regards the UN financing, the same is an existential issue. Basically UN's financial woes are due to non-payment of compulsory dues by the Member States, the main culprits are large debtors led by USA. Besides this, there are reasons of sub-optimal utilization of funds, wasteful/avoidable expenditures and the growing internal (implying office/ sustenance) expenditure. Following actions are recommended:-

(i) **Urgent Need.** There is an urgent need to take a fresh exercise of the assessment of ODA liabilities based on current NIEO realities and payment capabilities. Interest should be charged on late payments and non-payments should attract sanctions. In the new exercise, the single State dominance should be ended by the financial burden being shared by middle order economic powers.

(ii) **Re-align Priorities.** The UN led by UNSC must take a massive exercise in retrospection with an aim to reassess and re-align their priorities and learn to manage their finances with regular budgets. If rampant corruption, huge wastages and gross spending on non-essentials can be controlled, the same will be possible. There is also a case for winding down non-essential UN Bodies/Committees/ Commissions/ Organs whose independent and vertical tasking patterns can be dual/multi-hatted to a fewer essential ones.

(iii) **Alternate Sources.** An expert group under the UNSG should examine in a time-bound manner, various proposals for providing to the UN, access to alternate sources of funding for which many a practical financing options have been put forward by the experts (Tobin Tax/Tax on International Arms Sale/Global Resource Dividend etc).

Administration, Management and Co-ordination. One of the major factors impinging upon the failure of the UN in the 21st Century is its organisational viability. Further, there is a need to right size the UN

Secretariat, which has grown from 300 in 1946 to 14,691 in 1994 and is counting over since. An expert assessment says that the same must be cut down to less than 8000. In addition, there is a need to introduce best management practices in the functioning of the UN. These could include internal audits, performance evaluations, programme reviews, expenditure over sight committees checks on recruitments, promotion polices etc. The 'Quiet Revolution' started by UNSG Kofi Annan in 1997 to merge departments, cut costs and build a code of staff conduct needs to be carried forward. There is also a need for cleaning the mess of corruption by making people accountable and demanding a 'bang for each buck'. The establishment of 'Internal Oversight Services' in 1998 with a degree of operational independence is a step in the right direction. Also, there is a crying need to cut duplications (wastages), wherein, multiple agencies are doing the same task with no mutual co-ordination/cost – cutting etc.

UN-US Pas de Deux – Need for an Attitudinal Change. In the UN-US Pas-de-deux, (as Ramesh Thakur would prefer to call it), there is a lot of mind (attitudinal) change required. :-

(a) **Advantage US.** Firstly the world at large needs to realize that despite all the financial downturns, rising debts, mounting unemployment, galloping inflation and all the negative effects of GWOT, the US still has solid strengths. Economy will upturn (or at least its downfall will decelerate) , military and technological strengths will remain almost untouched and hence US will remain a deciding strength in what UN does, or fails to do. This is a fact, and we all have to live its reality.

(b) **Dominance.** On the other hand US must also realize that the days of its unquestioned global dominance with the UN at its leash are about getting over keeping in mind the realities of the new world economic and pegging order.

(c) **Unilateralism.** Another reality which must dawn on US is the fact that with the major portion of the world community standing in rebellion, unilateralism of the type in 2003, will largely become unsustainable. Such action will only end up alienating it more and more from the world community.

The MDGs. The MDGs will remain a major driving force in pushing many agendas round the globe and keeping the UN centre-stage in relevance and purpose. Some reflections in the prognostic mode are as under :-

(a) **Much is Required**. While the overall world poverty levels are on the wane, sustained and continued efforts would be required keeping in mind the fact that the quantum of humanity to be alleviated continues to increase, thanks to the double whammy of food and financial crises, the world over. Also, there are negatives of deficit governance, failing States, and continued atrocities by States on its own peoples. Women would require far greater support and help to take them out from their current state of social inequalities, lack of basics in life and many other vulnerabilities.

(b) **Primary Education**. Since the 2015 targets of achieving universal primary education for all boys and girls will slip, the MDG initiative will need to be extended with continued and renewed vigour well beyond 2015.

(c) **Gender Equality**. Like the above, the huge challenge of promoting gender equality and empowering women should remain 'work-in-hand' by the UN. The targets for special emphasis should be tertiary education for women, improving GPI figure for secondary education, promotion of equal opportunities for women and pushing for greater roles for them in the Parliaments of the world.

(d) **Child and Maternal Mortality**. While tangible progress has been made under this goal, a lot of ground still needs to be covered. Against the target of reducing the child mortality rate by two thirds (75%) between 1990 and 2015 the mortality rates had fallen by 35% in the period 1990-97 in developing world. While this target will slip by 2015, renewed efforts must continue in this direction. The same can be said for maternal mortality ratio as well, where also, the target will slip in 2015.

(e) **HIV/AIDS/Malaria**. There is a need to keep up the momentum in halting/reversing the spread of this menance especially in Sub Saharan Africa, North Africa, Caucasus Central Asia and some least developed countries where the rate of progress is slowing down.

(f) **Environmental Stability**. This must remain an area of priority and renewed action for the UN well beyond 2015 as all targets of MDG in terms of sustaining biodiversity, provision of drinking water and basic sanitation are way short of their desired destinations and are crying for improvement.

As can be seen from the foregoing, the UN and the world is thinking collectively and synergetically in multiple forums and along multiple dimensions on carrying forward the MDGs in their post 2015 avatar of Sustainable Development Goals. The MDGs are and will continue to be of great relevance in times to come. These also provide a degree of centrality to the UN System by placing it firmly at the fountainhead of the World Development Agenda.

On HLP Report

(a) **Co-Terminaty with MDG.** MDGs with a larger run time (2000-2015) and driven through Yearly Implementation Review actually overlap almost all the Recommendations of HLP. Therefore only linkages need to be drawn between the two where applicable. The same has been done while talking of recommendations in relation to the HLP Report.

(b) **Action Points – Relation to NBC Weapons.**

(i) **Additional Model Protocol.** The IAEA must put into effect, the said protocol which is capable of putting into place stringent vindication norms for deliberate non compliance of provisions by Member States.

(ii) **NPT.** International efforts must continue to get all the member States under the NPT regime; surely some dissenting voices (India) will remain (and for good reason). Effects must also continue to urge member States to voluntarily institute a time limited moratorium for any further enrichment/re-processing facility.

(iii) **Iran Time Bomb.** Though not strictly under HLP, a case in point is the ongoing 'time bomb' of the Iran imbroglio on its ongoing nuclear enrichment activities and the efforts of the world (read US) to draw the line with UN chipping in with sanctions and more sanctions. The Researcher feels that the desired (essentially a compromise) end state should be achieved through negotiations before another bloody (and unending) war unfolds between US (with coalition of the willing) and Iran, UN might be on board or may be bypassed.

(c) **PSI.** UN must strengthen and support PSI in its efforts to interdict the illicit and clandestine trade in nuclear proliferation. Member States should be encouraged to join.

(d) **Terrorism**. The comprehensive definition of terrorism as suggested by the HLP is recommended for acceptance. Member States who have not yet signed and ratified the 12th International Conventions and eight special recommendations on terrorist financing and money laundering should be urged do so at the earliest. The UN Counter Terrorism Strategy must move beyond the rhetoric of statements. Under the UN Counter Terrorism Executive Directorate, a Capacity Building Trust Fund should be made which should build the capabilities of global surveillance, seamless intelligence sharing, capacity for policing and deploying preventive force and legal and administrative mechanisms. State not complying with UN's counter terrorism resolutions should attract debilitating sanctions. All these efforts must end up into a Global Counter Terrorism Strategy covering all the four dimensions of prevention, protection, prosecution and response.

(e) On Use of Sanctions. While the credibility for the use of sanctions as international community's conflict resolution strategy is firmly established, the UN must be alive to its many shortcomings namely its tangible negative humanitarian impact, (populations victimised for actions of 'Governments'; Peoples and Governments are not the same), sub-optimal implementation, leakages, corruption and the like. There is a need for continuous impact assessment in the run-time of the sanctions.

(f) **On Intervention.** As a rule, UN must avoid interference in matters that are within the domestic jurisdiction of any member State. However in cases of humanitarian disasters and man-made catastrophes like mass murder, rape, ethnic cleansing, forcible exploitation, terror and genocide etc, which either befall upon the Peoples of a member State or are inflicted by the State itself, the question for the UN must not be right (or absence of it) of intervention but must be of the 'R2P' the lives of innocent peoples, especially when the State is unable and/or unwilling to do so. In the contemporary world, the concept of State sovereignty must not to be considered absolute or inviolable and the UN must come good in its responsibility to protect civilians from the man-made catastrophes. This 'R2P' is also to be seen as complimentary to UN's responsibility to protect Human Rights. Guiding rule for the use of force must be same as suggested by the HLP. Lastly, the key to allay the fears of the majority State of misuse of this provision lies wider representation of the world order at the UNSC.

(g) **On Use of Force.**

(i) **By State in Self Defence.** All cases of a perceived 'imminent threat' must be compulsorily referred to UNSC by member States. The latter without delay must deliberate and authorize a suitable action over the entire spectrum of persuasion, negotiation, deterrence, containment or even a military option as the last resort. The act of taking military action by a State against an imminent threat on the plea that it cannot wait for the decision of the UNSC must be UNACCEPTABLE to the International Community.

(ii) **By UNSC.** With the type of threats that we face in the 21st Century, it is not an option whether the UNSC may/may not use force to maintain international order, it will become a necessity. The criterion given by the HLP, if followed in the right spirit will indeed ensure that this provision is not misused. The apprehension in the mind of member States for its misuse is very genuine. It can only be removed in the bigger canvas of overall UN reforms of the UNSC and UNGA, where the UNSC, with a wider representation of the current world order, is likely to take representative decisions 'unbitten by the veto'. It is to be hoped that such an end-state is reached.

(h) **Peacekeeping/Enforcement.**

(i) **Recommendations.** Mandates need to be unambiguously defined having flexibility to adapt to the dynamic situations. The force must have the 'teeth' to execute the mandate. Status of Mission Agreement (SOMA) and ROE must be secured before the start of the mission. ROE must contain the procedure for graduated response escalation and must set the limit of action/operation by peacekeepers.

(ii) **Stand by Forces.** The member States should live up to their commitment of providing pledged forces.

(iii) **UN Rapid Deployment Force (UNRDF).** While the concept of UNRDF may be correct in principle, it cannot fructify unless the apprehensions of the developing world related to its misuse are removed through a wider representation at the UNSC, as explained earlier. It will be a good idea to consider basing UNRDF on regional groupings having the capability and wherewithal to provide such a force on specific authorization of UNSC. Alternatively, UNRDF can stand separately constituted and operate in synergy with regional groupings. With the UN-AU hybrid peace force becoming a reality in Darfur, the concept of amalgamation of UN and regional force is taking shape gradually. This needs to be further developed.

(iv) **Peace Building Commission (PBC).** PBC is a step in the right direction. The organization should be adequately resourced by the UN.

(j) **UNGA.** As explained, the need of the hour is to make the UNGA more functional, more democratic, and more representative of 'We the People' through greater engagement with NGOs and civil society organizations. The plenary session should be reduced to bring objectivity. Unwieldy agendas need to be shortened through prioritization and similar Resolutions need to be amalgamated. The ills of 'automatic majority', UNGA being an 'ineffectual talk shop' and 'democratic deficit' etc, need be remedied, as explained. There is also a need for smaller and more tightly focused Committees to help sharpen, prioritize and impress the resolutions.

(k) **UNSC.** In essence, the UNSC must have a wider representation in consonance with the current world order. The just aspirations of the majority world (developing) in having a say in the decision making organ of the UN must be respected. Those who contribute most to the UN financially, militarily and diplomatically must have a proportionate representation in its decision making process. Knowing the hard reality that the veto cannot be wished away totally, there is a strong case for limiting its application. Other recommendations like the inclusion of 'indicative voting', increasing the jurisdiction of the UNSC to include the threats of the 21st Century, need for 'informal consultations' to spotlight P-5 actions, 'right of troop contributors' to the details of deployment of their forces and obtaining 'professional military advice' etc, should all be considered seriously and implemented by the UNSC.

People Driven Revolutions. Starting from the Arab Spring and spreading across Egypt, Libya and new Syria a new found awakening is taking shape in the form of 'People Driven Revolutions'. It is becoming clear that riding on the wings of communication, connectivities, IT and ITeS, the collective will of the people can arouse such tremendous power that it can sweep away Governments/dictators/autocratic regimes and the like. Since this and more of it will be a reality in times to come, the UN is recommended to follow this line :-

(a) **Be Alive to Reality**. Be alive to the reality of 'People Driven Revolutions' which have massive earth-shaking powers due to their mass strength.

(b) **Impotency**. Never be a passive By-stander to the events unfolding under such revolutions. Pertinent to mention, that tell tail signs for such revolutions show up pretty early in the overall time line.

(c) **Maintain Importance**. Resist/pre-empt all efforts by the P-5 or any other member State being driven by the skewed verticals of its narrow national interest to override/bypass/trivialize the presence/effect of UN as the central node representing the voice of the civilized international community.

(d) **Peacekeeping Musts**. If peacekeeping/peace building/ peace enforcement becomes a necessity then the UN must ensure the following :-

(i) **In time** – not too late and too little.

(ii) **No mandate inadequacies**.

(iii) **Press for SOMA and ROE** in a time bound manner.

(iv) To have the requisite '**quantum and teeth**' as reqd by the mandate stipulations.

On NIEO. It is time, the UN (read P-5) realized the hard reality of the NIEO. The crises of global economic recession, crises in the eurozone, failing /failed economies, mounting US debt, waning unquestioned unipolar dominance alongside the rising sun in the Asian Century, the growing might of the dragon, the upswing of BRIC, ASEAN and Japan need to be appreciated by the UN. All this and more, simply boils down to the requirement of making the UNSC high table representative of the current realities of the world and the emerging NIEO. The need for the same cannot be over emphasised.

Requirement of Continued Centrality. Is UN the sole voice on the world stage today? Clearly no. With fast pace of globalization the phenomenal growth of the MNCs, emergence of many markets (especially in the third world), the race of NGOs and the dynamic role of Bretton Woods institutions, expert feel that UN has become 'just another player'. It is for the current hierarchy in the UN in particular and the member States in general to ensure that UN while remaining 'just another player' also remains 'the most central player' on the world stage. An adequately democratically represented UN will automatically ensure that it is not made irrelevant or bypassed at will or its resolutions thrown to the wind by the stakeholders. The researcher realizes that it is a tall and an utopian order, but their future survives and thrives on our 'hopes' for the same.

On Environmental Suboptimalities. What has actually been achieved in the field of environment and health is only high awareness and a visibility at the world state. There are still many action points which need to be attended to. Some details :-

(a) **Overlap**. The huge amount of overlap in UN agencies (UNEP, WHO, UNHCR etc) need to be addressed at the macro level and removed.

(b) **Environment**. The IPCC initiative is reaching nowhere. With the Kyoto process gasping for breath, it is a near dead issue. There is a requirement to take forward the Doha Climate Gateway. There is also a requirement for ratification of the entire process by USA and efforts need to be made to reverse the exit of Japan, Russia, Canada and New Zealand.

On Peacekeeping

The biggest challenge for the UN in the 21st Century will be to maintain its relevance and inevitability by effectively facing the numerous challenges of peacekeeping, peace building and peace enforcement. In this context, the following is recommended :-

(a) **Ineffectual Talk Shop**. UN must not be seen as an ineffectual talk shop which dishes out toothless peace plans/proposals that lack one or more of the following :-

(i) The collective resolve of the international community.

(ii) Power to enforce its will.

(iii) An unequal/irrational/one-sided/redundant end scenario which belies the revolution and the sacrifices made therein and/or does not address the key issue driving the conflict.

The above is a huge wish list which calls for many an ideal scenarios like the coherence in the will of the international community (or at least an overwhelming majority) on a crisis situation. This is seldom achieved (stand of Russia and China on Syria, is a case in point). Adequate teeth and an enabling mandate is also in the wish list, which may or may not happen :-

(b) **The P-5 Coherence**. For any peacekeeping/building or enforcement action to be successful the coherent nod of the P-5 (or majority) is inevitable. Dissenting vetos can kill missions and stymie them before they can take off. That such coherence may be achieved in times to come can only be wished.

(c) **Mandate Inadequacies**. Mandate inadequacies have been the cause of failure in many Missions. Mandate must be clearly and adequately defined, and it must have the required 'teeth' and inbuilt flexibility to adapt to the dynamic changes that may be reasonably believed to occur in the course of a mandated mission.

(d) **Status of Mission Agreement (SOMA) and Rules of Engagement (ROE)**. The SOMA and ROE must be insisted ab-initio with the host Government unlike in Rwanda where the UN Mission was in place from Jul 94; SOMA was not signed till late 1995. This may however not be possible where the Government in power is to be ousted (Haiti 1995). The ROE must contain the procedures for graduated response escalation and must set the limits of operations/actions by peacekeepers.

(e) **Inordinate Delay**. Due to inordinate delay in putting the mission personnel actually on ground, success has been allowed to slip away in many cases. A composite force of modest dimensions inserted into the conflict zone quickly can achieve much more than a much larger force introduced months later. One of the measures instituted by the UN to overcome this inadequacy is the earmarking of **'stand by forces'** pledged by member States. This concept is endorsed.

(f) **Case for Standing UN Rapid Deployment Force (RDF).** In order to further enhance the time response of peacekeeping forces to get a capability of deployment within a matter of days, **the HLP had recommended a Standing UN RDF**. This proposal was not accepted in the Outcome Summit due to the fears and apprehensions of majority of member States of misuse by the powerful States using the vehicle of a hijacked and hostaged UN. The concept is endorsed provided the genuine apprehensions are removed.

(g) **Post Conflict Peace Building**. In order to ensure that a nation does not slide back into chaos and disorder once the peacekeepers leave the country, the HLP has suggested the constitution of a Peace Building Commission (PBC). This has been accepted and a PBC stands established by the UN. What needs to be done now is to realize the administrative and the support structures required to operationalise the PBC.

Endnotes

1 Krishnan N, "Whither United Nations" The World Focus, Volume 24, 2003 in K R Gupta ed " Reform of the UN" (Volume 1) Atlantic Publishers and Distributers (P) Ltd New Delhi, 2006.

Bibliography

Primary Sources

Original UN Documents/Reports (Accessed through www.un.org)

UN, "The Blue Helmets : A Review of UN Peace Keeping" New York : Dept of Public Information 1996, page 134.

Chronology of Reforms since 1997.

A Programme for Reforms 1997.

Brahimi Panel Report: UN Peacekeeping Operations, UN Document Number A/55/305-S/2000/809 dated 21 Aug 2000.

UN Press Release SG/SM/7962/Rev.1 dated 18 Sep 2001.

Strengthening the United Nations: An Agenda for Future Change, UN Document Number A/57/387 dated 09 Sep 2002.

UN Civil Society Relations Report of the Panel of Eminent Persons, UN Document Number A/58/227 dated 18 Aug 2003.

Strengthened and Unified Security Management System for United Nations, UN Document Number A/59/365 dated 11 Oct 2004.

"Report of the Secretary General: High Level Panel on Threats Challenges and Change: A More Secure World - Our Shared Responsibilty" , UN Document A/59/565, Dec 2004, pages 24-26.

Kofi Annan, "In Larger Freedom : Towards Development, Security and Human Rights for All" Report of the Secretary General (New York : UN document A/59/2005, 21 Mar 2005) para-17.

World Summit Outcome, UN document Number A/RES/60/1 dated 24 Oct 2005.

Comprehensive Review of Governance and Oversight within the UN and its Fund Programmes and Specialized Agencies, UN document

Number A/60/883 dated 10 Jul 2006.

Report of the Redesign Panel on UN System of Administration of Justice, UN document Number A/61/205 dated 28 Jul 2006.

Report of the High Level Panel on UN System-Wide Coherence in Areas of Development, Humanitarian Assistance and Environment, UN document Number A/61/583 dated 20 Nov 2006.

Periodicals and Journals

Abdul Nafey, "Permanent Membership in the UNSC: India's Diplomatic Initiatives and Strategies." Journal of International Affairs, Indian Council of World Affairs, New Delhi Volume LXI, No 4, Dec 2005.

Amy Gutman and Dennis Thompson, "Democracy and Disagreement", Cambridge MA Harvard University Press, 1996, page 4.

Aryeh Neier, "The Quest For Justice", New York Review, 08 Mar 2001, page 34.

AJR Groom and Paul Tailor "United Nations and United Kingdom" UN University Press, 1995, pages 376-409.

Ann Kent, "China International Socialization : The Role of International Organisations" Global Governance 8 No 3, 200, page 34.

Ann Kent, 'Beyond Compliance China, International Organisation and Global Security" Stanford University Press 2007, page 63.

Chinmaya R Ghare Khan, "The Relevance of the UN Charter in the Contemporary World." USI Journal Oct-Dec 2003.

Donald J.Puchala, "World Hegemony and United Nations", International Studies Review 7, No 4(2005):575

Devaki Jain, "Women Development and UN; A Sixty Year Quest for Equality and Justice". Indiana University Press, Bloomington, 2005, page 157 .

Define S.Go, Richard Harumsen, and Hans Timmer "Regarding Momentum, Finance and Development" 47, No 3 (2010), pages 6-10.

Elizabeth G. "Economy, The Game Changer Coping with China's Foreign Policy Resolutions" Foreign Affairs 89, No 6, 2010, page 143.

Environment News Services, "08 Dec 2012 Doha Outcome : Kyota Protocol Lives", Global Climate Deal by 2015.

Ferrando R Tesorn, "Humantarian Intervention : An Enquiry into Law and Morality" New York Press, 1998, page 3.

Frank Biermann, "The Care for a World Environment Organisation". Environment 42 No 9 (2000), pages 22-31.

Gideon Rachman, "Think Again, American Decline", Foreign Policy, Jan-Feb 2011, page 63.

Greg Hittand Scot Miller. 'Booming Voice for New Block' Wall Street Journal Dec 17-18, 2009

Gupta KR, "Reform of the United Nations" (Volume 1and Volume 2), Atlantic Publishers and Distributors (P) Ltd, New Delhi 2006, page 43.

Hélène Gandois, "After Millennium Development Goals; What Next?" carried in Irwin Arieft (Ed), "A Global Agenda Issues Before the United Nations", 2011-12 United Nations Association of USA, 2011, pages 134-136.

Hans Dehlgren, "The United Nations and the Fork in the Road". USI Journal, Jan – Mar 2005.

Ian Taylor, "Millennium Development Goals and Africa: Challenges Facing the Commonwealth." The Commonwealth Journal of International Affairs, Routledge, Issue 385, Jul 2006.

Igancio Carido 'The Fight Against International Terrorism:Defence Aspect' EU5151 session Document A/1900' Report 14 Jun 2005 pages 162-168 . Accessed on 25 Sep 2012.

IDSA Publications – United Nations Multilateralism and International Security, page 580.

International Food Policy Research Institute 2010, "2010 Global Hunger Index".

Jetley VK, "Op Khukri- The UN Operation fought in Sierra Leonne," USI Journal Jan-Mar 2007.

Kanwal Gurmeet, "Emerging Trends in Military Interventionism." USI Journal, Apr – Jun 2004.

Madeeha Bajwa, "Situating UN Reforms in the Context of Cosmopolitanism: The Globalization of democracy." Quarterly Journal of Strategic Studies, Islamabad, Volume XXV, Number IV Winter 2005.

Michael Grossman, "Role theory and Foreign Policy Change : The Transformation of Russian Foreign Policy in the 1990s", International Politics, 42 Nos (2005), pages 334-335.

Michael Barnett, Eyewitness to a Genocide; the United Nations and Rwanda (Ithaca: Cornwell University Press, 2002).

Michael Barnet et al. "Peace building : What is in a Name?' Global Governance 13, No (2007), page 37.

Nambiar Satish, "Robust Peacekeeping Operations, Rapid Deployment Capability for the UN: An Indian Perspective." USI Journal Oct-Dec 2006.

Oran R. Young, "The Intermediaries : Third Parties in International Crises". Princeton University Press, 1967, page 283.

Prises, Gwyu it.al, "The Hartwell Paper – A new direction for climate policy after crash of 2009" London School of Economics May 2010 . Accessed on 18 Sept 2012.

"Platform for Action", An Agenda For Women's Empowerment : Report of the Fourth World Conference on Women; The Beijing Declaration. Un Document A/Conf/177/20. Accessed on 18 Dec 2012.

Report of the Commission on Global Governance, "A Call to Action" 1995, page 15.

Ramesh Thakur, "A United Nations for our Times." USI Journal Jan May 2003.

Report of the US National Intelligence Committee, "Mapping the Global Future", London 2003.

Richard Jolly and others, "The Power of UN Ideas : Lessons from the First 60 Years" New York, UN Intellectual History Project, 2005, page 34 .

Ramesh Thakur, "UN and the three Pillars of Arms Control." USI Journal Jan-Mar 2004.

Secretary General Kofi Anan, quoted in Millennium Report "We the

Peoples".

Sally Morphet, "Multilateralism and Non Aligned Movement" Global Governance, 10 No 4, 2004, page 553.

Satish Nambiar, "Robust Peacekeeping Operations, Rapid Deployment Capability for the UN : An Indian Perspective", USI Journal, Oct – Dec 2006 , page 257.

Teresa Whitfield, "Friends Indeed ? UN Group A Friends and Resolution of Conflict" Washington DC ; US Institute of Peace Press : 2007.

"The Millennium Development Goals Report 2012", UN Document 12-24532 printed at the United Nations, New York Jun 2012 Sales No E.12.1.4, page 72.

Timothy D. Sisk, "Introduction; the SRSGs and the Management of Civil Wars", Global Governance 16 No (2) 2010, pages 237-242.

UN General Assembly "Report of the Secretary General Pursuant to General Assembly Resolution 53/35 : The Fall of Srebrenica".

'UN Chronicle' Volume 13 No 1 Mar 1993, pages 13-16.

United Nations, "Report of the Panel in United Nations Peace Operations (Brahimi Report)."

UNSC Resolution 688 : A Reappraisal in the Light of Changing World, America University Journal of International Law and Policy, Volume 7 (1993), page 383.

UN Document Number A/58/817, UN Deptt of Public Information.

"UN Change Management Team" Spear headed by Atul Khare" http://www.decanherald.com/contact/165568/Indian-lead-un-change-mangement.html) Decan Herald 11 Jun 11. Accessed on 29 Nov 2012.

UN "World Summit Outcome?" Document No A/60/L.1 sec, 81, 82.

UN General Assembly "Report of the Secretary General Pursuant to General Assembly Resolution 53/35 : The Fall of Srebrenica".

'UN Chronicle' Volume 13, No 1, March 1993, pages 13-16.

United Nations, "The Blue Helmets : A Review of the United Nations Peacekeeping" 3rd Ed, New York, UN Deptt of Public Information.

1996.

United Nations "Peacekeeping Operation 'Principle and Guidelines' New York.UN Department of Peacekeeping Operations, 2008.

"UNSC Resolution 688: A Reappraisal in the Light of Changing World". American University Journal of International Law and Policy, Volume 7 (1993), page 383.

VS Mani, "Humanitarian Intervention and International Law", IJIL, Volume 33, 1993, pages 1-11.

W Andrew Knight, "The Changing Human Rights Regime", State Sovereignty and Article 2(7) in Post Cold" War Era, New York, 2005, pages 12-16.

William Malley, "The UN and Afghanistan : Doing its Best for Failure of Russia", New York, NYU Press, 2001, page195.

Newspaper Articles

Dmitry Shlapertokh, "Out side View : Russian Troops in Iraq" Washington Time, 2004

Joseph Nye,"Does the UN Still Matter?" Financial Express (US) 12 Jul 2007.

Kofi Anan's 'Six Point Plan For Syria' Al Zazeea, 27 Mar 2012.

Press Conference by Kofi Anan, Joint Special Envoy to Syria, UN HQ Geneva .

"Russia and China Veto UN Resolution in Syria", The Telegraph, Tuesday 08 May 2012.

Ramesh Thakur, "Financial Accountability at the UN" The Hindu, 15 Jun 2007.

S Nihal Singh, "UN – A Hostage of US." Tribune, New Delhi, 19 Jun 2007.

Sunday's Zaman, 13 Apr 2012.

Times of India, Bhubaneswar Edition, 05 Nov 2012.

Un Secy General Ban Ki Moon, quoted in Sidney Morning Herald, 31 Dec, 2010.

Secondary Sources

Books

Anthony Parsons, "From Cold War to Hot Peace", Penguin Books, 1995, page 73 .

Bijayalaxmi Mishra, "UN and the Security Council in the New Millennium", New Delhi Kilaso Books, 2004, pages 23-69.

Bijaylaxmi Misra, "UN and Security Challenges in New Millennium" New Delhi, 2004, page 48.

Bruce Jones, "Implementing the Secretary General's Report, "In Larger Freedom" carried in the Book "Irrelevant or Indispensable" 7 ibid page 33.

Brahma Chellaney, "Water, Asia's New Battle ground", Georgetown University Press, Aug 2011.

Barnet and Fennemore, "Rules for the World", pages151-152.

Cameron Hume, "United Nations, Iran and Iraq : How Peacemaking Changed", Bloomington's : University of Indiana Press, 1994, pages 81-82 and 88 – 100.

Courtney B. Smith, "Politics and Process at UN; The Global Dance", Boulder : Lynne Reinner 2006, Chapter 3.

Cudad Colon "Human Rights Reference Handbook" (3rd Edition.rev.ed), Costa Rica : University of Peace, ISBN 9977-925-18-6.

Chadwick F. Alger, The Future of the United Nations System : Potential for the 21st Century, United Nations University Press, New York 1998.

David Mc Dowell, "A Modern History of the Kurds" London I.B Tauris 1996 pages 357-36.

David Mc Dowd, "A Modern History of the Kurds", London : IB Tauris 1996, pages 357-363.

David M. Malone and Yuen Fong Khoong, ed. "Unilateralism and US Foreign Policy : International Perspectives" (Boulder :Lynne Rienner 2003)

David M Malone, "The International Struggle over Iraq: Politics in the

United Nations Security Council", Oxford University Press, 2006.

Dhirendra Dwivedi, "Collective Security under United Nations : Retrospect and Prospects", Kanishka Publishers, New Delhi, 2005.

Dimitris Bourantonis, "The History and Politics of UN Security Council Reform", Routledge Taylor & Francis Group, London and New York, 2005.

Dore Gold, "Tower of Babble: How The United Nations Has fuelled Global Chaos", New York, 2004.

Edward C. Luck, "The UN Security Council; Irrelevant or Indispensible? The United Nation in the 21st Century", ed. Paul Heinbeacker and Patricia Golf (Water loo, Canada, Wilfred Laurier Press, 2005, page 148.

Esther Boserup, "Women's Role in Economic Development" (London : George Allen and Unwin, 1970. Accessed on 18 Dec 2012.

Elizabeth R. De Sombre "Global Environmental Institutions", London Routeledge, 2006, pages 14-20.

Gupta KR, "Reform of the United Nations", (Volume 1 and Volume 2), Atlantic Publishers and Distributors (P) Ltd, New Delhi, 2006.

Hugh Smith, "Australia in Politics of peacekeeping in Post Cold War Era", Sorenson and Wood, pages 9-13.

Irus L. Claude Jr., "The Changing United Nations ", New York : Random House, 1965, page 32.

JC Hurewitz, "The Struggle For Palestine", New York, Schocken Books, 1976, pages 307-308.

John Allphin Moore and Jr Jerry Pubantz, "The New United Nations : International Organisation in the 21 Century" (Upper Saddle River, New Jersey) 2006, page 53.

John Allphin Moore, Jr, and Jerry Pubantz "Encyclopedia of the United Nations," Facts On File, Inc, 2002, pix.

Joshua Muravchick, "The Future of United Nations," Understanding the Past to Chart a Way Forward," The AEI Press, Washingtion, D.C, 2005.

Jarat Chopra, "The Obsolescence of Intervention Under International

Law", Miami, 1992, pages 1-129.

Julie Mertus, "The United Nations and Human Rights : A Guide for a New Era", 2 ed, New York, Routledge Chapter 2.

Irwin Arieff, "Global Agenda; Issues Before the United Nations, 2011-12" UN Association Press, 2011.

Kayathwal Mukesh Kumar, The United Nations : Retrospect and Prospects, Pointer Publishers Jaipur, 1997.

Karen A. Mingst and Margaret P Karns, "The United Nations in the 21st Century" Fourth Edition 2011.

Ken Mathews, "The Gulf Conflict and International Relations" London Rout ledge, 1993, page 81.

Keith Krause, "Canada, United Nations and the Reforms of International Institutions "Alger, Lyons and Trent, page 171.

Margeret. P.Karns and Karen A. Mingst. "International Organisations : The Politics and Processes of Global Governance", 2nd edition (Boulder : Lynne Rienner, 2009).

Margaret P. Karn and Karan A. Mingst "The United States as Dead Beat? US Policy and UN Financial Crises", Boulder : Lynne Rienner, 2002 pages 267-294. Accessed on 14 Jul 2012.

Mary. N. Hampton, "Germany, In Politics of Peacekeeping in the Post Cold War Era", ed Sorenson and Wood, pages 43-49.

Mark Malloch Brown, "United Nations and Changing World Policies", page 285.

MP Vorster, "UNSC Resolution 418 (1974)", South Africa Yearbook of International Law, 1978. Pretoria, pages 130-152.

"Men, Militarism and Peacekeeping - A gendered Analysis" by Sandra Whitworth , page 185.

Manoj Kumar Sinha, "Humanitarian Intervention by the United Nations", Manak Publications, New Delhi 2002.

Marten Zwanenburg, "Accountability of Peace Support Operations", Martinus Nijhoff Publishers Leiden Boston, 2005.

Nazrul Islam, "Reforming the United Nations", Viva Books Pvt Ltd New Delhi, 2005.

Paul Hienbecker, Patricia Golf, "Irrelevant or Indispensable? The United Nations in the 21st Century", Wilfred Laurier University Press, 2005.

Peter Weltensleen, "Representing the World; A Security Council for 21st Century" Security Dialogue 25 No 1 (1994) page 67.

Paul Hawken, "The Ecology of Commerce". Harper Collins, 1993, ISBN 978-0-88730-704-1.

Paul Kennedy, "The Parliament of Man: The Past, Present, and Future of the United Nations," Vintage Books, Random House, INC. New York, 2006.

Peterson M.J., "The UN General Assembly", Routledge Taylor & Francis Group, London and New York, 2006.

Richard Holbrooke, "To End a War" New York, Random House, 1998, page 99.

Ramesh Thakur, ed, "What is Equitable Geographic Representation in the 21st Century?", Tokyo, United Nations University 1999.

Ramesh Thakur, "The United Nations Peace & Security," Cambridge University Press, 2008.

Ramesh Thakur, "Past Imperfect Future Uncertain : United Nations at Fifty", Macmillan Press Limited, Great Britain, 1997.

Robert. E. Osgord, Woodrow Wilson, "Collective Security and Lessons of History in Dhirendra Diwedi, ed. "Collective Security Under UN : Retrospect and Prospect", Page 41.

Richard Holbrooke, "To End a War", New York, Rwandan House 1998, page 99.

Steward Patrick and Shephard Foreman, ed. "Multilateralism and US Foreign Policy : Ambivalent Engagement", (Boulder : Lynne Rienner, 2002).

Sadako Ogata, "Japan's Policy Towards United Nations", ed. Alger, Lyons and Trent , pages 231-270.

Saxena KP, Reforming the United Nations, "The Challenges and Relevance",

Sage Publications, New Delhi, 1993.

Thomas, G. Weiss and others, "The United Nations and Changing World Politics", Westviao Press, 2010, page 4.

Thomas G. Weiss, quoted in his book "Whats Wrong with the UN and How to Fix it", Polity Press, 2008, page 19.

Thomas G.Weiss and other, "United Nations and Changing World Politics". West views Press, 2010, pages li-liii.

Thomas G.Weiss, Tatiana Carayannis and Richard Jolly. "The Third United Nations", Global Governance 15, No 1 (2009), page 123

William Mallay, "The UN and Afghanistan : Doing its Best in Failure of Mission" in William Mallay, ed, "Fundamentalism Reborn! Afghanistan and Taliban" New York, NYU Press 2011, page 195.

Weiss, Carayannis and Jolly, "The Third UN", page 127.

www.ingramcontent.com/pod-product-compliance
Lightning Source LLC
Chambersburg PA
CBHW050233270326
41914CB00033BB/1889/J

* 9 7 8 9 3 8 4 4 6 4 6 9 1 *